Basic Book of
ANTIQUES & COLLECTIBLES

Basic Book of
ANTIQUES
& COLLECTIBLES

GEORGE MICHAEL

Wallace-Homestead Book Company
Radnor, Pennsylvania

Published in Radnor, Pennsylvania 19089, by Wallace-Homestead,
a division of Chilton Book Company

Designed by Anthony Jacobson
Manufactured in the United States of America

Library of Congress Cataloging in Publication Data

Michael, George.
    Basic book of antiques and collectibles / George Michael.
       p.   cm.
    Includes bibliographical references and index.
    ISBN 0-87069-649-1
    1. Antiques.   I. Title.
NK1125.M463   1992
745.1'075—dc20   92-50189
                                                       CIP

1 2 3 4 5 6 7 8 9 0   1 0 9 8 7 6 5 4 3 2

This book is dedicated to

Richard Carter Barret

whose knowledge of antiques
is exceeded only by
his friendship to all who know him

———————

Contents

Preface

Having been involved with antiques since 1946, I have witnessed many changes in tastes and collecting. In those early years, everything had to be in mint condition and of the period. Anything made after 1830, when machines began taking over, was not on the accepted list for true antiquarians. Even grandmother's grape carved sofas were not acceptable. Collecting was much easier then—one only had to learn seventeenth, eighteenth and early nineteenth century artifacts. When items from these periods diminished in availability and rose in some cases to astronomical prices, the later nineteenth and twentieth century items came into vogue. This demanded new scholarship and learning.

It would be impossible to list my many teachers. My PBS-TV programs, taped from the 1960s to the 1980s, brought me in contact with many scholars in the field, as well as a multitude of collectors who gave freely of their knowledge and experiences. Special thanks must go to Richard Carter Barret, the former director-curator of the Bennington Museum in Bennington, Vermont. He is a treasured friend whom we visit from time to time—he is still a font of knowledge. Others still on the scene are Ken Wilson, former director of collections at the Henry Ford Museum; Dorothy Lee Jones, director of the Jones Museum of Glass and Ceramics at Douglas Hill, Maine; Robert Bryden of the Pairpoint Company; Carl U. Fauster; Dr. H.A. Crosby Forbes; Sonia Paine and Eric de Jonge.

Gone, but not forgotten are Lowell Innes, Charles Montgomery, Philip Hammerslough, Marika, Tom Williams, Roger Bacon, Mary Earle Gould, and Ruth and Kenneth Wakefield.

Experience proves that the functional item is best to collect. Always, there is a ready market for chairs, tables, chests, china and silver services, oil paintings and prints for decoration; rugs, lighting devices, and the like. Many decorative objects have risen in value; more because of the maker and rarity than as a necessity in the home.

Dealers and auctioneers welcomed the acceptance of twentieth-century collectibles. This provided the spark for the many flea and antiques markets which appeared coast to coast. The 1960s witnessed the appearance of the group shops which allowed more freedom for dealers to be out buying. Antiquing became a twelve-month business. More attention was given to encourage the gift of antiques rather than new items for birthdays and Christmas—something unheard of but a few years back. Who wouldn't like to find a Queen Anne highboy next to the Christmas tree?

The rise in the number of auction galleries attests to this method of marketing. The major galleries proved that the majority of the large estates are liquidated via this method. The estate and farm auctions, which have always been with us, were stimulated by this new interest in collecting on the part of young and old alike. The treasures from these old places are dwindling, but somehow keep appearing, leading many to pursue the hidden rarity.

Most who collect eventually begin wheeling and dealing. One upgrades in this manner and it satisfies the gambling urge which is in most of us. My old travelling partner, Frank Rowe, once told me, "When you're out and around, you should always buy something to pay for your gas." And that was when gas was 25¢ a gallon. I recall his words well every time I go to an auction, flea market or show. Accept the challenge and see how well you will do in your travels. Maybe there will be some information here that will help you find the one great item which will make buying and reading this book very worthwhile.

George Michael
Merrimack, New Hampshire

INTRODUCTION

How to Enjoy Collecting

If you purchased this book with the intention of learning something about antiques and how to collect and enjoy them, you have just embarked on one of the most interesting adventures in your life. There is no mystery to antiquing. Newcomers to the field are fascinated by the actions and know-how of the old timers in the game, not realizing that once they too were taking the plunge which would involve them in a business which combines a form of gambling, suspense, intrigue, and adventure which is really quite harmless in its nature, yet very rewarding to those who have the fortitude to stick it out and learn the rules.

Before getting involved, you must judge just how deeply you want to get into the nitty gritty of antiquing, and then try to hold the line in conformance with your plans. Some have likened the antiques business to a disease which gradually possesses you, drawing you in deeper until there is no retreat or escape, but do not let this deter you. Along the way you will have lots of fun, meet many interesting people, win a little, lose a little, and above all, come away with at least one very important advantage—you will be more aware of the beauty in our art and antique objects. If this awareness is the only profit you receive, you will be well rewarded.

This quality of "awareness" is the most important asset you can have in the antiques field. Some people are born with it—they have an affinity for the arts and can translate and relate their feelings to them quite easily. Others have to acquire this affinity through study and hard work. Still others acquire it by buying and selling. My motto has always been, "The more rapidly you lose money on antiques, the more rapidly you learn about them. You never forget your lessons."

Everyone experiences a certain amount of this type of learning. No matter how long people remain in the antiques business, they find they make occasional mistakes. In many cases buying and selling is based on personal judgment alone, since one of a kind items keep turning up, and you must gamble on your feelings toward the piece. Frank Rowe once told me after such a losing experience, "When you find you have made a mistake, sell out, and get out." My father once told me, "You make your money when you buy, not when you sell; goods well bought are half sold." I keep this in mind at all times, but there are many occasions when factors such as a possible eventual buyer, personal emotion for the piece, or just the gambling spirit make me plunge into items which later prove to be duds. A dealer once remarked about one of his mistakes, "I showed it to the world, and nobody wants it." This is why it is so important that you judge the type of collector-dealer you want to be before you get involved in serious buying and selling.

There is no separation between collecting and dealing. Even though you may not have a shop with a shingle hanging out front stating that you are in the antiques business, you will find that before long you will be buying and selling to upgrade your collection. Items bought when money was tight will eventually give way to better items acquired through good buys or during a period of more affluency. This swapping off can make you money as well as providing an outlet for any gambling instincts you have, and will give you the satisfaction of creating a collection of which you can be proud.

Everyone has an instinct to collect something, and this urge can be directed in several ways. First, there are those who collect to impress their friends with something of interest or beauty which can also be used as decoration. There are those who collect only functional items, such as chairs, tables, chests of drawers, and beds, and those who collect decorative pieces like oils, glass, and fine porcelain. Others combine their desire to enjoy the items they buy with the idea of treating them as an investment, with liquidation for a profit in the future. Then there is the final category of people who are outright dealers, those who buy and sell for profit alone, along with the pleasure of having quality items pass through their hands. The person who stuffs cupboards full of creamers or salt and pepper shakers is a delight to auctioneers and dealers who otherwise would not know what to do with many of the items available for sale. Collections of this type are mostly dust collectors, and unless they are of really high quality can represent only the satisfaction of a squirrel-like need to stuff something away.

People who collect to impress their friends are usually affluent people who have little thought of buying or selling or upgrading their pieces. They collect art for art's sake and enjoy it on that level, which is a very good one if you can afford it.

Those who collect functional items probably make up the greatest proportion of buyers today. People have learned that if you are going to buy a table, chairs, chests, etc., it is much more sensible to buy old than new. New furniture is worth about half its price when it is delivered to your home, and it continues to depreciate rapidly. Good antique furniture will almost always rise in value, and you can usually sell it at a good profit if necessary. In the meantime, you can enjoy the pieces, whether they are furniture or decorative, since all of them have a much warmer and more comfortable look because of the patina which comes with age.

Those who treat antiques as an investment are wise in their choice. We are continually made aware of fantastic increases in value as auction sale prices are reported. Quality antiques have always risen in value faster than stocks, and provide a much greater return than bank interest. If you buy quality, you need have little fear of a decline in value. It is much more pleasurable to enjoy a fine oil painting on the wall than it is to read figures in a bank book, especially with the realization that the painting is increasing in value much more rapidly than your bank account. Quality

Auctions are a way of life in America. Most important is the period before it begins—inspection time—when one should inspect everything and have questions answered about the items going up for sale.

items can always be liquidated rapidly for cash, so they represent a very fluid form of capital investment.

People who buy and sell as dealers are the ones who do most of the work of acquiring good antiques for those who want them. They are the ones who scrounge about in attics, barns, and cellars and spend long hours at auctions, shows, and flea markets, searching out the means to their living. It is a rather thankless job in many respects, but the rewards are more than financial, and you must be willing to spend long hours at it. Many dealers have to empty attics which are roasting hot from the summer sun and no ventilation. Others have to paw through mountains of rusty junk in garages and barns, often risking their lives by lowering pieces down from haylofts. The best buys at flea markets are made when the dealers are setting up, sometimes as early as 6:00 A.M. and this means rising very early to be there for the first crack at the new merchandise when it is being unwrapped. Dealers will often spend long hours staffing booths at shows and flea markets as well as running a shop at home. You have to be quite dedicated to the field to be a dealer—you will earn everything you work for, but the work will be fun.

Perhaps the greatest introduction to antiques is professional instruction in the field in which you are interested. This is very important in developing the most important attribute in the business—being "aware" of what you see. If you want to specialize in collecting ceramics, it would be advisable to take an eight-week pottery course at whichever local school, university, arts and science center, or historical society sponsors one. Although you may never become a fancy or recognized potter, at least you will learn the makeup of ceramics, recognize the problems faced in making and decorating such pieces, and acquire a feeling for quality. And when you begin collecting, it will not be difficult for you to separate the good from the bad. This advice also applies to those who are interested in furniture, oil painting, pewter, brass, silver, copper, iron, jewelry, sewing, and rugmaking, or any other craft. Your courses of instruction will give you a better appreciation of the problems faced by an artist, and this will result in your being better able to judge quality work.

Above all, read the many good books available and become a frequent visitor to museums and restorations in order to see, firsthand, the items in which you are interested. An excellent place to begin your education is at an auction—you can sit and listen to the auctioneer describe the pieces sold, you can note the interest and activity in bidding, and you can learn the price at which representative pieces sell. Go to good shows and shops and talk with the dealers. You will find them friendly, interesting, and full of information. They are business people who want to cultivate you as a buyer and friend. The old clichés which deal with the reliability of dealers and auctioneers are as dead as dodo birds. There are scoundrels in every business—the antiques business should not be singled out as a particular area in which many of them are active. I find that dealers and auctioneers are much more reliable to do business with than people in private homes who often could care less if they never saw you again. The dealers and auctioneers want you to come back and they will treat you as a valued customer if you are responsible in your business dealings with them.

One of the most confusing aspects of the antiques business is determining just what constitutes an antique. There are many descriptions, but perhaps the following will clear up some misconceptions. In my view, an antique is an art object that is wholly or partially handmade. We buy the work of an artisan's hands and appreciate the feeling, depth, and dimension put into the work. This applies to all fields of art—furniture, glass, paintings, ceramics, silver, pewter, and the rest. One can draw a comparison with an oil painting which has depth, dimension, and feeling and says something to us when we look at it. One

Antiques shows grew in the 1950s to become a favored method of marketing antiques and collectibles today.

can purchase a printed colored picture and hang it as a wall decoration as well, but one can see instantly that the print stamped out by a machine cannot compare with the painting done by hand. This applies to all fields of the decorative arts as well. Quality is achieved only by handwork. Those items made by machine must fall into the collectibles category.

We must also talk about quality, as handwork alone is not enough. Quality is made up of three things—good taste, good design, and good construction. Taste includes form, proportion, color, and decoration. The form of any piece must be pleasing to the eye—such as the shape of a teapot, its handle, legs, cover, and finial. Proportions must be harmonious. Color is important, not only in glass and ceramics, but in the patina acquired by wood, brass, silver, pewter, etc. Early painted furniture must exhibit color which has aged naturally. In American furniture, decoration should enhance, not overpower, a piece.

When one looks at the French Louis furniture, the rococo carving meets the eye before the body on which it is done. This is all right for French and other continental furniture, but is not accepted as well on our native work.

Purity of design is most important. Furniture was the largest item in the home, so the decorative arts of any period were designed to conform to the furniture. Hence our design periods, which are indicated in the furniture chapter, outlining the span of years in which particular designs were most popular. As the artisans moved from one style to the next, many pieces were created with features from two or more periods, creating what we call transitional furniture. The purist will not want it as it is not pure in design.

The last requirement is good workmanship. Whoever creates the work must do it well. This sets the fine artisan apart from the untrained. All these features must be in harmony to create quality an-

In the earliest shows, it was customary to exhibit nothing but period antiques. Demand for less expensive fun items made the shows more enjoyable and affordable for everybody.

tiques. Your awareness of these rules will grow as you go from auction to auction, shop to shop, and show to show. Suddenly objects will speak to you rapidly—you will recognize quality items at a glance where once you needed to study them.

I have not mentioned age. Most think that an item a hundred years or older is an antique. This rule was established back in 1930 only to determine if duty had to be paid on purchases made overseas. The year 1830 was selected because at that time machines began taking over many of the chores for artisans. The year 1830 was used as the determining date until 1966, when President Johnson signed a law which uses the 100-year rule not to designate an antique, but rather to indicate

when duty should be paid. In other words, if you leave the country for more than 48 hours and return with something more than a hundred years old, you will not be required to pay duty. This does not necessarily mean that the item is an antique.

Some prized items such as pressed glass (see Chapter Two) have value in the context of rarity and design. Much handwork was involved in making pressed glass. Some items, such as mechanical banks, have risen greatly in value, but only because they are rare and perform an interesting function. On the whole, you will find the handmade item is much more desired than its machine-made counterpart.

At the beginning of the industrial age, in the 1820s, manufacturers found that

Visiting museums and historic restorations is the best way to learn and understand antiques. This seventeenth-century kitchen exhibits much of what was used during the seventeenth and eighteenth centuries.

machines could turn out products more rapidly and were willing to sacrifice quality for speed and quantity to satisfy growing demand. In rural regions, however, away from the seaports and large cities, we know that many relied on handcraftsmanship as late as the period of the American Civil War, as most could not afford the new machinery and perhaps they did not want to use it either. Handcraftsmanship has never died—it is still with us today.

A paperweight made by Domenick Labino at his home in Ohio in the 1970s will command far more money than most made in the last century. When the Dedham (Mass.) Pottery closed in 1948, you could have bought fine handmade and hand-decorated plates there for but a few dollars; today, most are worth hundreds. The Dorchester Pottery, near Boston, closed its doors in 1978. Its work is commanding many dollars more than much older work. The famed Mount Washington–Pairpoint Factory of New Bedford,

Mass., closed in 1958, left behind a heritage of glass, porcelain, and silver which is eagerly sought by collectors. These are but a few examples that show that age alone has little effect on the desirability and price of antiques.

Something that was a monstrosity 200 years ago may be just an older monstrosity today. Age is a factor that affects the law of supply and demand. The work of a fine eighteenth-century cabinetmaker is valuable not just because it is 200 years old, but because of the quality which creates desirability. This is what sets the price—desirability, not how old it is.

If the piece meets the requirements of being handmade and of good quality, one cannot always be sure it is worth more than contemporary work. I applaud collecting the work of today as we enjoy the creations of artisans whose skills are equal to or even better than those of artisans who worked years ago. The handmade item of today can very well be the desired antique of tomorrow. Many museums are adding contemporary work to their collections now, rather than waiting years when the price most surely will be higher. If your grandfather had purchased a Winslow Homer back when they were selling for $50, you would be a very happy heir, today. A lot of what is collected today was saved by chance. So many pieces were thrown in the dump or disposed of in other ways. Today, educated as we are in the field of collecting, we can call the shots much better on what will survive into the future as desirable items.

Educated collecting is a little like betting on a horse race by studying the past performance of the participants. You should check on the awards and recognition won by the artist, and check each particular work in the light of good taste, good design, and good construction. You can then visualize if it meets what you feel will be the desires of collectors in the future, since they will be little changed from what they are today as far as art appreciation is concerned. You can then begin buying the works of those you feel meet the test with

the hope the artist will some day "arrive" and be recognized, thus making his works more desirable. In the meantime, most such investments are small when compared to investing in antiques, and the items can be enjoyed just as much in your home. Whether the artist "arrives" really isn't of great importance as long as you enjoy his work. You can only hope for the other.

When collecting either antiques or contemporary work, insist on all the documentation of the piece which is available. The past history of ownership of an old item can help in tracing its maker someday. Insist that present-day artists sign their work in some manner, and preserve this documentation. We must begin creating birth certificates for our antiques and collectibles so research on them in the future will be made easier. It also helps to raise the value when works can be traced to important craftsmen as well as important owners. Borrowing an etching pencil from your local policy department to inscribe your social security number on your valued possessions is becoming popular today. This should not hurt the value of it if the number is put in an inconspicuous place, and it will aid in identification and help curb the increasing wave of fine arts thefts. The name of the maker can be put on with the same etching pencil if need be.

Collecting antiques should be fun and owning them should be even more pleasurable. Yet there are very few people who really know how to enjoy antiques. Many people worry about them because of their value and the thought of possible fire and theft is always in their minds. If you cannot enjoy an antique, you should sell it to someone who can. If you find that any items are a source of concern when you are away from your home, or when there are children about, it is high time you sold them. Some people are so concerned that they hire "antiques sitters" as a protection when they leave their homes. This defeats the idea of enjoyment and if you are going to get this involved with material possessions, think twice before embarking on a collection. You should have your items appraised; use the appraisal to insure them under a less expensive fine arts policy, and then let your insurance agent worry about them when you are away. This is why you are paying for insurance.

At the back of this book is a bibliography of the latest available books which will be of great help to you in pursuing further information and instruction in your chosen phase of antiquing. This book is intended as an introduction to the identification, collection, and enjoyment of antiques and collectibles. I hope it lays a good groundwork for you to use in the future. Above all, if I have been able to make you more aware of what you are looking at and have shown how to judge the piece in the light of its contemporaries, I will feel I will have accomplished this goal. Personal tastes in antiques and appreciation of them differ sharply. Just as you would not attempt to buy such a personal thing as clothing for another, neither can you presume you know his artistic tastes, since these may vary greatly from yours. Learn, look, and examine. Do not be casual in your appraisal, as many good pieces are passed over because of this.

The possible fields for antiques and memorabilia collecting are limitless. Let your eye be your guide to quality, and let your experience at shows, auctions, and flea markets be your guide to values. You must be immersed in the business to buy and sell wisely—a part-time, on-again, off-again collector will not keep himself advised sufficiently to do well at it. Talk to dealers and collectors in the field in which you are interested. Go to museums to see the objects on display and study their characteristics. Above all, read good books on the subject. You will find that there is a wealth of material that will help you, if you will only seek it out.

CHAPTER ONE

Furniture

Introduction

Historical Overview

To attempt to explain the various details that must be studied in furniture of all areas would require space far beyond the bounds of this book. Its purpose is to make you "aware" of what you see. You must study history, for even the simple revelation of dates will prove instantly when the first example of a style or period was produced.

In seventeenth-century America we managed to keep abreast of the motherland in design, since commerce brought with it manufactured items which could be copied. Design books became plentiful in the middle of the eighteenth century, and we were faithful in following these so that the settlers here could live in the manner of their forebears. The original thirteen colonies were the center of production until about 1820. The colonization beyond into Ohio, Indiana, Illinois, and the Louisiana Purchase (which became U.S. property in 1803) meant that craftsmen of all kinds helped in creating new settlements. It is unlikely that highly styled furniture would have been made until affluency was there to support it. You must content yourself with the study of the country pieces made during this time, gauging when the first real prosperity hit a community and cre-

ated wealthy patrons who would demand the latest and best. The machine age began at about this time, and with the exception of those who still worked apart from modern civilization with hand tools, you may run into the mass production pieces which saturated the country—especially after the railroads came in and made mass distribution possible.

An unusual situation occasionally comes about because of an event in history. At the time of the Revolution, Connecticut owned a strip of land which extended from its western border all the way to what is now Ohio. Congress later granted parts of this land to New York and Pennsylvania as it intersected their borders and then granted new land at no charge to the Connecticut residents who wanted to pack up and move West. This land in the northern Ohio area is now known as the Western Reserve. Much fine Connecticut and other New England furniture can be found in this part of Ohio, since it was taken there early in the nineteenth century. Some claim the first Hitchcock style chair was made in Ohio, but research shows it more likely that it was made up of parts furnished by Lambert Hitchcock from his factory in Connecticut. He is known to have made chair parts and shipped them unassembled from about 1815 to 1825, when he decided to make complete chairs at his factory in Riverton. Much early Ohio furniture has the look of New England, as it was made by the Connecticut craftsmen who moved there.

Pennsylvania was dominated by a fine school of workmen who worked in strict adherence to English design. This work reached its greatest heights during the Chippendale era, and some feel the finest work in this country was done there and then. Baltimore housed many fine craftsmen who gave birth to ideas in style and veneering which were soon copied all over the colonies. One has but to see the elegant inlay work, the dainty Pembroke tables, and the magnificent banquet tables to realize how important Baltimore was as a center of fine furniture. Charleston and Annapolis had the wealthy clients a community needs to inspire great cabinetry, and the amount of it left in those areas speaks for itself. A trip to the area's museums and historic homes is highly recommended for further study of this work.

The growing ports of Mobile and New Orleans were definitely influenced by the French and Spanish furniture and artifacts which were easily imported over the sea—a much easier method than overland transport in those days. It inspired local cabinetry in the same style, and much study is now in progress to document such work.

We have read that John Alden was our first cabinetmaker—whether this is true or not is academic. What is most apparent is that if the Mayflower had been loaded with all the furniture and artifacts attributed to it, it could never have left the dock. The Pilgrims came with the barest of necessities and it is unlikely there was any furniture aboard. Actually, not much of our seventeenth-century furniture has survived. Most would have been made from the easily worked pine and some from the plentiful oak, birch, and maple. I would refer to the early part of the century as the Pilgrim period, for want of a better designation. Furniture would have been quite crude, yet functional. More time was needed for tilling the soil and hunting than for decoration of household artifacts. Much early furniture has probably been lost through attrition and over the years just thrown out as old and out of style. Most of what has survived has been snatched up by museums and for use in restored homes.

Toward the latter part of the century (at the time of the restoration in the 1660s) we were influenced by the prevailing English Jacobean styles of heavily turned oak furniture, and its counterpart was made here. The rest of the periods came under the influence of cabinetmakers who worked independently, though some were fortunate enough to have their names attached to the styles in which they worked and which influenced cabinetry on both sides of the ocean.

Identifying Furniture Style Periods

DO YOUR LEGWORK

Throughout furniture identification we see the importance of leg design in each

Design Periods in America	
Pilgrim	1620–1670
Jacobean	1670–1694
William and Mary	1694–1710
Queen Anne	1710–1750
Chippendale	1750–1775
Federal	
Hepplewhite	1775–1800
Sheraton	1795–1830
Empire	1810–1840
Victorian	1840–1870
Renaissance Revival	
Eastlake	1870–1890
Misson	1890–1920
Art Nouveau	1895–1920
Art Deco	1920–1940

Seventeenth-century carved chest of the type made in New England. The ball foot is but one example that might appear on such a piece. One might find a hoof, hoof and ball, turnip, mushroom, or other turned design.

Pair of Italian rococo carved walnut armchairs, mid-eighteenth century. Sold for $18,700 by Butterfield & Butterfield, Los Angeles. Photo courtesy of Butterfield & Butterfield.

period. This is perhaps the most important feature for rapid identification. I have explained these leg stylings with accompanying illustrations and further explanation of design techniques. We must be careful in using the word "style" as there is evidence that cabinetmakers, especially in the country, refused to let go of some designs and continued to work in them long after new styles came into popular use. It is best to refer to a piece as being of "Queen Anne style" since we know that such pieces were made almost until the nineteenth century, though the most popular years for it were during the first half of the eighteenth century. Some changes in methods of workmanship might give an indication as to whether the piece is early or late, but sometimes this type of attribution can be hazardous.

Leg designs graduated from the heavily turned ball-type construction to the more graceful yet ruggedly designed William and Mary legs, whose turnings were influenced by Dutch design. Early in the eighteenth century, at the time of Queen Anne, the graceful cabriole leg and varied type pad feet were conceived as a breakaway to light and airy furniture, more in keeping with the delicate monarch herself.

There are many leg variations in this period more fully explained in the illustrations.

Noted cabinetmaker Thomas Chippendale was the son of a cabinetmaker, and his son followed in his footsteps as well. He was influenced by his contemporaries and freely copied their ideas. His first work, *Cabinetmaker's Guide*, published in 1754, influenced work on both sides of the Atlantic for many years. In fact, his designs are the most reproduced today. Names such as Matthias Lock, Batty Langley, and Sir William Chambers are less known to collectors, yet all pioneered forms adapted by Chippendale for which he was credited.

Chippendale continued to use the cabriole leg but gave it a new look with a ball and talon or ball and claw foot. The idea for the claws embracing the ball came from the Orient, where it was symbolic of a dragon's claws encompassing the earth. Most refer to this as the "city style" Chippendale, whereas the simpler country pieces featured nothing more than cutout boards, often called a bracket base, for legs. This can be found on cased pieces, such as chests, desks, bookcases, and the like. There are short cabriole legs with talons or claw feet, and these are referred to as bandy legs. These designs lasted until about the time of the American Revolution, though some country cabinetmakers

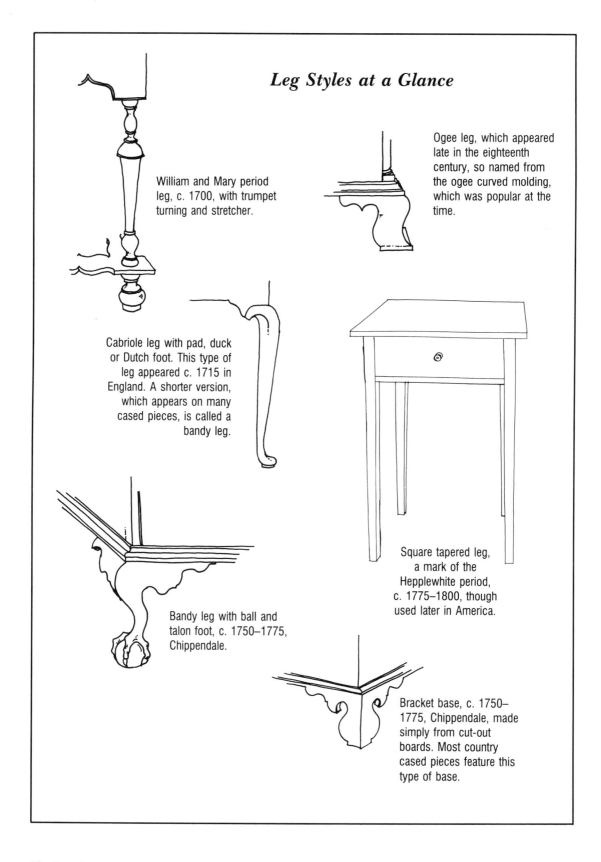

Leg Styles at a Glance

William and Mary period leg, c. 1700, with trumpet turning and stretcher.

Ogee leg, which appeared late in the eighteenth century, so named from the ogee curved molding, which was popular at the time.

Cabriole leg with pad, duck or Dutch foot. This type of leg appeared c. 1715 in England. A shorter version, which appears on many cased pieces, is called a bandy leg.

Square tapered leg, a mark of the Hepplewhite period, c. 1775–1800, though used later in America.

Bandy leg with ball and talon foot, c. 1750–1775, Chippendale.

Bracket base, c. 1750–1775, Chippendale, made simply from cut-out boards. Most country cased pieces feature this type of base.

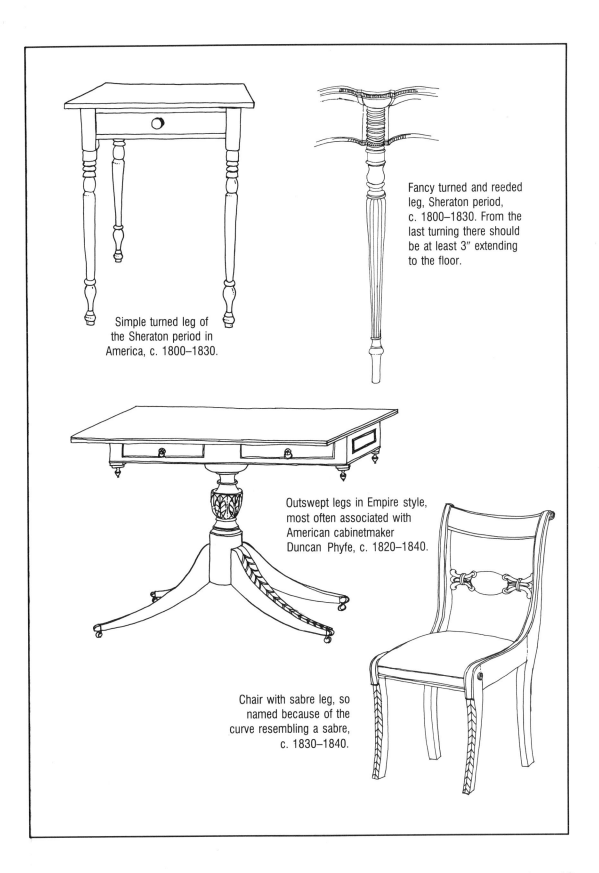

Simple turned leg of the Sheraton period in America, c. 1800–1830.

Fancy turned and reeded leg, Sheraton period, c. 1800–1830. From the last turning there should be at least 3″ extending to the floor.

Outswept legs in Empire style, most often associated with American cabinetmaker Duncan Phyfe, c. 1820–1840.

Chair with sabre leg, so named because of the curve resembling a sabre, c. 1830–1840.

Maple Queen Anne highboy with cabriole legs and pad (or duck or Dutch) feet. The bottom section features a molding and the the top section fits into it. The molding should be no more than an inch wide; otherwise you must suspect the piece is married.

less handling; others may have been left on dirt floors in cellars, and some were too tall for their new surroundings, so out would come a saw to take them down to size or even them off. This hurts a piece of furniture as the change is quite visible to the eye, which is interested in good proportion. There are no set rules for the height and width of most furniture, so you must judge the piece with your eye—either the proportion is pleasing, or it isn't. You may find evidence of new wood where the saw has been at work. The cutting may be very evident unless the legs are cut properly at the termination of a turning. No one can help you on this, so use your own judgment and it will not be long before your eye will make you suspect tampering.

MARQUETRY AND VENEER

Not long ago, the public was indoctrinated with the idea that the only good furniture was that made of solid wood. The horrible veneering of walnut and oak on our twentieth-century furniture gave rise to this idea. With older antiques, however, you will find that veneered pieces will usually command a higher price than solid wood. In the Queen Anne and Chippendale periods, when veneering was at a minimum, there is naturally little comparison

Italian neoclassical marquetry writing table, last quarter of the eighteenth century. Sold for $15,400 by Butterfield & Butterfield, Los Angeles. Photo courtesy of Butterfield & Butterfield.

worked with them until the new design books found their way to the rural areas.

The Hepplewhite period is characterized by the simple square tapered leg, which many feel is the purest in design. These are found on chairs, tables, and some of the delicate cased pieces, such as a lady's secretary. The large cased pieces are equipped with French legs, as illustrated. These are the only two legs identified for this period.

Leg heights are important in all pieces of furniture. Many were damaged in care-

Slant-top desk in solid tiger maple wood, New Hampshire, late eighteenth century. This is the country-style bracket base, made simply from cut-out boards (no carving), which is often found on cased furniture of the period.

cially in northeastern Massachusetts and southern New Hampshire, show evidence that they are English. There must be exceptions, but in my long experience, I haven't seen one to convince me it is American. However, George Hepplewhite in his *Cabinetmaker and Upholsterer's Guide* freely used marquetry (veneering and inlay) to beautify his pieces. In America, eighteenth-century furniture was beautified with carving. Many feel that this late eighteenth-century furniture is more beautiful with the highly grained woods veneered to dress it up. Nowhere did this style reach greater heights of expression than in the northeastern section of the country, where such woods were plentiful. Fine figured maple furniture was found as far south as Pennsylvania and west to Ohio. The ultimate work seems to have been done during this period in the Boston to Portsmouth, New Hampshire, region, where classic pieces were made to satisfy the retiring captains, shipowners, and wealthy merchants along the seacoast.

to be made. The Federal period brought with it a revival of this work, and in this era comparative pieces are valued according to the beauty and workmanship in them—not on whether they are veneered. The striking figured maple and birch most often used made furniture works of art, not just functional pieces. In this respect, I feel that Federal period furniture is still highly underrated today, and before long will, in many instances, surpass the value of comparative pieces from the preceding periods. Age alone does not make a desired antique. Artistic beauty as a result of fine handcraftsmanship will become more and more of a deciding factor in value. We are at the threshold of this renaissance now, so Federal furniture represents a much better buy for investment than the furniture which preceded it.

In American furniture, it is unlikely that one will find marquetry work in the Queen Anne and Chippendale periods. Some early Queen Anne pieces are veneered, but those I have examined, espe-

Hepplewhite banquet table which is in two sections, rounded at the ends, with deep leaves at center. Mahogany, late eighteenth century. Chairs are shieldback of the same period. Upholstery covering the seat and frame are permissible in this period.

Tambour desk, four graduated drawers, French legs, mahogany-stained birch, figured birch veneer, Hepplewhite, c. 1800–1810. The tambour doors are made by gluing strips of wood to canvas; they slide back into the case. Others were made with doors and are called cupboard desks. This is a New England form.

Charles Montgomery in his *Federal Furniture of the Federal Period* (Viking) indicates that one should be careful in indicating that a wood used for veneering in American furniture is satinwood. While he was director of Henry Francis DuPont's Winterthur Museum in Delaware, he had samples of veneer chemically analyzed. No satinwood was found. Practically all of the furniture was decorated with figured birch, one of the many maples, holly, or, in some cases, aspen. Though satinwood was used in foreign furniture, it was not in favor with American cabinetmakers. This is largely because satinwood comes from the Caribbean and was expensive to import. Also, it does not have the striking graining of North American wood.

Separate shops were set up to make inlay and veneer woods. These were sold to many cabinetmakers in the same area. Such marquetry may help confirm attribution to a maker, but cannot be used as the only guide.

In some pieces the woods have been shaded to a black color to highlight the design. This was done by toasting the pieces of wood in hot sand to acquire the desired tonal quality. Few cabinetmakers had the time to devote to such specialized work, so were very happy to have someone else do it.

CONSTRUCTION AND DESIGN

Bowfront chests were constructed in a manner that made it impossible for them to lose their shape. First, three or four two-by-six-inch pieces of lumber were stacked one atop the other, the length of the drawer. The boards were then glued together with animal glues, after which the craftsman outlined the curve of the drawer front on the top board. He then sawed through the several boards, cutting the front in the exact shape desired. Because there is no stress on the wood, it never attempts to straighten itself. The front was then veneered with the desired wood. To determine that a chest is an early piece, look at the back side of the drawer front: the lines of the several planks glued one atop the other are very evident. If they are not, the piece is probably not of the pre-1830 period.

Chairs became quite comfortable in the eighteenth century and the upholstered wingback with overstuffed cushions were the rule. To be proper, American side chairs of the Queen Anne and Chippendale periods should feature removable slip seats. If one is upholstered around the framing, so that the seat cannot be removed, it is either European or a reproduction. Often, one will see an American chair of these periods authentic in every detail except the slip seat, which may have been reupholstered years later and done improperly. (I have seem this in several major museums.) Removing upholstery will leave tack holes around the frame, so most slip seats are left alone.

Backs of side chairs may be shaped in

Chippendale side chair in country style with squared legs. The ribband back and extended crest rail are marks for identification. In this and the preceding Queen Anne period, American chairs such as this must have slip seats.

were more widely spaced than those of later years. Pine was most often the secondary wood used in America whereas deal or other soft wood not native to our shores appears in the English furniture. Little walnut was used in England at the time, as blight had hit the trees in France, where most of them grew. Perhaps the most telling feature is the width of the boards used in drawer bottoms and on the backs of cased pieces and the direction in which they run. England had long before run out of wide boards, as their trees had suffered indiscriminate cutting for centuries. As a result, they used two or three boards to

a "spoon" fashion for greater comfort. Others may feature a split spindle or bannister back, which is nothing more than a combination of upright supports. Drop-leaf tables were very popular as they conserved space. The cabriole leg was the rule in fancy furniture. Some of these legs appear on late Queen Anne furniture, though most are ascribed to Chippendale. One must identify what surrounds the ball before identifying its type. Those with animal claws or hairy paws may be identified as ball and claw, but when surrounded by birds' talons, the proper designation is ball and talon.

During Queen Anne's time, the English gradually did away with pegging the joints whereas American craftsmen pegged into the beginning of the nineteenth century. Dovetail joints in cases and drawers

Design Periods in England

Until the middle of the eighteenth century, the names of furniture styles and periods had been taken from those of monarchs. Actually, most dealers in the British Isles still identify eras according to the ruler's name at the time. The following chart will help if you wish to do the same.

Elizabeth I	*1558–1603*
James I	*1603–1625*
Charles I	*1625–1649*
The Cromwells	*1649–1660*
Charles II	*1660–1685*
James II	*1685–1689*
William III	*1689–1702*
Anne	*1702–1714*
George I	*1714–1727*
George II	*1727–1760*
George III	*1760–1820*
George IV	*1820–1830*
William IV	*1830–1837*
Victoria	*1837–1901*

(George, The Prince of Wales, became Regent in 1820 at the time of his father's great illness.)

make up a drawer bottom, with the grain running from front to rear in the drawer. The Americans still had huge pine boards available and usually used a single piece with the grain running from end to end. These would be chamfered or chiseled down at the edges and slid into slots in the drawer sides and front. Also, most English case work has the back boards running vertically, while the Americans ran them horizontally. Some vertical work was done in Pennsylvania and states farther south where the English influence was great. Actually, if you could study pieces side by side, you would note that American furniture is basically lighter and more graceful than English counterparts of any period.

Identifying Regional Styles

Once you have learned your periods, you may accept the new challenge of studying the regional characteristics of furniture. The different cultures abounding in America resulted in the variety of tastes evident in many types of artifacts. New England furniture is characterized by its delicate style, slender legs, and good proportions. When it is veneered, it is done in good taste with highly figured woods. Dimensions are very important to this aesthetic, and this detail was unsurpassed elsewhere. New England sideboards feature more leg and less body, whereas those from Philadelphia are heavier bodied with shorter legs. Much carving was done, but not in the heavier rococo style that was the mark of Philadelphia work. Southern craftsmen relied heavily on dark stains in the manner of English work, but northern craftsmen were more content to use natural finishes and allow the wood grains to show in their own color. Northern five-legged game tables are a rarity, whereas they were the rule in the South. Charleston furniture is styled much like that of Boston, since many cabinetmakers from New England sought the more temperate climate and carried their influence with them. New York cabinetry was influenced

Chippendale secretary, eighteenth century, cherry, Connecticut. Bracket base is country style. The interesting interior is quite well done. (Bourne Gallery.)

for years by its Dutch heritage and culture, and the designs approximated much of what was being made overseas—much heavier in concept than that in New England.

Regional tastes are strong, and dealers travel all over the country buying pieces that are not appreciated in one area and selling them in areas where they are sought after. New England furniture has little appeal in New Orleans, yet the French furniture from overseas finds a ready market there. One will hardly ever find French furniture in an old New England home—it just does not look proper in the colonial setting.

For years, Empire and Victorian furniture was shipped by the truckload from New England to the South, where there was a ready market. It is only within the last twenty years that pieces from these periods began to find favor in the North.

Much fine furniture found its way overseas. Benjamin Frothingham worked in Charlestown, Massachusetts, and labeled his pieces as Charlestown N.E. Some years ago, a fine labeled highboy from his shop turned up in Cophenhagen, Denmark. Another great highboy now in an American museum was found in South Africa, and in 1952 a fine slant-top desk bearing his label showed up in England and was brought back to be sold at an auction in New Hampshire.

WOODS AND DECORATION

Woods may help in provenance. You will find upper New England furniture in pine, maple, and birch. Mahogany was favored in the coastal cities of New York, Philadelphia, Baltimore, and Newport (where it appealed to the wealthy). It was easier to obtain by sea from the Caribbean than other woods which were transported overland by ox cart. Cherry was used extensively in Connecticut and it was in favor as well in New York and Pennsylvania. Walnut was in use from New York to the South as this was a common wood in these areas. Beech, poplar, and hard pine were used in the South as well.

Pine William and Mary chest with ball feet, New Hampshire, c. 1700. Original condition except for pulls. Sold in 1968 in New Hampshire for $2,600.

Mahogany secretary, graduated drawers, French legs, Hepplewhite, c. 1800–1815. The Gothic arch doors are related to Portsmouth, New Hampshire, which helps confirm construction characteristics from the shop of Judkins and Senter. Photograph courtesy of Israel Sack, Inc., N.Y.C.

Historians tell us that stringing (a striped inlay), flowers, eagles and other decorative devices were used just about everywhere, but the cabinetmakers in the major cities of Portland, Portsmouth, Salem, Baltimore, Annapolis, Boston, Newport, New York, and Philadelphia brought the style to perfection.

Walnut and mahogany were favored woods in England early in the eighteenth century, but in this country, the artisans skillfully used the lighter-colored and highly figured maples, mahogany, cherry, and birch in their work. American craftsmen used little or no marquetry, preferring to paint or japan (lacquer and gild) the cased pieces for beautification. Carving was relegated to fans or shells on drawers and perhaps some cutout work on the tops of highboys and fancy finials. Late in the period, Philadelphia craftsmen carried this even further with carvings on the knees of the legs.

SIZE

Dimensions are important, as good proportion makes for a good-looking piece. Dimensions also affect value. Perhaps the most desired width for a slant-top desk, five- or six-drawer chest, or highboy top of the eighteenth century would be an even 36″. Those that are wider command less money and smaller ones usually command more. You must be careful in any "just like" attributions, as the width of the piece is very important in relation to value. Short, squat legs, which lower the body of a chest to the floor, do not give the graceful proportion of a tall, well-defined leg. Perhaps the greatest expression of this is in the

Six-drawer chest, Dunlap Circle, New Hampshire, c. 1790s. This is the shortened cabriole leg, which is called the bandy leg. Though the Queen Anne designs were pretty much phased out after 1750, country cabinetmakers still used this leg until the end of the century at customer request.

Mahogany Chippendale slant-top desk, serpertine front, Massachusetts, c. 1770–1790. In early cased furniture, it is important that all four legs be alike. These are bandy legs with ball and talon feet, all alike. (Butterfield & Butterfield.)

cased pieces made in New Hampshire, which, for some reason, feature high legs, which enhance the dignity of the pieces to which they are attached. Another New Hampshire characteristic is the wide moldings, which are apparent at the tops of highboys and chests-on-chests. Traveling a few miles over the border in any direction will reveal narrower moldings made by nearby contemporaries. Maine furniture is styled very much like that of Massachusetts, as Maine was part of Massachusetts Commonwealth until 1818 and must have been influenced by this.

Knowledge of these kinds of details can help you make reasonable attribution in the light of known facts. In a region that was full of fine cabinetmakers, the work on some pieces of furniture is so similar that you would be hard put to specify the area of craftsmanship.

Identifying Pre-1830 Handmade Furniture

CONSTRUCTION TECHNIQUES

You should always get beneath any piece of furniture to examine the leg and base structure, since this is the first place that will receive damage in moving or handling. You must examine the age (or patina) of the wood, to make sure it is the same in all sections and that there are no replacements. Wood reinforcing blocks are glued at important joints to strengthen them. If corner blocks are held in with screws, you must determine if this is later construction or merely bracing which was added later to reinforce a weak spot. If screws are used, they must be of the handcut variety, usually with the point tips cut off. In the old days, holes were drilled before the screws were put in, removing the necessity of a point. The slits in the screw heads will usually be off center as they were made quickly by hand. Machine screws are cut dead-center; this gives them away.

The drawer bottoms should preferably be single board and the grain should run from side to side in the chest. If the bottom has several boards running from front to rear, be suspicious, as you are most likely looking at an English piece. The drawer bottoms should be chamfered, or narrowed down at the edges, and should fit into slots at the drawer sides. The drawer sides should be dovetailed to the front and rear boards—generally, the wider and cruder the dovetail, the older it is. By the Federal period, dovetails were highly refined. The front dovetail is often hidden with a molding or cockbeading which surrounds the drawer front. This is referred to as a "hidden dovetail," and it does not detract from the piece. The drawer bottom boards should show signs of hand planing or rough saw marks. Saw marks which are straight up and down and parallel to each other are evidence that the board was cut on an up and down jacksaw. This was a two-man saw manipulated by a man standing atop the log and a man beneath in a pit, with the saw stroke moving up and down. The circular saw was reinvented by the Shakers in the 1820s, so boards which show the marks of a circular saw must have been cut during that time or later.

Some experts can feel the leg of a piece and determine if the piece is old. New wood will still be quite round, while wood which has aged over the years will dry, with wood cut against the grain drying more slowly than wood cut with it. As a result, there is a slight oval shape to a turned leg if it is old, but you must sharpen your senses to work with this clue.

In American work, back boards on cased pieces should run horizontally, and usually are of pine, hewn and chamfered. They are generally held in by rough handcut nails. However, such nails are now being duplicated, so do not use this as an absolute means of attribution. In Centennial furniture, the back boards are often a dead giveaway to the age of the piece. Many pieces were made with thin machine-cut wood, and they most likely came this way. You may suspect that fakers later replaced these with old hewn pine to mislead unwary buyers.

Examine Pieces Closely—Determining the age of a chair poses particular problems. You cannot merely examine it from the outside. You must examine the frame construction, since this is where the truth lies. This often means ripping out a dust cover. If you are not permitted to examine the interior framework, stay away from the chair, unless you are paying a reproduction price. Reinforcing blocks to strengthen the legs against the frame were glued on early pieces; in later construction corner blocks were fastened with screws. The age of the wood is important. Look for many tack marks where the upholstery was changed over the years. Look for hewn marks on the inside wood, as most were left a little rough and are not as smoothly cut as a machine-driven saw would have left them. To judge by the leg backs alone is hazardous unless you know your woods and patina, and have a feel for the correctness of the piece. Even collectors this knowledgeable turn the pieces over.

It is difficult to determine the age of wingback chairs when one cannot cut the dust covers beneath to examine the construction. One can be fairly safe if you find the chair quite heavy when you lift it. Most likely this is a repro, perhaps a hundred years of age, but nevertheless not in period. After lifting literally hundreds of these I have found that the eighteenth-century chairs had much less wood in them, which has dried out considerably, making the chair much lighter than the repros. You can get the feel of the weight by going to auctions where authentic chairs are sold. Once you lift a few, you will feel the difference.

"MARRIED" PIECES

If you are buying a chest-on-chest or highboy, you should check to make sure it is not a married piece. Due to family disagreement on who should get the furniture, it would sometimes be divided, with separate halves going to different owners. A new frame would then be built to hold the upper half, creating a phony chest and a top would be put on the lower section. In the case of a highboy, this lower unit is often miscalled a lowboy. Over the years, dealers and buyers have been reuniting sections, even though they are not original to each other. You should pull out a drawer from each section and examine the dovetailing to make sure it matches perfectly. Moldings and beading on the upper and lower cases should be checked. Back boards must be identical and must show the same age. The base should show no signs of tampering. Holes for the brasses or pulls should be cut or drilled identically. Above all, the proportions must be right—be sure the molding supporting the top section on the base is not too wide, and that the height and width of the top is proportioned well in relation to the bottom. Of course, the wood must be the same, but

Mahogany, bonnet-top chest-on-chest, Goddard-Townsend school, Newport, Rhode Island, c. 1760–1785. The ogee legs were used in the second half of the eighteenth century. Sold for $264,000, June 1990, by Butterfield & Butterfield, San Francisco. (Butterfield & Butterfield.)

diligent refinishing can make them match. Study the wood in both sections and make sure they originated in the same cabinet shop. It has been suggested that more than one man may have worked on such big pieces, so there may be variances. Although this was very likely, the work would have been divided by specialty—with one person cutting, one dovetailing, one carving, etc.—so all similar work on the two pieces should check out as the same.

HARDWARE

The type, age, and condition of brasses is important. From the teardrop pulls of the late seventeenth century, the turn-of-the-century style advanced to bale handles with brass plates behind. The pre-1830 brasses or knob pulls featured a threaded post. This was inserted from the front of the drawer to the inside, where it was held on with a hand-cut nut, often round. Later brasses would be held by a bolt, which would be inserted from the inside of the drawer and fastened to the bale handle or knob at the front. After you have seen really old brasses, you will have little difficulty in telling them from the new. However, new brasses do not fault a piece too much, as most collectors will accept them as long as they are in the proper period style. Many museums have new brasses and knobs on their furniture—perhaps because they came that way, and perhaps because of the problem of theft.

Wooden and brass knobs were used extensively in the eighteenth century, especially during the last quarter. They were very popular all through the Federal period, and a great deal of Empire furniture appears with them. Glass pulls were introduced in 1825 by Bakewell of Pittsburgh when he developed a pressing machine to make them. The Boston and Sandwich Glass Company of Cape Cod is known for its fiery opalescent drawer pulls. These became quite popular and appear on much late Sheraton and Empire furniture. After this time all sorts of metal, wood, and glass pulls and handles with back plates were used. There is such a variety that I would be lost in attempting to discuss them. Since most were not handmade, they have little importance in the collecting scheme.

You should check the inside of the drawers to determine if the pulls are original. Pull knobs were quite often replaced

Simple desk on frame, William and Mary, late seventeenth century. The H stretcher made its appearance about this time; the teardrop pulls are proper for this period.

with bale handles and an additional hole would have been drilled. Early artisans hollowed out the holes on the drawer interiors so that the bolts and nuts would not tear clothing. If you find a drawer with one hole hollowed and one just drilled to accommodate the bolt, it is obvious that the brass is a replacement. Sometimes two new holes have been drilled to accommodate a bale handle, and the single hole that once held the pull knob will be quite obvious from the interior, though it will be covered by the back plate at the front of the drawer.

American Style Periods

Pilgrim

During the Pilgrim period (1620–1670), cabinetmakers used whatever woods grew locally. Oak was favored in England at the time, so it is only natural that this wood was used here as well. A clue to provenance is that white oak prevailed in England while in America both red and white were used. Furniture made from red oak is most likely American, since it is doubtful that anyone would have shipped this wood back to England at the time.

Naturally, pine was a favorite as it was plentiful and easy to work with primitive tools. Oak gave way to walnut and mahogany early in the eighteenth century due to the demand of the wealthy for fine furniture such as that made in England. However, out in the country, maple, hickory, birch, cherry, and other fruitwoods were utilized, as they were readily available at literally no cost.

Jacobean

The Jacobean furniture of the early seventeenth century was rectangular and low in proportion, reflecting the low ceilings popular at the time. Most legs were straight with some turnings, and a melon shape was popular. Legs were braced with stretchers and were most often close to the floor. The later Jacobean period brought with it much carving and even caning of chairs.

Some refer to the Jacobean period as the Carolean period, which was characterized by the introduction of S and C scrolls with mixed Dutch, Portuguese, Flemish, Spanish, and French-Italian influences. Spiral turned legs appeared, and geometric moldings were favored. The Dutch had perfected the turning lathe, which made the spiral moldings possible, at a time when the English and other artisans were still carving them totally by hand. At this time, padded backs appeared on chairs and bun or ball feet were the rule. Needlepoint, velvet, leather, and brocades were used for upholstering. The great wood carver Grinling Gibbons left his mark with work which has perhaps never been duplicated. Motifs included acanthus leaves, roses, crowns, and scrolls.

During this time, artisans produced crude stools; benches; trestle tables, which were long dining tables; low box type chests; bible boxes; and simple bed frames with rope supports for a feather or corn-

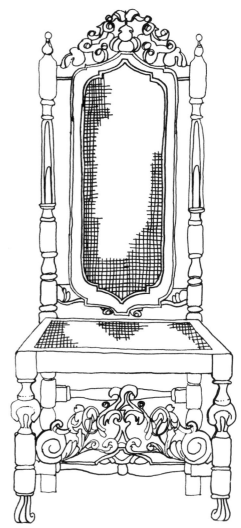

Chair of the Jacobean period, English, around 1670, when caning was popular. The design and carving were influenced by work done in the Mediterranean area at the time.

husk-filled mattress. There was little attempt at beautification, but we do find good examples of carving in specific areas. In the western Connecticut–western Massachusetts sections, a school of carvers is recorded near Hadley which left us a fine heritage of their work. Some pieces are called "sunflower" chests because of their floral decoration, and others are simply called Hadley chests as a means of identifying the school of work they represent.

Oak was a popular wood for this work, and because of this many pieces have survived. English counterparts of these chests are also collected, and you must determine their provenance by the decorative motifs. Study of the decoration that existed at the time both here and overseas is a great help, as this can help in attribution. To do it solely by workmanship at this early period is hazardous.

Historians tell us that the term "Jacobean" might be applied to several periods in the seventeenth century. The name is loosely adapted from *Jacobus*, the Latin name for King James I, who reigned early in the century. James I was succeeded by Charles I, who was later beheaded by Cromwell and his associates. Some refer to the years 1649–1660 as Cromwellian, as they feel there was a definite change in design to reflect the absence of the monarchy, which until then had supported and inspired craftsmen. Furniture from this period is characterized by stiff lines, with little embellishment, but this should be of little concern to the American collector as there is little available either here or in England.

Until recently, styles of this period were not much in favor here in America, since the cased pieces are bulky and the chairs and settees are quite uncomfortable. Also, one would find it almost impossible to acquire a complete set of chairs, or other multiple items, as time has taken its toll of many of them. Our practice of wanting complete sets held down interest in such seventeenth-century furniture. The English reproduced much of it in the nineteenth century, and you must be careful in your purchases if you want the early work. Perhaps the best clue to look for is pegs in the framework. The English were using pegs to join furniture right into the Queen Anne period early in the eighteenth century, but at that time such work began to disappear. However, almost all seventeenth-century work should show pegs. Also, you should check the underframe of any furniture to look for new screws or angle-cut braces. In the early days, craftsmen glued crude blocks of wood at joining points, whereas later work shows machine-cut braces held in by screws. You should look for early marks left by saws, planes, and chisels. Later work done by machine will be perfectly smooth, with very tight joints.

William and Mary

James II, the son of Charles II, seemed to have little better luck in ruling than Charles I, and he fled the country, leaving his daughter, Mary, to rule with her husband, William, who was Dutch. Though they ruled only from 1688 to 1702, William and Mary managed to have an influence on furniture and other art styles. Many Huguenot craftsmen were coming into England at this time to escape religious persecution caused by the revocation of the Edict of Nantes. The Dutch and French influence was immediately felt, and for the first time furniture took on graceful lines and proportions. It featured a combination of curved and straight lines and chair backs were heightened. The seats

William and Mary style pressed cupboard, late seventeenth century. The heavy ball feet and split spindle turnings are characteristic of the period.

were most often square, with backs slanted for comfort. Turned legs with vase and ring, trumpet and inverted cup designs became the rule. Ball and bun feet were still used on low chests for strength, but longer legs with stretchers framing them became the rule for the taller cased pieces. The chests and highboys were soon decorated with inlay, painted decorations, and well-grained veneers. Some royal furniture was gilded, and some appeared with marble tops. The cockleshell was popular in carving, and some chair legs had feet with toe and even ball and claw carvings. China cabinets were popular, as antique collecting became a pastime for the wealthy. Tall clocks appeared, and the game tables introduced at the time of Charles I became the rage as cards and other games of chance swept the nation. The long, rigid refectory tables of the preceeding years gave way to graceful gateleg and other drop-leaf designs. One of the most important designers of the period was a Huguenot, Daniel Marot, and as a result his work shows the influence of the Louis XIV styles then prevalent in France. This was a period of high style and represented the transition from the rigid and functional to the graceful and beautiful in furniture.

William and Mary highboy with burled veneer. This features the ball and hoof feet, and legs with trumpet turnings. This is the only period in which more than four legs are connected by stretchers on a highboy.

Queen Anne

The advent of Queen Anne to the throne in 1702 brought with it a further refinement in style, with the pieces becoming perhaps more delicate and beautiful than those of any other period. The heavy underbracing of the preceding periods gradually disappeared, and graceful cabriole legs, designed from the architectural cyma curve, became the rule. Anne ascended the throne after the death of William of Orange, who had given Parliament the power of absolute rule in England, reducing the monarchy to a titular role as far as governing was concerned. With the monarchy no longer dictating style, cabinetmakers exercised their own imagination, yet most came up with a refinement of the continental styles which were still most appreciated. The Dutch influence was strongly felt during Anne's reign, and we are fortunate that it was, since it left us with a heritage of fine furniture. In America, cabinetmakers in Boston, Portsmouth, Newport, New York, and Philadelphia rivaled their counterparts in England. The Americans were able to work with a wider selection of woods, using native woods as well as mahogany and other exotic woods from the Caribbean. Proportions were more delicate to fit the smaller homes in this country.

Some feel that little or no furniture in this style was made in America before 1730—that it would have been shipped from England. As I have written, veneered Queen Anne highboys are in the older settled sections of the country, so many must have been shipped here.

Bannister back of a country Queen Anne chair, early eighteenth century.

Queen Anne desk on frame, c. 1720–1750, New England. Wing brasses appeared late in this period and were used in the Chippendale period as well.

Unusual blockfront Queen Anne lowboy with cabriole legs. The first recorded blockfront, made in 1731 by Job Coit in Boston, is currently displayed at the Henry Francis DuPont Winterthur Museum. Most likely, the one pictured here would date from between 1731 to 1750.

Chippendale

Until the middle of the eighteenth century, the names of furniture styles and periods came from the monarchs. It was about this time that the name of Thomas Chippendale became quite prominent in cabinetry. He borrowed designs from others and carried them to perfection in a blending of functional use as well as beauty. Chippendale might be called the first true English style which evolved from many others, and which was carried to perfection by other cabinetmakers as well. Here in America, the craftsmen seized on this departure from the reserved Queen Anne style, and turned out classic pieces using our beautiful woods. This was the era of the famous Goddard and Townsend families in Newport, and their creations in the Chippendale style are considered to be the epitome of cabinetmaking in this country.

Chippendale favored mahogany and used curves freely. He continued the use of the cabriole leg and placed the ball and

Chippendale mahogany block-front chest of drawers, Boston, c. 1750–1780. Sold for $52,500 by Butterfield & Butterfield, San Francisco. Photo courtesy of Butterfield & Butterfield.

claw and the ball and talon foot firmly in leg design. He favored carving over veneering for beauty. The back rails of chairs were most often serpentine or of curved shape, and many are characterized by pronounced ears at the juncture of the side posts and crest rail. Chair arms were curved and often flared at the ends, and the supports were angled forward at the

Chippendale chairs with cabriole legs and ball and talon feet, c. 1750–1775. The chair at the right bears the label of Benjamin Randolph, a Philadelphia maker, but is a phony. The chair at the left is authentic. The former could be a reproduction from the Centennial period of the 1870s. Do not trust all labels, which may be duplicated.

Festooned looking glass of the Chippendale period, third quarter of the eighteenth century. This is in unusually good condition; most are damaged.

side rails of the seat. The ladderback design was carried to its greatest height, and many featured intricate piercing and carving on the rails. Chippendale's carvings featured acanthus leaf (which was brought to its fullest fruition early in the nineteenth century), scrolls, French rococo, fruit and flowers and even lion heads. The breakfront made a dramatic appearance in Chippendale's time, and he furthered the making of sideboards, which are generally credited to Thomas Shearer, another English designer.

Other designers of note were also in great favor during this time. Perhaps Chip-

Unique mantel mirror in Chippendale style, c. 1750–1775. It is bordered by gilt and features an urn finial.

Perhaps the ultimate slant-top desk is this carved ivory example, which is kept in the summer palace at Push-kin, near St. Petersburg. It is a superb example of French artistry done at the time of Catherine the Great, late eighteenth century.

pendale was most influenced by Thomas Johnson, a well-known designer and carver in London. Johnson was a master of the French styles which we label as Louis XV. Sir William Chambers went to the Orient, and on his return pioneered the use of oriental influences in furniture, and this caught Chippendale's fancy. The "Chinese Chippendale" design was created as a result. Chambers published his *Designs For Chinese Buildings, Furniture, Dresses, Etc.* in 1757, and Chippendale was quick to use it. Robert Manwaring published the *Chair-maker's Guide* in 1766 and this, along with a furniture style book done by Matthias Darly, had great influence on Chippendale. Robert and James Adam were primarily architects, but wealthy patrons had them design furniture to match their house designs. The shops of Chippendale and another up-and-coming cabinetmaker, George Hepplewhite, were used for its manufacture. Needless to say, both were

Transitional chair with Queen Anne base and Chippendale back. Period would be about the middle of the eighteenth century, when designs changed.

Very desirable six-drawer chest, Chippendale, bracket base, third quarter of the eighteenth century. Note the graduated drawers, which heighten value. Best width is 36"—if they are wider, value goes down. Oval bale handles are not proper; they should be wing brasses for this period. Wood is maple.

Game table with square country Chippendale legs, c. 1750–1775. Its blockfront design makes for an interesting top. (Photo courtesy of Shelburne Museum, Inc., by A. S. J. Mengis.)

Chippendale carved mahogany card table, by Thomas Willing, Philadelphia; carving attributed to Garvan Carver, c. 1760–1770. Sold at record auction price for a card table, $1,045,000, on February 2, 1991. (© 1991 Sotheby's, Inc.)

influenced by the Adam styles, about which little is known in this country as so little of it was made or sent here. The Adam brothers returned to the use of fluting in legs after excavations in Greece had uncovered such designs and they are also credited with stressing the use of veneers and inlays to beautify furniture.

Federal

HEPPLEWHITE

George Hepplewhite, another noted London cabinetmaker, was responsible for

a radical departure in furniture style, doing away with the curved legs and fancy carvings of Chippendale's time. Though contemporary with Chippendale in his early years, Hepplewhite took his inspiration from the then recent excavations at Pompeii, which prompted a revival in interest in the classic lightness, grace, and elegance of pieces unearthed. He did away with bizarre decoration and trusted to purity and simplicity of line to create a whole new idea. Louis XV had died, and across the channel the French designers noted the change in tastes and paralleled Hepplewhite with their version of the Louis XVI

Card table, Hepplewhite, late eighteenth century, mahogany with bird's-eye maple veneer. The cuffed leg—the added taper at the foot—is typical of Salem, Massachusetts, design.

Tilt-top candlestand, mahogany, bird's-eye maple veneer in diamond inlay, reeded post, Dunlap Circle, New Hampshire, c. 1800–1820. The spider legs (with spade feet) came into general use after 1800.

style. Both featured the slender tapered leg, often with a spade foot. Bowfront chests made their appearance and the convex fronts were often terminated at concave corners, another Hepplewhite form. A favorite of the Prince of Wales, Hepplewhite utilized a feather carving on many pieces, inspired by the feathers on the prince's hats. He adapted the Crusader shield as a shape for the backs of chairs and also for mirrors. Short, curved arms were used on chairs, as was a rail above the seat to reinforce the back. Chairs were usually upholstered with the material extending over the frame and covering it entirely. If you should find a Hepplewhite designed chair with slip or removable seat, be cautious, as this is not the norm. Some say Hepplewhite's styles reflected the austerity of the period after the Revolutionary War. Be that as it may, there are students today who consider his styles perhaps the most classic of all. Such beauty was created with simplicity, using the coloring of well-grained woods, either veneered or solid, along with restraint in any carving. New appreciation is growing for work done in this style in America, since from Boston

north to Portsmouth, New Hampshire, it was brought to full development in beauty and fine cabinetry.

Chests of this period most likely would feature the "French leg," or outturned tapered leg, often reinforced with a pronounced toe. The cutouts on the skirts of such pieces are important, as this work determines much of the value, based on the ingenuity of the maker. Though we generally record that the Hepplewhite style was going out of favor in America at about 1800, we have found documented pieces made in this fashion as late as the 1830s, despite the advent of two period changes at the time. This was still an era of hand construction, and one would go to a cabinet-maker and order the pieces made up as he saw fit. It would not be unusual to have pieces made to match earlier ones handed down in a family. Because of this, it is much safer to refer to a piece by style, such as "Hepplewhite style," as you cannot be sure whether a piece was made during his lifetime or during the time his designs were most popular. This would apply to all periods. The Dunlap family (a group of cabinetmakers in New Hampshire from 1740 to 1830) is known to have worked in the Queen Anne style as late as the 1790s, as this is what their customers wanted.

Several features in Hepplewhite furniture should be mentioned. The long, tapered legs on tables and chairs often boast an enlarged square foot. This is called a spade foot and was used on both sides of the Atlantic.

While the preceding periods had produced tall chests and highboys, they went out of favor during Hepplewhite's time, and none has appeared in his style. Some of the four drawer chests made in the north-shore Massachusetts and Portsmouth, New Hampshire, areas are fast approaching (and in some cases have exceeded) the values of chests of previous periods. These are outrageously beautiful pieces most often made in mahogany, or mahogany-stained birch, and veneered with striking figured birch or maple woods. Those featuring a drop panel, which is nothing more than a decorative rectangular or oval veneered decoration beneath the bottom drawer, are highly sought because this distinctive feature is rare.

Research I have done on this drop-panel feature has uncovered the names of several makers: Joseph Clark of Greenland, New Hampshire; Judkins and Senter of Portsmouth, New Hampshire, and Nathaniel Appleton of Salem, Massachusetts. Fewer than 100 cased pieces featuring the drop panel have turned up in the country. There are clock cases which have it. The research has indicated that this drop-panel decoration did not appear on any Boston

Four-drawer, drop-panel chest with French legs, serpentine front, mahogany-stained birch case, figured birch veneer. Mahogany banding and cross banding. It has construction details found in Judkins and Senter furniture, Portsmouth, New Hampshire, early nineteenth century. (Art Institute of Chicago, Gift of the Antiquarian Society.)

furniture, but cabinetmakers there, such as the Seymours, featured a raised-panel decoration at the tops of secretaries. Portsmouth furniture of this type did not feature a raised panel, but Salem work featured both upper and lower panels.

Decorative drop panels have appeared in furniture outside New England, but most are circular in design and are not veneered with the same woods as found in New England. More research should be done on these as the decoration has shown up on pieces made in Philadelphia as well as Baltimore. One known chest made in Tennessee features a semicircular panel with rayed veneer suggestive of the sun.

Duncan Phyfe—In his wildest imagination, no one could conceive that a baby born at Loch Fannich in Scotland in 1768 would grow into a craftsman who would revolutionize the style of furniture not only in this country but throughout the world. This small town, but thirty miles from Inverness, was hardly known until Duncan

Thomas Shearer

Thomas Shearer worked in the 1760s in England. Along with the Adam brothers, he popularized marquetry decoration on furniture and the turned and reeded leg that was to become the mark of the Sheraton period, which began in 1794 when Thomas Sheraton, a contemporary of Hepplewhite, switched from the tapered leg to the one that would eventually bear his name. Shearer gets no credit for it, nor do the French who used it during the time of Louis XVI. The legs were turned on a lathe and, in country furniture, were left this way when added to the furniture. The higher style, made for the more wealthy, featured reeding or fluting. This is

Sheraton fancy armchair, which features bamboo turnings popular during the early part of the nineteenth century.

Sheraton side chair, c. 1790s. Though the legs are tapered, the back is gometric, which indicates the period.

what appears as a ribbed carving, almost the length of the leg. If the carving is convex, with the rounded area extended toward you, it is reeding. If the rounded carving is done into the leg in concave fashion, it is called fluting. Often, old furniture landed in the cellar or barn, where a leg may have rotted, so all were sawed to a matching length to restore the piece. However, this destroys the form and proportion. It is easy to determine if this has been done on a Sheraton leg. One should measure the distance from the last turning to the floor; it should range between 3 and $4\frac{1}{2}$ inches. If it is less than 3, one must suspect that the leg has been cut. If the leg has button feet, this rule does not apply, as the button is the last turning, which meets the floor.

Phyfe left it and came to Albany, New York, in 1783. During the long voyage with his family, a brother and sister died, reflecting the hazards of travel at that time.

When Phyfe was sixteen, he entered a cabinet shop as an apprentice. When he was qualified, he opened his own shop. He was lured to New York City early in the 1790s as he was told this was where the money was. Located on Broad Street, among many other cabinetmakers, he was hard put to make ends meet until a member of the John Jacob Astor family saw and liked his work and gave him orders. Soon other wealthy people became his patrons; by the turn of the century, he may have been regarded as the outstanding furniture craftsman there.

New York was a growing community after the Revolutionary War, and our increasing trade with the French brought with it the latest styles from the continent. Phyfe worked from the design books of Hepplewhite and Sheraton, but soon turned to the incoming French Directoire style. Gradually, he developed his own ideas and incorporated them in his furniture. In this later work, one rarely sees a straight line. He is best remembered for his curves and reverse curves in chair and table legs and backs to chairs and sofas. His decoration included carving, marquetry, and reeding. Many of his pieces feature brass paw feet. Most of the furniture was mahogany and featured carved acanthus leaves, which were popular at the time. The outswept legs often rode on casters, and the pedestal-based table in this design is felt to have made its first appearance in his shop. His imagination in carved decoration ran from the lion mask to the cornucopia and oak leaf. Many panels are done in drapery, whorled fluting, thunderbolt, wheat ear, leaf and dart, and palm leaf. The rotating-top, tilt-top game table appeared during this period; it is possible Phyfe helped pioneer it. Phyfe liked the lyre design and often used it in the base of a table and on the backs of chairs. Often, the strings are of brass or whalebone, and some features highlighted with ebony.

His sofas featured short legs that most often terminate in a bulge. Most seats were upholstered, but some were caned. Carved eagle and lion heads were features, but not limited to his furniture alone.

The Phyfe style has never died. Many furniture firms feature reproductions in their catalogs and showrooms. Naturally, because this style has been popular since the beginning of the nineteenth century, one must learn how to identify the period pieces. In Phyfe chairs, the seats were always curved or rounded; apparently he designed them this way to allow for the elasticity of the cane. The supports underneath the cane were mortised into a dovetailed groove in the seat rail which gave it the strength he wanted. If the cornucopia motif is used, it is generally accompanied by the laurel, which complemented it.

If a chair features the reeded Sheraton leg, most often the back carving includes the thunderbolts, wheat ears, drapery, and fluting. The joining of the chair legs to the frame is most often reinforced with glue blocks, whereas the more modern brace is nearly triangular and screwed with relatively new looking screws.

Phyfe made many Pembroke-style ta-

Sheraton drop-panel chest, cherry with bird's-eye maple and mahogany banding on drawers, c. 1820–1830. Attributed to Spooner and Fitch, Athol, Massachusetts. (Garth Auctions.)

bles and many worktables but most featured the reeded Sheraton leg and not the pedestal base for which he is best known. He made an early extension dining table which was the forerunner to those we enjoy today. They did not appear until about 1820.

The furniture purist does not pay much attention to the Phyfe style unless it is labeled by the master himself. Most of his pieces were well labeled, generally along the inside of a framing member. Chairs and sofas may reveal this labeling if the dust cover is pulled back, but since most people do not want to disturb the cover, it is possible there are many authentic Phyfe pieces whose owners do not know their importance or value. Most competent appraisers can tell from the outward appearance if the piece is old or new and if it should be checked further.

One feature which seems native to Phyfe and New York State is the winged claw feet that appear front and rear on sofas of the period. If you see one with feet like this, it's time to lift the dust cover to look for a label.

SHERATON

The name Thomas Sheraton looms large as one of the foremost eighteenth-century cabinetmakers who worked in London. He issued *The Drawing Book* in 1794, which set a pattern of style in furniture that was to remain quite popular until about 1830. At first, he used the tapered leg, which had been popularized by George Hepplewhite, another London maker, but soon brought forth his own design—the turned and reeded leg. This was patterned after furniture designs uncovered in excavations taking place at that time in Italy and Greece. It was a return to a more classic style.

During this period, the trade between this country and the Orient began to grow, and soon the Oriental influence was felt in our decorative arts. Bamboo furniture became popular, and soon furniture makers were turning our local woods out to resemble the bamboo in legs, arms, and spindles of chairs and other pieces. Rush seats were most popular on the chairs, and soon the name "fancy chair" was applied to those with this Oriental look. Because they were popularized during the Sheraton period, it was only natural that the term "Sheraton fancy chair" came into being.

Actually, there is not much fancy about them—they were low in cost, and had greater appeal to those of limited incomes. They found their way to the common homes, to the farms, and in the servants quarters in the wealthy homes. Today they are more highly regarded, as they are handmade, rugged, and of quite good quality to use. Age is in their favor, for those who wish to equip their homes with period pieces. It would be safe to say that all were painted originally, and some will be found with decoration and stenciling. The front legs must have button feet and must be in good shape. The bolder the turnings, the better.

This is a period worth collecting right now. Prices have not yet ascended beyond the cost of much of today's fine new furniture. The carving as well as the marquetry, using many beautifully grained woods, can be considered works of art. There are many Sheraton tables selling for relatively little money. Bowfront chests have become more expensive, but there are many flat-fronted examples of the period which are quite beautiful and will have excellent value 20 or 30 years from now. Some of the prettiest work tables are Sheraton; many were made to hold candle holders as well as whale oil lamps, which appeared in the period.

The Sheraton designs overlapped with the incoming Empire designs, and many transitional pieces incorporate features of both. Rope legs, acanthus leaf carving, and scroll backs are most often ascribed to Empire design, but these appear on otherwise identifiable Sheraton chests. Actually, the designs were used as late as 1840–1850, when in New York State, Pennsylvania, and Ohio, cabinetmakers refused to work with the fancier legs and decorations

Decorated Pennsylvania blanket chest with drawers, second quarter of the nineteenth century. Often these are called dower chests. The bird's-eye maple veneered drawers and floral painting enhance the value.

that had appeared as early as 1810 in the Empire style.

EMPIRE

By about 1810, a European influence of design was felt in America. Cabinet-

Arrowback-thumbback armchair, second quarter of the nineteenth century. The flattened spindles distinguish this from the plain thumbback form.

makers had been content to work with English styles to the end of the century and beyond, but gradually they entered into the early nineteenth-century period, which is called "Empire." A variety of leg styles appeared—the curved curule of the Roman magistrate chairs; animal dolphin and fish legs, inspired by the Egyptians; rope, twist, and carved legs; outswept legs with brass paw feet; and other variations. This is the last period with distinctive feet; furniture from later periods is not nearly as easily identifiable by its feet. Leaf and fruit carving became popular. The scimitar or sabre leg, patterned after the Roman swords, is a design used to this day. Though some very graceful pieces were made in the Empire period, the earlier gave way to some rather horrible ideas such as the scroll leg or elephant trunk style. This plagued the upper sections as well as the bases, on pieces that otherwise are good in design. It was during the Empire period that the machine age set in so that less handwork was required. Good taste and design seem to have gone out the window. During this and the later Victorian period there was much carving, but most of it was done by machine.

Prior to our Revolution, our furniture was inspired by the tastes and styles of our mother country, England, and it was not until after our separation that we began to develop our own tastes. After 1800, American tastes leaned strongly toward the French. France and America entered into trade, to the discomfort of the English and soon our seaports were deluged with the latest fashions from France. New York became a leader in the furniture revolution, and soon the best of the French Empire or Directoire styles were being copied here. Decorations in carving featured the acanthus leaf, pineapples, animal and bird feet, flowers, lyres, cornucopia, and scrolls. Heavy cornices and moldings were prominent. This is a rather enigmatic period since some good furniture was created, as well as some that was outright monstrous. In the early part of the period, which extended from about 1810 to 1830, furniture

Characteristics of Empire

The style is an amalgamation of Greek, Egyptian, and Chinese motifs along with the inspiration of the French who put it all together. English furniture was inspired by cabinetmakers in Europe, notably France, during the eighteenth century. Excavations in Greece and Egypt unearthed styles which were immediately copied.

The sabre and reeded legs of the chairs and the dolphin feet of the table are marks of the period. The S shape found on the dolphins as well as the footstool are marks of the period. At the time, much furniture was made in mahogany and rosewood, but was then painted and gilded to reflect the esoteric tastes of the very wealthy. Brass inlay replaced the bronze doré mounts which decorated earlier eighteenth-century work. The dolphin was a favored decorative device, but one can find crocodiles as well, since they were a symbol of the Nile and were very evident during the British occupation there. Rope carvings were symbolic in this maritime nation. The oval mirror virtually disappeared in this period to be replaced by square and rectangular examples. The outswept curved legs which we identify as Duncan Phyfe style in this country, still appears on much reproduction furniture made today. Here, we call it Empire; in England it is Regency.

Pair of caned Empire side chairs, unknown maker, Philadelphia, c. 1825–1830. Black ash, poplar, and pine. (Gift of Marie Josephine Royet and Rebecca Madeville R. Hunt. Philadelphia Museum of Art.)

Chests with corner columns and large overhanging top drawer indicate the Empire period. Cherry with bird's-eye maple drawer fronts, pressed glass pulls. New York State. The small chest at left features scroll feet, also of the period.

Fine and rare pair of Regency carved and gilded beech armchairs, c. 1815. Sold for $46,750, Nov. 5, 1990 (Butterfield & Butterfield.)

Secretary by Isaac Miles and Joel Livingston Lyons, Greenfield, Massachusetts, c. 1845–1855. This is the first labeled work by these makers. Mahogany, mahogany veneer, butternut, yellow poplar, and eastern white pine. (Museum purchase with funds provided by Dr. and Mrs. Michael W. Swanson. Courtesy Historic Deerfield, Inc., Deerfield, Massachusetts.)

with tasteful proportions and decoration was made by such artisans as Duncan Phyfe and Henri Lannuier in New York and Anthony Quervelle and Henry Connelly in Philadelphia. When machines came into general use, about 1830, the art of hand-craftsmanship began to die out, and with it the true lines of beauty in furniture. The Empire styles that came after began to show the effects of poor design and construction, and by the time the Victorian designs achieved a foothold, the look of fine furniture had all but disappeared.

During the Empire period, mahogany was most favored as a wood. When it was not available, country workmen would often veneer simple pine with mahogany to create a more expensive look. Four-poster beds were quite popular. Some were made

with a simple tester frame on which a skirt would be hung, while some were made with the full canopy. The poorer people settled for high legged beds made with posts as much as four or five feet from the floor, and those which featured pineapple or cannonball carvings at the tops were popular. The tall posts were often reeded in Sheraton style, and acanthus leaf carving was used to beautify them. You may see canopy topped beds with reeded posts at the foot and tapered posts at the head—this is perfectly all right, as reeded posts were difficult to make, and the artisans possibly felt the head posts were pretty much out of sight anyway. Sleigh beds made their appearance, and set the stage for the look of future beds. Until the appearance of the Hollywood style bed in this

Bookcase/secretary, mahogany, Anthony Quervelle, Philadelphia, 1825. Though it features many Empire design motifs, one can find several Revival motifs. (Philadelphia Museum of Art. Photograph by A. J. Wyatt.)

New York State chest, cherry, bird's-eye maple veneer; secondary wood is pine. Claw feet indicate c. 1830–1840; pressed glass drawer pulls. Chests with large drawers at the top are not a form made in New England, but appear in New York State, Pennsylvania, New Jersey, and other states.

century, most beds were very conventional, with a headboard, footboard and spring and mattress of some kind. Rope springing beneath the mattresses gave way to coil springs and flat springs at about the time of the Civil War. A man by the name of Samuel Pratt is credited with inventing coil springs for furniture in the 1820s, but they did not seem to make their appearance as bed springs until the aforementioned time. At least we know that furniture upholstered with springs did not come before the 1820s. Attribution as to the age of chairs and sofas can often be based on this, unless there is evidence that springs were added later.

Horsehair as an upholstery material came into full use, though it is known that

Thomas Shearer featured it in the third quarter of the eighteenth century. The fetish for putting animal paws and bird feet on chairs, sofas, and cased pieces has never been explained. Some approximated the grotesque and in later years—in fact right up until the 1950s—many pieces were thrown into dumps and otherwise disposed of. Renowned cabinetmakers like John and Thomas Seymour, who worked in Boston during the Federal Period (1770–1830), left some elegant works of construction for us to marvel at today, but some of these have animal feet which detract from the aesthetics of the whole piece.

Victorian

Queen Victoria was a buxom woman and some feel that her ascent to the throne prompted the massive furniture that appeared at about the same time, 1840. Some designers reverted to the styles of Chippendale and the cabriole leg with ball and talon foot made a dramatic return. Others were plainer in concept, but carving,

Victorian dressing stand with marble top and mirror. Vintage, c. 1840–1870

mostly done by machine, became the favored decoration. Decorative veneering and inlay all but disappeared. The machines made mass production possible and reduced the output for fine handcrafted furniture to a few scattered shops throughout the country. However, away from the cities, good furniture of this period was still made by the country cabinetmakers who could not afford machinery, or would not bother to use it. Such pieces may show evidence of good handwork and may be prized accordingly.

There was much delicate Victorian furniture, and much that was heavy and cumbersome. You must judge it on the merit of quality as outlined in the Introduction. However, a problem exists so far as age is concerned. As this styling extended for such a long period and has been reproduced so much in this century, you cannot always be sure in judging age. This

merely underscores the problem of collecting machine-made items which may be reproduced at will. Several large furniture companies in the 1920s and 1930s did nothing but make fine reproductions of Empire and Victorian styles, and many of these pieces are now touted as 125-year-old originals based solely on the fact that someone's grandmother owned them.

This was a period popular for its marble-topped pieces and you should insist on pure white American marble as opposed to the often used colored marbles from overseas. Mahogany and walnut were the most popular woods, but some rosewood has appeared on American pieces. Secondary woods were pine, ash, poplar, chestnut, and elm. Much elm wood was used than is generally realized, as it was an inferior wood for burning, and could not be relied on for surface construction of any furniture. However, once dried properly, it was strong and fairly stable. If elm is used on a surface, and exposed to the elements of heat and cold, it is prone to split. Leg styles reverted back to the late seventeenth and mid-eighteenth centuries, reviving the heavy ball and cabriole leg with various styles of feet. The graceful sweep of the Louis XV leg of the mid-eighteenth century is very evident. Rounded forms were

Victorian recamier with carving and cabriole legs, c. 1840–1870

used on chair backs and carvings of grapes, flowers, swags, and even rococo motifs were used for adornment.

The increased affluence of the populace in the growing industrial complex brought the need for more closet space in which to hang clothing. Since such space was at a premium in older houses, the wardrobe experienced a great revival. The Dutch and Germans had been making their *kas* and *schrank*, the French, their armoires, since coming to this country and settling outside the New England area. The Northeast had few counterparts of these until the Victorian period. The well chest became popular, with raised small drawers offsetting the larger ones. Mirrors became a part of almost every bureau. Dark stains which hid the beautiful wood graining, were the rule, as some felt it would make the massive pieces look smaller.

While fine furniture was being made for the well-to-do, there was a lower quality being turned out for the masses. Little has

Pine dry sink, mid-nineteenth century, of the type that was found in most country homes of the period. Most often, the sink area was lined with zinc. The hand pump would be mounted on a fixed cabinet at the right, with the spout over the sink section.

been written about the pieces then being made for the industrial worker, whose funds were limited. To lump this furniture together with Victorian-style antiques is not wholly appropriate. At least one historian, years ago, suggested classifying the entire Empire and Victorian periods into an American theme, calling it American Home. However, others had grouped the

Hutch or chair-table, mid-nineteenth century, pine. This was a space saver in a small home—the top tilts out of the way and the table can be used as a seat.

Pennsylvania pie cupboard, pine and punched tin, nineteenth century. The decoration on the tin helps set the value.

Hepplewhite, Sheraton, and Empire periods together as the Federal period, and this is generally accepted today. This encompasses the work between about 1770 and 1830, when the machines began to take over.

The reasons are many. It is not easy to classify this pine furniture—bedroom sets, drop-leaf tables, kitchen chairs and benches—as Victorian. Can we honestly identify sleigh beds and rockers, Morris chairs, and platform rockers with the basic Victorian furniture? There were many oddities created, such as beds which dropped out of phony chests of drawers and even a set of shelves on an iron frame which could be swung parallel to each other to form a table top. There were shapes in chairs and settees not found in Europe; such as arrowbacks and Hitchcocks and the Shaker style, created by the well-known religious sect. Painting and

This is a help in dating chests of drawers. To replace the hand dovetailing of earlier years, a machine was invented in Fitchburg, Massachusetts, in 1865 to make this scallop and dowel method of joining drawer fronts to the sides. All furniture with this detail must be dated after 1865.

Revival marble-top table, attributed to Joseph Meeks, New York City, c. 1850. The carving reflects the artistry of this noted concern.

stenciling furniture were quite popular, and often one will see a bedroom set decorated with the scenes at a farm, where an itinerant painter might take lodging in return for his work. Is this a technique which can be ascribed to those who did honor to Queen Victoria? The last of the monarchs to lend a royal name to a period style cannot be credited with (or blamed for) all that was done then.

In short, I feel that the era from 1830–1890 could be designated the American Home Period, leaving the more classic designations to those who enjoy them overseas.

Renaissance Revival

As early as the middle of the nineteenth century, there had been a revolt against the massive Victorian designs. Cabinetmakers such as John Belter, Joseph Meeks, and the Herter brothers in New York City stimulated a revival in earlier forms, notably those of the renaissance period. Meeks and Belter changed more slowly, being content to work at first with the rounded forms, but highlighting them with graceful design and carving. Belter pioneered the use of laminated wood—what we call plywood today. Backs of chairs and settees were steamed and bent under pressure. While in the proper curve, they were carved, which in turn released the pressure of the wood fibers to attempt to straighten themselves. None has gone out of shape since then. One may examine such fancy chairs to see if the laminations are visible at the edges of the backs.

The Herter brothers and others worked toward the end of the century in

American Renaissance inlaid maple and rosewood tall chest of drawers made by the Herter brothers of New York, 1872. Sold for $20,900, June 17, 1991, by Butterfield & Butterfield, San Francisco. (Butterfield & Butterfield.)

Carved side chair, John Henry Belter, New York City, c. 1840–1850. The back is of laminated wood, which is evident upon examination of the edges.

the Renaissance Revival forms. It was not until 1972 that the public became much aware of the furniture made during the period 1870–1890. Charles Eastlake had refined the Gothic Renaissance Revival forms into furniture which would fit into the average home. Jonathan Fairbanks, curator of the American Decorative Arts at the Museum of Fine Arts in Boston, staged an exhibition of pieces designed by two noted architects, Henry Hobson Richardson and Frank Furness. He suggested the use of the term "Eastlake" to denote the furniture of the period, setting it aside from the term "late Victorian" which had been used until then.

EASTLAKE

The period between about 1870 and 1890 must be assigned to the influence of Charles Eastlake of England. His *Hints on Household Taste*, published in 1868, refined the Gothic Renaissance Revival forms into usable household furniture for the average person. The Eastlake style was characterized by decorative panels and carving, both by hand and by machine. Rounded forms were out and the architectural Gothic

The architectural quality of the base of this walnut table and the intaglio carving mark it as Eastlake. This may have been part of a bedroom set made in the same style.

The cylinder desk in walnut made its appearance c. 1870–1890. The original form appeared late in the eighteenth century, but was revived by Charles Eastlake in his book Hints on Household Taste.

styling was in. Some of the designs approached the grostesque, which held back appreciation of them for years.

Actually, the Gothic Renaissance Revival style was a revival of Gothic, Italianate, and ancient Greek and Roman forms. Some suggest it was a wedding of Gothic and Jacobean styles of the sixteenth and seventeenth centuries. Walnut became the favored wood. Mahogany, cherry, oak, and pine were used as well during the period. Furniture is characterized by its architectural look. Factories in Michigan, New York, and the South began making poor man's Eastlake and, until recently, this has been regarded as the bottom in design, compared to all the periods.

Other identifying features are the tear-drop pull, which reappeared after an absence of about 200 years (it had last been seen during the William and Mary period) and carved "acorn" pulls. Also, bureau drawers grooved horizontally, most often

"Texas highboy," Eastlake style, c. 1870–1890. Made of walnut, it features the locking corner post, which is hinged. When closed and locked at one point, none of the drawers can be opened.

in oak, are a mark of the period. However, one cannot identify Eastlake from leg design, as all types were used.

One of the most interesting pieces made in the Eastlake period is the "Texas highboy," so called, because it was made of walnut, one wood the termites in the Lone Star State did not like.

I have seen these highboys with six and seven drawers, with a corner post attached to a piano hinge. There is one keyhole in this post. When it is closed against the drawers, all can be locked from this single point. In the 1950s, most sold for five to ten dollars apiece. They are well into three figures now. They are much in demand everywhere, as they offer a lot of drawer room in such little floor space. The bracket-based five- and six-drawer chests of the late eighteenth century have risen so much in price, buyers are settling for the walnut version. Most are decorated with

burl walnut panels in lighter woods, almost the color of bird's-eye maple, though some maple was used to decorate the interior of desks.

Many of the pine sets from this period were decorated at the factory. This decoration will heighten value if well done and in good condition. Out in the country, some pieces can be found which were decorated by itinerant artists or even by an artistic member of the family. I have seen some with scenes of buildings on the farm along with trees, flowers, and animals. These must be treated with the same care as oil paintings. They can be restored by a good artist if there is not too much deterioration.

Wooten Desks—The Wooten is called the "King of Desks" by none other than Eileen Dubrow, who is known as the country's foremost collector of them. Having a close association with Wells Fargo, as one was in each office, they have been spread all over

Eastlake lady's desk, c. 1870–1890. The burled walnut panel on the drop lid and the acorn pulls and walnut case are marks of the period.

the country since they were made in the 1880s. The form is Gothic Revival, which translated to simpler terms is Eastlake, as his design features appear on them. Most were made of walnut, and often inside drawers were veneered with maple as well as burl walnut. An interesting note is that Wells Fargo is known to have marked all its possessions in all its offices, yet no Wooten desk has yet turned up so identified.

Wooten desks were made in Indianapolis. The first patent was issued October 6, 1874, and by 1875, the company was in full production. Businesspeople as well as presidents were among the first customers. The desks were made in three grades—standard, extra grade, and superior. The latter featured exquisite carving. Hardware was of Berlin bronze.

Some of the Wootens were built with cylinder tops; these came in twelve styles. In 1877, Joseph Moore, former Wooten

Wooten desks are in the Gothic Renaissance Revival design, refined in household furniture by Charles Eastlake of England. Most of these desks were made in the 1880s in the heart of the period.

Very ornate in its Eastlake design case is this pump organ of the 1870–1890 period. The inexpensive electric organs have diminished interest in them.

manager, obtained rights to make the desk, and also in the same year, Henry Wiggers of Philadelphia patented a desk closely allied to the Wooten. One of these is in the Heinz House at the Henry Ford Museum. The desks were last advertised in 1885, with the company going out of business. Some say the walnut trees needed to make them were disappearing, but history tells us there was a great recession in the mid-1880s—perhaps this is more the reason. Wooten desks have turned up in England, as well as in barns out on old country farms, all covered up.

Mission

About 1890, the oak period began, lasting until about 1930. It was inspired by the simple, straight-lined furniture found in the Spanish missions on the West Coast and in Mexico. Made on square lines, the pieces are rugged indeed. Many town halls and other public buildings are still outfitted with Mission chairs, desks, and tables, since they are functional and nearly indestructible. Most of the pieces would not win any beauty awards, but the clean lines are reminiscent of the comfortable Hepplewhite, which is enduring in quality.

The oak period began about 1890 and lasted until about 1930. This huge carved oak sideboard sold at auction in 1969 for only $350.

The most conventional furniture for the home was made in this period. The round oak table, pressed back chairs, side-by-side cupboard/desk combinations; Hoosier cabinets; entire bedroom sets, ice boxes and sliding door bookcases were in disfavor until the early 1970s. Then, the values of furniture from the previous periods had risen dramatically. Those who wanted to outfit their homes with nostalgic pieces from the past began to take an interest in oak.

Later, attention was directed to the arts and crafts production which had been limited to but a few makers. The names Gustav and L & JG Stickley of Fayetteville, New York, Limbert in Michigan, and the Roycrofters in East Aurora, New York, began to assume importance as collectors recognized the superior design and craftsmanship. Since then, many books have been written, analyzing the good, better,

Carved oak table, four chairs, claw feet. Custom oak furniture of this type is much in demand today.

Early in the twentieth century, the Arts and Crafts movement became a reality. This Stickley-style sideboard is an example of the high style of the period.

and best of oak furniture, and these serve as good guides to buyers.

One must pay attention to labels and marks to determine maker. Gustav Stickley not only made furniture, but published *The Craftsman* magazine in which he detailed the measurements of lumber and offered to sell fittings, pulls, textiles, and other parts and pieces so his furniture could be copied exactly, at home. He indicated in his own writing that each piece of his furniture bears a shopmark, which is a pair of joiners' compasses enclosing the motto "ALS IK KAN," along with the written signature, Stickley, within quotation marks. The original name of the community in which he did his work was Eastwood, New York. Further, he stated that he had no connection with any other factory, to dispell any thoughts that his brothers Leopold and J. George were part of his concern.

Early in this century, Elbert Hubbard assembled craftspeople who worked in furniture, pottery, lamps, ceramics, and metals, making some of the most desired pieces

of that period. The factory went out of business in 1940, but has been revived as the Roycrofters at Large Association in East Aurora, New York. The early Roycrofters furniture is well marked, either by carving on the wood or by a diamond-shaped bronze plate—an R within a circle, topped by a double cross. Mission-style oak was the mainstay of the business, but under Mr. Hubbard's direction, new ground was broken in designs which contributed to the direction of the Art Nouveau and Art Deco periods. Hubbard was a philosopher and his wife, Alice, fought zealously for women's rights. In their memory, the Elbert Hubbard Foundation was formed and the original "campus" which the Roycrofters inhabited is alive again. The location has been placed on the National Registry of Historic Places. One should note the new Roycroft mark features R's back to back. Hubbard is known to have developed the Larkin Club, where he worked before going out on his own. On May 7, 1915, the press announced that the Lusitania had

Common oak furniture was mass produced in many states. This side-by-side is of the type manufactured by the Larkin Company in Buffalo, New York, to be given as premiums for the purchase of Larkin Soap. This is quite a nice example with curved glass door, carving on the legs and top rail, and beveled plate glass mirror.

collected today came from the Larkin factory in Buffalo.

The pieces were marked with a paper label, many of which, unfortunately, have come off because of improper care. After World War II, the furniture made its way to cottages, cellars, and chicken coops, as well as the dump. Oak was not in favor. However, with the renewed interest since 1970, the Larkin pieces are considered very desirable today. Copies of the catalog reveal that a round oak table could be had for sixteen soap wrappers. The other premiums are astounding when considered against today's prices.

There is English oak in this country as well. One designer, who is quite well known, was William Morris. An artist and

been sunk by a German submarine. Hubbard was on it.

One cannot talk about oak without mentioning the Larkin Soap Manufacturing Company. It began operations in 1875, marketing soap, then eventually branching out into other products. One could exchange soap wrappers for premiums, which included furniture, lamps, rugs, curtains, silverware, linens, and china. The Buffalo Pottery Company was organized in 1901 and began firing in 1903, making pottery items to be used as premiums for the soap wrappers. The furniture work extended into the 1920s, and much of what is

Pressed back oak rocker. The design was imbedded in the wood, which was first soaked, then stamped with the design.

writer from a wealthy family, he was born in 1834 and died in 1896. Morris was interested in design and in 1857 opened a studio with several partners. Here they designed stained glass, tiles, tableware, textiles, and furniture. This work was the forerunner of the arts and crafts movement. Morris was a contemporary of Charles Eastlake and was influenced by the revival forms popular at the time. The Morris chair is named for him, as he designed it. The favored wood was oak, though mahogany and other hardwoods were used on both sides of the Atlantic. Morris perceived furniture that was suitable as well as functional—well designed, in a way that could be mass produced. The name "Morris" is generic now. None will be found with his name, as his studio only designed them; others did the manufacturing.

Art Nouveau

Late in the nineteenth century there was a growing interest in designs from the Orient. Trade with Japan brought new ideas in forms and decorations and the Europeans were the first to incorporate them in their decorative arts. Even the entrances to buildings captured the spirit of what was soon to be called the Art Nouveau style. Flowing lines, floral decoration, and a sculptured look became the rage with architects as well as with decorators and artisans.

Louis Comfort Tiffany studied in Paris and returned to create some of the best pieces in this period. One could list the names of many lesser-known designers but their work is not as well recorded, making identification of the artist almost impossible. During this period, the arts and crafts movement flourished, creating much which is high on the collecting list, today. These designs persisted until the 1920s, when new ideas originated after World War I.

Twentieth-century Art Nouveau chair by Friedrich Adler, Munich. (Philadelphia Museum of Art.)

Art Deco

In 1926, an exhibition was staged in Paris, titled, Arts Decoratif, which introduced new forms into the art world. Nudes appeared in bronze, glass, ceramics, and wood. Photography came into its own during this period and those who typified the "flapper" era have left a profound record of clothing, artifacts, furniture, and decorative objects which exhibited free flowing forms and great nuances in color. Walnut waterfall furniture was in vogue and blonde oak was soon to follow. The years 1920–1950 are designated as the deco period, which was phased out after World War II in favor of much experimentation in design which has yet to be labeled.

Other Styles and Influences

Shaker

To broaden our knowledge of the Shakers, whose industry helped create many artifacts that are high on the collectible list today, we must recall the movement started here late in the eighteenth century when Ann Lee left England with a band of followers and founded the first colony at Mt. Lebanon, New York. A celibate sect, it grew nevertheless, and locations for colonies extended all through New England and as far away as Kentucky. The Shakers supported themselves as food and herb growers, and also by the manufacture of furniture and other household items. Their furniture is light and delicate, yet very strong. The lines are simple with no ornament, and in this simplicity project

Shaker furniture is appreciated for its simplicity and function. Very desirable is this chest with six graduated drawers which came from the Enfield, Connecticut, colony. Nineteenth century.

great beauty. They worked with the woods at hand, and created pieces like chairs, cupboards, desks for the Eldresses, tables of all kinds, and just about everything which was made of wood. Their buildings, which still stand today in some places, were designed with strength and durability in mind. They can be found in their original state at Canterbury and Enfield, New Hampshire; Sabbathday Lake, Maine; Hancock, Massachusetts; Chatham, New York; and Pleasant Hill, Kentucky. Most of the groups sold off their material possessions as their numbers dwindled and during the Depression. Shaker furniture is high on the desired list today, not only with private collectors, but with those who are busy restoring Shaker buildings to their original look. The largest colony is in Canterbury, where twenty-seven buildings have been preserved by a foundation set up for this purpose.

At a seminar in Canterbury, New Hampshire in 1991, June Sprigg, curator of Hancock Shaker Village, gave much insight on Shaker artifacts. According to Ms. Sprigg, there were never more than 6,000 Shakers in the movement in this country, in villages stretching from Maine to Kentucky. Thus, if they made everything attributed to them, none would have ever slept. Some oval boxes made as recently as 1987 have been doctored with red paint and aged. Reproduction Shaker seed packets are being made, wrinkled and aged to fool most anyone. Baskets are altered with Shaker style handles.

A popular item is the Shaker oval box. The walls are a single piece of thin wood, bent and joined with overlapping "fingers" which are nailed (most often with copper nails) to fasten them. Some feel the fingers should point only to the right, but it was affirmed they could point in either direction. Iron nails were used early in the nineteenth century; the copper nails came later. It is possible there are some cribs and cra-

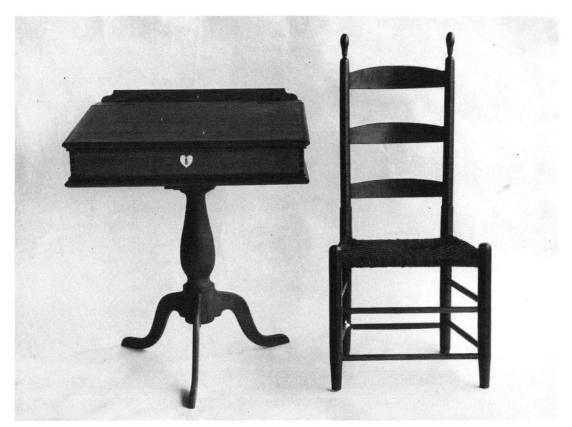

Rare Shaker writing desk and ladderback chair, nineteenth century, Enfield, Connecticut colony.

Shaker shawl-back rocker. Canterbury, New Hampshire, colony, nineteenth century. This form is native only to the Shakers.

dles, despite the Shaker vow of chastity, as they often took in young children to raise them.

There are no Shaker decoys, card tables or game boards. They did not decorate buckets. Samplers with birds or crowns are not theirs. Double beds were made until the 1830s but not after that. The Brother Gregory rockers with ten spindles are being reproduced. Practically all Shaker ladderback chairs have inclined backs.

Moravian

Anyone who has visited Bethlehem, Pennsylvania, marvels at the early stone architecture; some of it dating back to 1741. Buildings here and in nearby Nazareth marked the founding of the Moravian colonies in the new world. Later, this religious group expanded its missionary work to

Winston-Salem, North Carolina and into Ohio.

The history of the Moravians goes back to the fifteenth century when an independent religious community was set up under the guidance of Johan Hus in Germany. August 13, 1727 is celebrated as the foundation day of the renewed community at Herrnhut, not far from Dresden. The oppression of religious groups prompted many to migrate to the American colonies.

In Bethlehem, the Kemerer Museum has many items attributed to the Moravians. As with most furniture items made by religious groups, the designs are quite austere. There are not many clues to determine provenance as many other religious groups who settled in Pennsylvania made similar pieces.

Bethlehem is the home of the Moravian Archives, a place where one can research and study the history of this movement. The cemetery is revealing; the stone markers lie on the ground and reveal that anyone, including blacks, were welcome as members. Some are identified as such on the stones, evidencing the all-encompassing work of the Moravian brotherhood. Moravian antiques are not plentiful, but one can study their form and proportions at the Kemerer. It is well worth a visit.

One may visit a settlement overseas at Christianfield, Denmark. The architecture is much like that in Bethlehem and many artifacts made by the Moravians are displayed. It is preserved as a national historic landmark.

Biedermeier

When a piece of nineteenth-century furniture sells for $154,000, a lot of interest is aroused as to what it is and why it brought so much money. In this case, at the November 21, 1984 Butterfield & Butterfield auction, a rather heavy "Biedermeier-style" secretary realized the highest price ever received for something not commonly found in America. Most know little about this Continental style, which was popular

Unusual Biedermeier ormolu-mounted and parcel-ebonized inlaid walnut secretaire à abattant, c. 1815–1820, Austria. Lyre-shaped form with molded rectangular cornice, well carved with stylized leaves. Sold Nov. 21, 1984, for $154,000. (Butterfield & Butterfield.)

during the first half of the nineteenth century in Germany and Austria. The term "Biedermeier" actually originated from a popular cartoon character who came to symbolize the German bourgeoisie of that period. Eventually, the term was applied both to the period in general and to the period's social, political, and decorative style.

The Biedermeier design was adapted from French Empire style, but is characterized by a less formal simplicity. The pieces are smaller in scale, made of light-colored indigenous woods; surface ornament such as ormolu mounts were used sparingly. One of the reasons this secretary brought such an extraordinary price is that it broke all of these rules. Its architectural style and walnut wood are unique. Although the piece was identified as Austrian, some Austrian museum curators suggested it is not Viennese, but provincial. Inlaid with a coat of arms of a baron, it was probably commissioned by a newly enobled baron, explaining its opulence of scale, ornament, and design.

One will find Biedermeier furniture in this country, but it is not plentiful. The best places to look are where the Germans settled: New York State, Pennsylvania, Ohio, and the Carolinas. I have seen some in Denver and on the West Coast.

Zoar

In 1817, a group of separatists from the Lutheran Church in Germany, came to America and eventually created Zoar Village in Ohio. The group was active until 1898. Since this was a river town, those who stopped there on ferries and freight launches became customers for the furniture, pottery, and other artifacts made in the community. Zoar furniture is quite rigid and stiff in appearance and is rugged. Unlike the Shakers who developed their own designs, the Zoars, along with other religious sects, generally made furniture in the style of the day, not bothering to beautify it with marquetry or carvings.

The community is being restored today and more is being learned about what was made there. There is a limited amount of furniture that can now be documented, so you may never know if you possess a Zoar piece unless you do your homework. There are pieces at the Cleveland Museum of Art, where a booklet is available on the history of this sect.

Wallace Nutting

Few people involved in antiques and collecting do not know the name of Wallace Nutting. A Congregationalist minister, he began collecting American furniture and

Wallace Nutting is responsible for very good reproductions of period furniture. This is one of a pair of beds custom made to match the Windsor chairs in a bedroom in Massachusetts.

decorative arts as early as 1905. His first book, *Furniture Treasury*, published in 1928, is well illustrated and shows a wide range of what to collect. It is still available in bookstores, which testifies to its value as a guide to collectors.

In later years, Nutting acquired the Wentworth-Gardner House in Portsmouth, New Hampshire, and used it as a showroom in which to sell antiques to museums and other serious buyers. This led to further acquisitions, such as the Saugus Ironworks in Saugus, Massachusetts, and the Webb House in Wethersfield, Connecticut, both of which have since been fully restored and opened to the public.

In 1917, Nutting began making reproduction furniture, and it is said that he lost a fortune in the venture. However, many of his pieces are turning up today and are highly sought, though none is much more than 60 years of age—dispelling the notion that something must be old to be good. I have seen what I feel is a rarity in Nutting furniture, a marked pair of beds made to resemble the backs of Windsor chairs. These were done on special order for someone who wanted to have them match the other Windsor-style furniture in a room. The beds are in a home in Holyoke, Massachusetts.

Nutting is best known to some collectors for the color photographic prints that bear his name. They give us a look at life as it was, and are still as decorative today as when they were issued. The Wadsworth Atheneum in Hartford has a permanent installation of Nutting's collection of early American furniture.

Centennial

During the third quarter of the last century, there was a revival of interest in the styles prevalent during the Revolutionary period almost a hundred years before. Fine reproductions were made of period styles popular then, using the same woods and same types of veneers and inlays. Another revival took place during the 1920s and 1930s, and the work was so good that anyone but an expert can be easily fooled. Old handmade drawers were often taken from undesirable Empire style chests and incorporated into good period frames made from old wood. Appraisers long ago labeled such work "Centennial," and the name is in general use today. Many a poor chest or desk was altered with a new base, frame, legs, or feet, and was completely restyled to make it more desirable. Unscrupulous dealers have passed these on without saying too much about them—in one estate appraisal in Boston, eleven of the twelve cased pieces of furniture were Centennial, yet they were bought as antique. There must be some dealers who genuinely do not know that they are handling a reproduction, so they cannot be accused of misdealing. Actually, in many cases the furniture is just as finely made as its predecessors and should be regarded as fine work. It should not command the same value, but you should not ignore it as it represents that which was classic in form and work. There are Centennial collectors who want nothing else, and they must confine their buying to the Boston and Philadelphia

areas since this is where most of this work was done. What our Bicentennial has produced to match it is anybody's conjecture. The rule in buying is to look for as much handwork as possible, and to buy only quality in taste, design, and construction.

Twentieth Century Furniture

Not much can be said for the styling of furniture during the late twentieth century. America's burgeoning population gave growth to mass production, which inundated us with very mediocre pieces, and supply seemed much more important than quality. The walnut waterfall, blonde oak, and gray oak became the hallmark for those who wished to be modern. The era spawned a host of factories which brought back "colonial" designs in maple and birch, but the reproductions left a lot to be desired as the workmanship was not good and the wood colorings ranged from red to very light blonde. Quality furniture has always been made, but buyers have always been limited because of cost. Concerns such as Paine in Boston and Mayfair in Albany continued to turn out impeccable pieces, and their work is gathering a lot of attention today from those who regard it as classic in the same manner as you would assess a classic car, boat, or airplane. Private cabinetmakers have always been at work, and from time to time these individual pieces turn up to please their new owners. Those which are labeled are a prize, and if you should locate some of these, attempt to document their history if at all possible, while information might still be available. These pieces may be classics in museums someday, and such documentation will be very important.

It is not likely that there will be a return to the golden age of anything, as quick sale and profit seem to be the motivating force in our economy. Handcrafted furniture will always be with us and there is great interest in it today, but we can never hope to enjoy it on the scale it reached before 1830. You must live with your nostalgia if nothing more.

Areas of Collecting Interest

Chairs

BRANCH

There is no question that many years ago, crude chairs were made with available materials. One of the most interesting is a type of chair that was popular in the nineteenth and early twentieth centuries. Made of branches from which the bark has been peeled, it offered utility with very little comfort. Most had a simple handmade cushion to soften the bumps. Many of this type were made all across the country, though in the East they appeared most often in New York State. Some say branch chairs gave rise to what is known as the Adirondack chair. The mountainous areas of New York State were full of vacation hotels and homes for which local craftsmen created low-cost furniture.

The tradition for this design seems to have originated in central and eastern Europe, as far back as the sixteenth century. They appear in paintings and sketches of the period. Hardwoods, such as walnut, hickory, and, in this country, maple, seem to have been the favored woods. Oak does not bend well, so the makers did not use it.

When the West was settled in the last century, branch chairs, or twig chairs as some call them, made their appearance in abundance. There were no furniture factories out there, and what came in by railroad was too expensive for the average settler. Each is a unique piece as the design conforms to the wood used in the same way

Branch chair made by Clarence O. Nichols of Ossining, New York. (New York State Museum, Albany.)

that the shape of a stone wall depends on the shapes of the stones available. A chair like this is not overly valuable, but it is a good conversation piece. All should be saved as early examples of our culture.

WINDSOR

All through the eighteenth and nineteenth centuries, various types of country chairs appeared. Earliest of the type we can collect easily is the Windsor. According to one story, George III in England saw a spindle-back of this type in a farmhouse near his castle and became so enamored of its beauty that he commissioned many to be made for Windsor Castle. This is unlikely, as he did not ascend the throne until 1760 at the age of twenty-two. Historians tell us the Windsor chair form has been with us since about 1740 and well executed in both England and America. The Windsor is one of the most popular to collect today. Identified by its multi-spindled back, it comes in many forms and shapes, and it seems to have been adapted to just about every functional type of side chair or armchair known. The spindle-back chair is not original; counterparts have been identified in early Greek and Roman civilizations. That it was successfully revived in England is not disputed, but most feel it was brought to its fullest form in America. The rarities are the fancy writing armchairs which were made originally for use in classrooms and public buildings where political and public meetings were held.

Some call the bowback armchair a "sackback," but I have never found out why. Some of the best examples were made in Connecticut with knuckle arms and boldly turned legs.

The earliest American Windsors were of loopback, bowback, or what some call horseshoe back style, just a simple bowed structure. The straight line backs seem to be of later origin. They range from three spindles to as many as thirteen, which I saw on an English chair, and are valued accordingly. There is a basic rule that the greater

Bowback Windsor side chair, late eighteenth century. The more spindles, generally, the greater the value. Note the legs are doweled through the seat, then sheared off.

amount of handwork expended in making a piece, the greater the value, so those with more spindles are more expensive.

Some historians contend that Thomas Chippendale popularized the first straight crest rail top chair in the middle of the eighteenth century and since this is not disputed, we can assume that those with straight backs came after this time. The straight rail was popular in the seventeenth century in the Jacobean and William and Mary styles, but during the Queen Anne period (early eighteenth century) and into the Chippendale period, the rounded back was the accepted form.

A theory has been advanced that the Windsor chair actually originated in Windsor, Connecticut, in the seventeenth century and that the style was adopted in Britain. Some feel it was not fancy enough

Rare writing arm Windsor chair. These were used in classrooms and public buildings where meetings were held. Early nineteenth century.

Birdcage Windsor chairs on either side of a Sheraton dressing stand. All are early nineteenth century.

for the English home, but more suited to the colonies. Some feel they were the outgrowth of the Carver and Brewster chairs; the former feature spindles above the seat and the latter, spindles above and below.

The most popular type collected today is the birdcage Windsor, which features a series of squared spaces at the top. Spindles are doweled into the seat back and through the crest rail where they are sheared off. On the birdcage, another rail is installed beneath the top rail, several inches below. The spindles run through this rail as well, but are cut alternately to form the squared spaces. Some call these chairs pigeonhole or pigeon coop Windsors, but birdcage is the more accepted term. Windsor chairs with legs coming visibly through the seat plank are generally attributed to pre-1800; those with the ends of the legs hidden in the plank should be dated after 1800.

The most popular Windsor chair is the seven-spindle, but it appears with five to eleven spindles. The eighteenth-century forms feature widely splayed legs and H stretchers, whereas those after 1800 most

often have leg-to-leg stretchers. None has been found with button feet. Those with heavy bulbous turnings on the front round, with the large carved disc between—called the baluster turning—are not from New England, but rather show the Dutch influence in New York State and Pennsylvania. Any Windsor with a cabriole leg most likely comes from overseas. Early examples were constructed of durable oak, which gave way to pine plank seats and hardwood spindles and legs. These would be hickory, oak, ash, maple, or birch. Usually they were painted, but bringing them back to natural wood, if properly done, does not depreciate their value—that is, if they are nineteenth-century. If eighteenth-century, they should be examined to make sure refinishing does not destroy a good patina. Quite often, a chairmaker would use many different woods to use up stock in his shop, knowing all would be covered by paint anyway. Be prepared for surprises if several woods show up in the chair you refinish.

Another popular form is the step-down Windsor, whose crest rail is cut into a series of steps at the ends. These are not as valuable as the birdcage, but are found in many interesting varieties.

The desirable raised comb back is most often found in rockers.

The fan back is quite good—simple straight spindles fanned out to meet the crest rail. One with nine or eleven spindles is quite valuable.

Jelly Cupboards

Almost every nineteenth century home has a jelly cupboard, either in a breezeway or cellar. These were used for storing fruits and vegetables, which were canned on the premises to stretch the food budget. One old timer told me years ago that doors were put on them to prevent mice from building nests behind the jars. The doors were an assurance that when you reached in for a jar of jelly, you would not be greeted by a furry creature. Another told me that it was to keep the dust off the jars so they would look better when brought to the kitchen. I have never seen one with locks on the doors, so robbery seems not to have been a problem.

The most common wood is pine as this was plentiful all over the country, and this softer wood could be worked easily. Most workers liked wide boards so they could make solid sides and door panels. Farther south into New York State and Pennsylvania, as well as into the Carolinas, where walnut is plentiful, this seems to have been a favored wood. Jelly cupboards were made in cherry, birch, maple, chestnut, and oak. Sizes varied according to where they might be used, so there are no eagerly sought dimensions. Most were painted in the old red, blue, or green. If you can live with the original finish, it is best to keep them this way.

Some people converted their jelly cupboards into open-shelf hutches or pewter cupboards by removing the doors and scrolling the side boards. If you are buying an open-shelf hutch, make sure it is not a conversion.

Lacquered Furniture

When trade with the Orient began centuries ago, the Europeans brought back many decorated pieces of furniture as well as other decorative art objects. They found great favor on the Continent and in England, so it was only natural that this style was duplicated. Artisans were taught to beautify furniture in England in oriental design, but the wealthy wanted none of that. When furniture was ordered from an English cabinetmaker, quite often it would be sent by clipper ship to the Orient to be lacquered and gilded in this fashion. One might wait two years to end up with the piece in his home.

Here in this country, this was too much of a luxury, and the Orient was too far away. So in our seaport cities, japanners, as they were called, were trained to do such work locally. Today, this furniture is as highly prized as the oriental. Black japan lacquer was made from linseed oil, umber, asphaltum, and turpentine to thin

Very fine and rare Chinese red lacquer cupboard (sijianggui), Wanli Mark and Period. Sold for $99,000 by Butterfield & Butterfield. Photo courtesy of Butterfield & Butterfield.

it. The gilding was done with gold leaf or powder, then protected with a mordant varnish. Some refer to this type of decoration as chinoiserie. It became a favorite not only on furniture but on woodwork, silver, porcelain, pottery, wallpaper, cotton, linen, and other textiles as well.

Some historians believe that all Queen Anne furniture came painted, japanned, or decorated originally. Pieces that do not have this or other painted finish, in their opinion, have been refinished to the detriment of the piece.

Sliding-Door Bookcases

Very popular with the collecting set today is the sliding-door bookcase. Most were made in separate sections so that one could add them to create any height desired. The door lifts and slides to the rear over the books, making it self-storing and handy. One will find a drawer in the bottom section quite often, though many bookcases were made without them. Oak is the favored wood; most such cases were made between 1890 and 1930, when oak was very popular.

Oak fits in with the decor of many homes where this is the wood collected. Also, it is easy to move these cases, as each section lifts off. I have never seen one with locks, so one assumes that most books were not considered valuable enough to steal at the time. Most popular widths range between 36 and 42 inches. They were made by several companies, so it would be difficult to assign provenance if they are not labeled.

I have seen these bookcases in walnut and mahogany, but these do not have the value of oak. One will find them when law offices are sold out at auction, and they turn up in house auctions as well. Remember, though, that these are being reproduced today, in oak as well as other woods. Prices of new ones are about the same as the old, which means the value of the old ones should stabilize. Best advice is not to buy old or new for investment, but rather

for use, as reproductions generally diminish the value of the old. Many buyers prefer the new ones, which do not need to be refinished.

Spool Cabinets

Collectors seem to like any furniture which has a lot of drawers. They are put to use to hold collections or as storage chests that take up a minimum of space with maximum capacity. One of the favorites at auctions just about anyplace is the spool cabinet. The earliest seem to have made their appearance in the Eastlake period, c. 1870–1890, and were made extensively into the 1930s. Years ago, most communities had at least one dry goods store, which sold towels, sheets, and pillowcases along with yard goods, patterns, thread, and needles. The spool cabinet was a necessity as a storage and display piece of furniture. The earliest were made in walnut and oak and seemingly these woods continued to be the favorites. One will see them mahogany stained, but most likely less expensive woods were used underneath this coloring.

These cabinets range from the tabletop type to those that rest on the floor. The more drawers the better. Some spool cabinets from the Eastlake period feature acorn carved handles and teardrop pulls, while most feature knob pulls. I have seen them in wood, brass, and glass. Those with the original lithographed labels on the drawers and especially those in good condition will command more dollars.

If you purchase such a cabinet, it is best to leave it in original condition. Restoration might hurt its look and the interest in it if you ever wish to sell it.

Tea Wagons

The small table on wheels is called a tea wagon. Its history is not clear. We do know that tea drinking did not come into vogue until the seventeenth century, and most vessels, utensils, and furniture relating to it did not appear until then. The early tea table is small, often with a tilt top, and in many shapes and forms. None from our colonial period had wheels. The caster did not appear until the middle of the eighteenth century but was not used on most small utility tables. Casters were generally reserved for larger pieces, making them easier to move. The tea wagon seems to have appeared late in the nineteenth century, perhaps as late as the 1890s. No manuals on the preceding Eastlake and Victorian furniture picture them. Hence the term "antique" can be only loosely applied. Tea wagons are machine produced and have been made extensively right up until today. Most are in mahogany or walnut finish, though they can be made of almost any wood stained to resemble mahogany or walnut. Early in this century they could be found in almost any furniture store. Their popularity experienced a revival as the TV snack table during the early days of TV. This was nothing but a modern version of an older form. The dark colored woods disappeared, and the sleeker Scandinavian modern design took over.

Older tea wagons are judged by their style, wood, and condition. The fancier the better and true mahogany or walnut makes them more valuable. Wheels have narrow solid rubber tires and these must be in good shape. Some were painted and stenciled by owners over the years. Good decoration may enhance value.

Wicker

Wicker is a generic term, not a raw material, that includes wood, rattan, and manmade fibers. Very little is known about wicker furniture, though it is collected readily today. The earliest pieces, made as far back as the time of the early Egyptians, were made of rattan, and this material was used extensively into this century. New developments in the industrial age changed the way wicker and rattan furniture were made, so be aware of the different types and weaves when buying.

Late in the last century, it was felt that tightly-woven wicker furniture (known as Cape Cod style) was the best because it was stronger. A machine was invented to twist paper on wire into a cord which could be woven on yet another machine, developed by Marshall B. Lloyd in Michigan. Much of what is called wicker today is really this kind of tightly woven papier mâché. That is why knowledgeable buyers look for the open weave, sometimes called a Bar Harbor weave. Paper is not strong enough to be woven into an open design, so if you want rattan, look for the open weave. Naturally, the arms of a chair and other areas where reinforcement is needed will be tightly woven, whether the chair is made of rattan or paper. But if the nonstress areas, such as the back of a chair, are made in an open weave, you can feel safe that the chair is not made of paper. The Bar Harbor weave was used at first to cut down the cost of manufacturing wicker, but today it assures the material used, which is most important.

One danger in buying a paper wicker

Wicker with an open weave, called the "Bar Habor weave," is the best to buy. It is made of cane or rattan.

is that it cannot be dipped to remove paint. The paper will soften in the mixture, causing it to lose its strength. If you have tightly woven pieces, you can check to see if they are wood or paper by getting underneath and piercing with a knife blade. This is advisable before any restoration is undertaken.

Glossary

Acanthus—A plant native to southern Europe used as a motif in carving throughout civilized history. Very popular in French Empire style furniture.

Acorn—A turning based on the shape of the acorn.

Apron—A board which joins the understructure of cased furniture, tables, and chairs—often cut out for beautification.

Armoire—A cupboard for the storage of clothing.

Ball foot—A simple ball turning which was joined to the bottom of chests by a turned dowel.

Baluster—A turning, often done with bulbous swellings. Very popular in the late seventeenth and early eighteenth centuries.

Banding—A contrasting narrow stripping of veneer used for beautification. Popular during the Federal period, especially on drawer fronts.

Baroque—The Italian equivalent of French rococo, defining quite busy carvings and decoration.

Bombe—A chest or secretary base with a rounded bulging front and sides. Believed to have originated on American furniture in Boston.

Bun foot—A flattened ball with slender ankle above.

Cabriole—A shaped leg based on the cyma curve, with wide knees and narrow ankles terminating in various feet. Used extensively in the Queen Anne, Chippendale, and Victorian periods.

Caryatid—A carved human figure used as support for an upper pediment or shelf in furniture.

Court cupboard—Late seventeenth or early eighteenth century cased piece used for linens and dining areas.

Cyma curve—An S-shaped double curve.

Dentil molding—A series of carved rectangular blocks with spaces between. Often called hound's tooth molding if shaped to points.

Dutch foot—Often called a duck foot. A simple pad used on cabriole legs during the Queen Anne period.

Escritoire—A simple writing desk, with drawers, pigeonholes, secret drawers, and the like. The secretary was derived from this.

Escutcheon—A brass plate used for decoration or to surround openings such as a keyhole.

Fiddleback—A violin-shaped splat found as early as the time of Queen Anne, but revived during the Empire period.

Figured—Highly grained wood used in Marquetry.

Finial—A turned decorative device usually found atop cornices of high chests, or even as drops at the front lower section of highboys and lowboys.

Fluting—A channeled carving which is done in straight lines parallel to each other.

Fretwork—Ornamental work created by cutting and perforation.

Highboy—A tall chest of drawers, originally called a tallboy in England; usually standing on high legs and made in two sections.

Kas—A Dutch cabinet or sideboard painted with primitive figures.

Ladderback—A chair back with the cross splats arranged in ladder fashion.

Lunette—An ornamental design in half moon shapes. Often used in veneering in the Federal period.

Lyre—Design patterned after the instrument of that name. Popularized during the Empire period.

Marquetry—Decorations formed by inlaying various woods, shell, bone, or metals into a wood surface. This is often done in a thin wood veneer, which then is glued to the surface of the piece to be decorated. The rarer "intarsia" is veneering directly to the main surface.

Ogee—A shape made from two cyma curves with their convex sides meeting.

Patina—An aged surface.

Reeding—Convex grooves, carved parallel to each other.

Ribband—A reference to a carved or cutout "ribbon" chair back.

Rococo—From the French *rocaille*, literally meaning "a pile of rocks." Carved ornamentation full of curves and other fancy carving motifs.

Schrank—A German cabinet or sideboard painted with primitive figures.

Serpentine—A serpentine curve used on the fronts of furniture.

Spindle—A turned round such as that used on chair backs and frames.

Splat—The central figure in a chair back.

Stretcher—An underbracing beneath case pieces, chairs, and tables, with reinforcement joined leg to leg.

Swag—A carving of leaves, draperies, or flowers.

Tester—The frame of a high four post bed, to which a decorative skirt is attached at the top.

Veneer—A thin ornamental wood with desirable graining which is glued to a surface of lesser wood.

CHAPTER TWO

Glass

Introduction

Historical Overview

Glass reputedly originated on the shores of the Mediterranean when a group of Phoenician sailors built a fire to cook their evening meal. In the morning they found that the hot coals and flames had melted the sand beneath and this had hardened it into a crude form of glass. There must have been a quantity of soda mixed with the sand, since soda is necessary as a flux to form the melted silica. Since that time various minerals and elements have been mixed with silica to produce different types of glass, each with its own peculiar qualities. Lime, ashes, lead, and even gold have been used to produce glass ranging from the inexpensive to the exotic. Little is recorded about early glassmaking until the time of the Romans.

Roman civilization developed every known method of making glass objects until refinements in the making of plate glass were discovered in France in the seventeenth century, and the pressing of glass was developed in America early in the nineteenth century. At first, vessels were made by molding forms of sand or clay, and hot threads of glass were spun around these in spiral fashion. These were then

The most famous piece of glass in the world—the Portland Vase at the British Museum in London. Roman, first century A.D. It was acquired in the mid–19th century by the Duke of Portland, who presented it to the museum. It was smashed, then totally restored.

smoothed out as much as possible, joining the threads in the process. When the blowpipe was invented, artisans soon learned to form pieces and even add decorations, handles, spouts, etc., using crude tools, most of which changed little until the early nineteenth century.

From a collecting standpoint, you should concentrate on those items made after the Revolutionary War since there is not much pre-Revolutionary American glass, as England supplied most of our finished glass, and very little of this has survived. New Englanders like to take pride in the fact that theirs was the earliest settled part of the country and that the region preceded the others in the manufacture of all types of goods. However, it was quite late in producing one glassmaking concern that remained in business for an appreciable length of time. This was the New England Glass Company, located in Cambridge, Massachusetts, operating between 1817 and 1888. The concern then moved to Toledo, Ohio and today is known as Libbey Owens, Ford.

The earliest production of glass which might be collected today was made in the Pittsburgh region. Glass factories had operated in many places during the eighteenth century, but little can be attributed to them. After the Revolution, glass works began to appear in the Western Pennsylvania region, notably in what is now the Pittsburgh area. As early as the 1790s, factories were shipping glass via riverboat all the way to New Orleans. It was not until 1817, when the New England Glass Company was organized in Cambridge, Massachusetts that any long term production of glass originated in New England. The Marlboro Street Works was organized in Keene, New

Crown Tuscan made by the Cambridge Glass Company of Cambridge, Ohio. Jabe Tartar.

Sugar and creamer, cut and acid-etched by the Dalzell Glass Company, Findlay, Ohio, c. 1885. Butterfly and cosmos motif. Jabe Tartar.

Hampshire in 1817 but was quite small. Still, flasks from that company are high on the collecting list today. Inkwells and decanters are about the only other items made there that can be found and attributed to that works.

The center of glassmaking in the nineteenth century, as well as today, is in the region which comprises western Pennsylvania, Ohio and West Virginia. There were many fine companies in this area, making glass in similar metal content, designs and decoration. Years ago, historians referred to this region as the Midwest or Pittsburgh

Decorated custard glass made by the Cambridge Glass Company, Cambridge, Ohio. Similar glass was made by many firms in the Midwest. Jabe Tartar.

Some of the greatest forums and seminars held over the past years have featured glass as their subjects. This is where one learns the tidbits that make collecting fun and, at times, confusing. Back in 1978, at the Midwest Forum held at the Henry Ford Museum, Kenneth Wilson, then director of collections, showed a Syrian made bowl from the 1st century A.D. which closely resembles that work done in New Jersey late in the 18th century.

He also demolished the conception that the name "flip glass" should be applied to the large hand blown tumblers made on both sides of the Atlantic. Flip is a drink made with rum as its base and it is unlikely such a glass, quite large in size, would be used in drinking flip, as a small tumblerfull would suffice to put one under. Mr. Wilson stated that he feels the term is a twentieth century connotation, merely invented to identify the form.

area when discussing the output of the factories there—just as we make reference to Staffordshire County in England when identifying provenance of pottery which was not marked by the factories in that region. To identify all of these glass companies would require many books. Several are listed in the bibliography. One book in particular that I would recommend is *Pittsburgh Glass* by Lowell Innes, who is credited with bringing attention to the glass made in the Midwest and Pittsburgh areas and assisting in many museum exhibitions which helped identify it.

GLASSMAKING TECHNIQUES

Glass is a combination of sand, flint, and spar or some other silicous substance with an alkali or some other material added as a flux (a substance used to promote fusion). Of the alkalies, soda and potash were the first used successfully. Lead, borax, arsenic, nitre, and lime were used later. Sometimes pearl ashes, sea salt, and wood ashes were used. When red lead was used it gave the glass a yellow cast which could be corrected with nitre. If arsenic was used in excess the glass would turn milky. Pearl ashes were first used to make perfectly transparent glass. Borax was just as good, but it was more expensive and its use was mostly confined to making looking glasses.

The materials used for making glass were first reduced to a powder, either by pounding or by grinding in a horse mill. Then the powder was mixed with flux and calcined under intense heat for five or six hours. The resulting product was called "frit" and could be easily melted in the glass pots, with workmen skimming the scum from its surface. A typical mixture for a fine grade flint glass would be 120 pounds of white sand, 50 pounds of red lead, 40 pounds of pearl ashes, 20 pounds of nitre, and 5 ounces of magnesia. With the addition of a pound or two of arsenic, the material would fuse much more quickly and at a lower temperature. A cheaper mixture could be made by substituting sea salt for the arsenic. Crown glass (a popular product in the eighteenth century) was made from the following ingredients: 60 pounds of white sand, 30 pounds of pearl ashes, 15 pounds of nitre, one pound of borax, and a half pound of arsenic.

COLOR AND ETCHING

There were many "green glass" factories set up as early as the eighteenth century. A common mixture was as follows: 120 pounds of white sand, 30 pounds of unpurified pearl ashes, wood ashes well burned and sifted, 60 pounds of common salt, and 5 pounds of arsenic. In the rural glassmaking plants, a good green glass might be made by mixing 200 pounds of wood ashes with 100 pounds of sand.

Colored glass has been with us for centuries, and the formulas have undoubtedly changed over the years. The following formulas come from recipes in use at the turn of the eighteenth into the nineteenth centuries, and in general use for many years after that.

To a glass mixture (such as the one outlined for flint glass above) add 9 pounds of copper precipitated from aqua fortis and 2 drachmas of precipitated iron for green. To 10 pounds of glass add 6 drachmas of zaffre (oxide of cobalt) and 1 drachma of gold precipitated by tin for bright purple. Varying these formulas, you will find that for amethyst, magnesia was used; for black, magnesia and calcined iron; for white opaque, calcined horn, ivory, or bone; for ruby, gold precipitated by tin; for blue, calcined bones, horn or ivory, magnesia, and zaffre; for yellow, calcined iron or crude tartar and antimony.

After glass is formed, either by blowing or pressing, it must be annealed (heated) in an oven in which it then cools gradually in order to retain its temper and strength. Etching was originally done by dipping the glass body into ordinary melted wax. After the wax hardened, an artisan would etch the outline of a decoration or picture into the wax on the glass body. It would then be dipped into a lead lined box which contained a fluoric acid which would etch the glass wherever it was not protected by the wax. Initials and monograms could be put on glassware in this manner. After a rinse in neutralizing water to flush away the acid, the remaining protective wax would be removed by dipping the piece in hot water and melting it away. A varnish coating was sometimes applied.

Engraving on glass is generally done by a spinning cutting-wheel, with the artisan holding the glass body against the wheel to produce the desired decoration. The term "copper wheel cut" refers to such a method, with the wheel most likely sprinkled with diamond dust to speed the work. However, back in the early part of the nineteenth century, you could have purchased glass engraved in a more radical, simpler method. While the glass piece was hot, it would be dipped into a mixture of red lead, sand, and borax, heated and fused with what was called a menstrum—a mixture of pure cane sugar, water, and common writing ink, which would hold some oxide of manganese. The mixture might have also been painted on with a camel's hair brush or squirrel's foot. A simple etching or engraving tool would be used to cut away the desired decoration. The etching would appear in reverse, with the cut areas smooth and clear and the untouched areas appearing to have been roughened with a tool. Some artisans felt that clearer cuts could be made in this manner, with less possibility of unwanted glass

Nineteenth-century glass: flasks, log cabin bottle, hat, and ink bottle.

powder being ground into the body at the edges of the cuts by the wheel.

Identifying the makers of early glass is quite difficult, as most melted the same metals according to the same or very similar formulas. Colors and pattern designs were copied freely, and neighboring concerns would often help each other when large orders came in, with each making up part of the order in similar molds. Workers in this industry were quite transient and always in demand, so they might take their own trade secrets with them from plant to plant, which would account for the similarities of workmanship.

18th Century Glass

Glassmaking Pioneers

CASPAR WISTAR

Glassmaking in this country was introduced in Jamestown, Virginia, as early as 1608. There were window glass and bottle-making houses in New England and other settled parts of the country after that time, but it was not until Caspar Wistar, a Dutch inhabitant of Pennsylvania, went to Salem County in New Jersey and opened a glassworks there in 1739 that America had a company whose product became well known by name and survived for some years. Wistar made glass in what is now termed the "South Jersey tradition," and under his direction and that of his son's, it survived until 1780, when the fires of the Revolution put them out of business. Not one whole documented piece has survived intact from this output. Designs like the lilypad, cross ribbing, and swirled ribbons originated here and spread throughout the colonies.

HENRY WILLIAM STIEGEL

Next to Wistar in influence was a very colorful character named Henry William Stiegel. He came to this country from Germany and managed to marry the daughter of the ironmaster of the Elizabeth Furnace in Lancaster County, Pennsylvania. He opened his glasshouse in 1763 and began turning out pieces in the German tradition of glassmaking, which makes it difficult today to tell his work from the imported glass made at that time. Stiegel became wealthy,

and the title of "Baron" was bestowed on him as a measure of respect by his fellow townspeople. His high spending habits resulted in his being thrown into debtor's prison, which brought a halt to a very colorful career and the very interesting quality glass for which he was responsible. After the demise of his plant, about 1773, Pennsylvania remained prominent as a location for glassmaking due to the availability of coal and silica. The Philadelphia Glass Works was organized at that time with many of Stiegel's former workmen and this company prospered under varying ownerships well into the nineteenth century.

ROBERT HEWES

Collectors must take note of an early glass works which, though not successful, established the industrial concept of building not only a factory, but the homes and store for supplies to accommodate the workers. In 1780, a Bostonian, Robert Hewes, selected a site in Temple, New Hampshire which is in the Southwestern area of the state. The site was chosen because of an abundance of firewood to heat the pots and good silica which melted well for the production of bottles and window glass. It had been rumored that many of the workers were Hessian soldiers who had deserted earlier in the Revolution. The factory was started in May of 1780 and burned shortly after construction. It was rebuilt during the Fall of 1780–81. Ten days after firing, the main furnaces col-

Crown Glass

In the days when fashioning glass at the end of a blowpipe was the method of manufacture, everything, including flat pieces such as window panes, was made in this manner. It is believed the blowpipe was known to the Romans as early as 50 B.C. and remained the best way to fashion the metal (glass in its molten state) into desired forms until the French and English learned to form glass in sheets by pouring it into molds in the late 17th century. This was done to make the looking glasses from then into the early part of the 19th century and was a very expensive process.

The glass blowers who prevailed throughout the countryside both here and overseas still fashioned their flat glass by first blowing the metal, then spinning the rod in their hands to flatten the bubble at the end of the pipe. When this was extended as far as possible, the flattened glass was further smoothed with simple tools to widen it as much as possible. Once annealed, the cutters would slice it into the small panes, treasured by owners of period homes. However, the center piece, where the pipe had been attached, was always raised and often showed the spiral marks as evidence of the spinning. This center cut, often called the bullseye pane, is what gave the name "crown" to the glass made in this manner.

lapsed due to moisture and frost in the stones. In March of 1781 the Temple selectmen gave Hewes a loan to rebuild and organized a lottery to help, which failed. In the summer of 1781, the furnaces were rebuilt and by the fall of 1781, was in production of crown glass, philosophical glass (glass made for laboratories, i.e., beakers, test tubes, piping, etc.), bottles and window glass. This was the first crown glass made in America. In 1782, Hewes gave up the experiment and returned to Boston to open the Boston Crown Glass Company.

In 1976, the site was excavated under the direction of Frederick Gorman and Dr. David Starbuck—an undertaking sponsored both by the Boston University Department of Classical Studies and the Corning Museum of Glass. Hessian belt buckles were found to confirm the existing rumors. There is no authenticated piece of Temple glass in existence, though many feel some windowpanes in the old houses in the area could well have come from there.

JOHN FREDERICK AMELUNG

Another early glassmaker was John Frederick Amelung, who set up his New Bremen Works at Fredericktown, Maryland, in 1787. Lured here by promises of opportunities in the new world, he encouraged other workers to follow him into the venture, which survived only until 1795. America had not instituted tariffs against imports which would have given local manufacturers protection from overseas competition. However, Amelung's glass won great favor and there are good etched and signed pieces which have survived.

After the Revolution, many glassworks were built, but there are few records of what they made. Some did not survive long enough for documentation of their activities. It was not until the beginning of the nineteenth century that any really large, successful firms were established—with examples of their work documented. At the end of this chapter, I have listed the names of some whose work might be identified and collected.

19th Century Glass

We might categorize American glassmaking into different periods as an aid to identification. Nineteenth century glass must almost be lumped together so far as content and quality are concerned. Different blowing techniques and types of decorations might aid in determining the origin of some pieces as far as regions are concerned, but due to continuous importation, it is quite difficult to tell American work from that which came from overseas. When mechanical pressing of glass was developed about 1825, glassmakers were able to run wild with mold designs, and the industry diversified as it never could before. Suddenly, shapes, forms, designs, and pressing techniques could be identified, and glass from the Pittsburgh area took on a completely different look from that made in New England. New England benefited from the likelihood that immigrants would settle at their first port of call, where work might be available, rather than head into the less developed areas in the midwest. However, many workers got their start in New England and then went on to factories in the Pennsylvania, West Virginia, and Ohio areas, taking inland techniques and ideas learned on the coast. It is amazing how much we do know about the origin of American glass, when so little of it was marked or otherwise documented.

In collecting glass, you will find it is best to concentrate your efforts in the regions where it was made. If you collect Hobbs and Brockunier, you should look

Early nineteenth-century snap-case wooden mold, used to blow early bottles in the shape desired.

for it in the Wheeling, West Virginia area. If you desire Sandwich glass, there is more of this on Cape Cod and in eastern Massachusetts than anywhere else. You will find the prices are generally lower in such areas since the law of supply and demand keeps them stable. You should look for Keene and Stoddard historical flasks in New Hampshire—looking for one made in Mantua, Ohio, might be rather futile. However, shipments of glass were made to different parts of the country, so you might examine the old records of companies preserved by historical societies and researchers, and you may locate what you are looking for elsewhere. The Boston and Sandwich Glass Company shipped glass to the west coast, so a lot of it can be found there. Some was even sent to Russia and other European nations. However, I have looked for specimens all over Europe (even in Russia) to no avail.

Pressed Glass

In 1825, a patent for pressing glass by machine was issued to Benjamin Bakewell at his plant in Pittsburgh. This was first used for pressing solid objects such as drawer pulls. In 1827, a further patent on pressing was issued to Deming Jarves at Sandwich for an improvement whereby hollowares might be made. The new technology was adopted around the world, and the resulting mass production created so much glass in so similar a manner and look that most historians qualify their opinions on origin unless absolutely sure.

There are some who feel that glass should be judged by its quality and not by the name of the maker. Unfortunately, most dealers and collectors do not agree with this premise. Documentation of glass is most important as much is collected by the maker's name. Early colored pressed glass is desirable but patterns were copied on both sides of the ocean, which makes positive identification difficult. It was not until Ruth Webb Lee published her *Handbook of Early American Pressed Glass Patterns*

Blown and Pressed Glass

In the early days of pressing glass, it was found to be easier to make a larger piece in two sections. For example, the base of a whale oil lamp, such as those made in the 1830s, would be pressed in a mold. These could be done in many colors, but all would be in the same form. A top section could then be made either in a mold or by hand blowing. After cooling this could be attached to the base by means of a small hot glass wafer—the two pieces were just pressed together and on hardening, would be joined. In this manner, the same base might be used for candleholders, compotes, cake plates and the like—the wafer made it possible to join any two sections together.

What is interesting is that the base can be pressed, while the font is hand blown; hence the term pressed and blown glass, as both techniques are combined in the same piece. This can be puzzling to the novice glass collector, who can recognize the two ways of forming it, yet know that they can't be done together. A good glassblower could make the top section more quickly than it could be molded in a press, and at that time, there was still a lot of pride in doing hand work. Check any glass to see how it was made and decorated, you might be surprised at the several different techniques performed on the same piece.

Cologne and perfume bottles come in many sizes, shapes, and colors. These date from mid- to late nineteenth century.

Pressed glass of the c. 1830–1840 period, Boston and Sandwich Glass Company. Top, left to right: *a rare translucent blue acanthus pattern whale oil lamp; blue and white clam water dolphin candleholder from the earliest mold; a rare whale oil lamp with translucent blue base and opaque white font.* Bottom, left to right: *purple blue Three Printie vase; a translucent blue candleholder cast in one mold; and a dark blue blown and molded decanter with shell and ribbed pattern. (Bourne Gallery.)*

you discern the differences between original and reproduced glass pieces.

After the War Between the States, industrial plants had to turn from making military items to consumer production and glass companies struggled for their survival. Victorian England had been making fancy colored glassware which found favor here. It was not long before this was challenged with local production. America entered what often is called the "Art Glass period," when artistic design and color were the subject of much experimentation. In the 1860s, William Leighton left the employ of the New England Glass Company for a new job at Hobbs and Brockunier in Wheeling, West Virginia. He pioneered in the use of inexpensive lime as a flux for melting the silica. Until that time, glassmakers utilized lead and crushed flint to make what is a superior product. Lowell Innes, in his book *Pittsburgh Glass* (Houghton Mifflin, 1976), indicates that as early as 1850 John Adams was using a lime flux. He felt that Adams and Leighton may have worked together on this, with Leighton getting the credit for it.

The New England Companies

New England gave birth to the Boston Crown Glass Company, New England Glass Company, the Boston and Sandwich Glass Company, Portland (ME) Glass Company, and the Mount Washington-Pairpoint Company which was a marriage of the Mount Washington Glass Company and Pairpoint in New Bedford, Massachusetts. Another lesser-known company was the Union Glass Works which operated between 1851 and 1924 in Somerville, Massachusetts. Much that was made there is mistaken for New England Glass Company products or Sandwich glass. (There were about thirty-five businesses devoted to the making and cutting of glass which operated in Sandwich over the years, so one must read the books done by Barlow/Kaiser which are listed in the bibliography to learn of the wide range of work done in that community.)

in 1931 that collectors had a common glossary to use so items could be advertised in a manner that all could understand. Other patterns have been discovered since the book was published, but it remains an excellent guide. To this day, pattern glass is still made by basically the same mechanical means as that devised early in this century. This has made a faithful reproduction of many of the old designs possible, much to the consternation of collectors. Collecting an item which can be reproduced has its own built-in set of hazards, so you must arm yourself with great knowledge before venturing far into this field. Read the available literature and talk to dealers to help

The Boston and Sandwich Glass Company operated between 1825 and 1888 when it closed due to labor problems brought on by its inability to compete with the cheaper glass shipped to New England from the Pittsburgh region. The New England Glass Company closed the same year and its owner, William Drummond Libbey moved it to Toledo, Ohio, where it still operates as Libbey, Owens, Ford. Portland operated between 1863 and 1873. This left Pairpoint and Union as the two remaining works. Pairpoint was closed in 1958, with another works by that name opening in 1969 at Sagamore, Massachusetts under that name and the guidance of Robert Bryden, who was the last manager at the original plant. The present factory is still working and one may purchase fine glass there.

One could devote an entire book to studio glass makers—the individual people or small concerns which made much in decorative and functional wares. Since glassblowers today have benefited from the experience of the masters who have gone before them, it makes sense to collect new glass as well as old. Museums are doing this—check what you see on display in some of them and let this be your guide.

I have mentioned the New England factories—it would be impossible to list all of those which worked in New Jersey, New York and especially the Midwest or Pittsburgh region, which encompasses much of Ohio and West Virginia, as well. So many good books have been written about particular makers and types of glass that one should pursue these for specialized collecting.

Glass engraved by Louis Vaupel, New England Glass Company. Much decorated in this "Bohemian" style was made in America.

Silvered glass, miscalled mercury glass. The thin double walls are coated with a silver solution, then the blowpipe hole at the bottom is sealed to keep out moisture. Much was made at the Union Glass Company and Boston and Sandwich Glass Company.

Diamond banded, maiden's blush cranberry goblet, Portland Glass Company, 1863–1873. This banding appears on other Portland pieces—a good glass to collect.

The type of glass painted by Mary Gregory and her sister, Emma. Both worked at the Boston and Sandwich Glass Works in the 1880s. Their diaries reveal they painted winter scenes such as those pictured here, with an occasional variation, such as birds, for family and friends. These pieces were handed down in Emma's family, along with the diaries. Ray Barlow and Joan Kaiser.

THE MARY GREGORY STORY

Unless you have a copy of *The Glass Industry in Sandwich, Volume IV*, by Ray Barlow and Joan Kaiser, perhaps the true information about "Mary Gregory" glass has passed you by. Until its publication, rumor, stories and tales debunking the existence of Mary Gregory were rampant. Proponents said she painted white enamel figures on glass at the Boston and Sandwich Glass Company on Cape Cod in the 1880s. Others felt she never existed at all except in the minds of collectors and dealers who used her name to create a demand for late nineteenth century pieces which had enameled decorations, most often figures and background in classic form. Various rules were created to authenticate her work. The four generally accepted rules are that the figure had to be a child with only one arm showing; one leg should appear longer than the other; the child should be standing on a patch of fog or clouds; and there should be foliage, fernlike in appearance, in front of and at the rear of the child. These figures were supposed to be a takeoff on the Kate Greenaway figures which were popularized in her books. The final rule stipulated that all the enameling should be white—any color indicated the piece was not done by Mary Gregory.

In their extensive research, Barlow and Kaiser acquired the diaries of Mary Gregory and her sister, Emma, from the descendants of the latter's family. Indeed, Mary Gregory did exist and she did paint at Sandwich, though she did other painting work at home for other companies in various mediums. She painted between 1880 and 1883. Emma painted for a brief period in 1880. Mary never married—she spent

If Not Mary Gregory, Then Who?

When asked the provenance of all the enameled glass with figures, if they were not Sandwich, Dorothy Lee Jones, director of the museum and former president of the National Early American Glass Club, said, "All of you who have been my friends for the past twenty years know that I have always stated such glass was not made in America—it came from Europe."

More professionalism can be shown by identifying the figured pieces as enameled glass, with no reference to Mary Gregory. It has no resemblance to the work she did. The quicker we relieve this fine painter from any responsibility for much of the shoddy work on such glass, the better.

Enameled figures on glass most likely were made in Europe. This is not Mary Gregory glass; her diary reveals she did not paint figures at the Boston and Sandwich Glass Works.

This is often called a Currier and Ives lamp, because of the winter scene, which resembles the work of George Durrie. The scene, in warm tones of brown, black, and gray on an opalescent glass, also resembles the work of the Gregory sisters.

most of her life caring for her mother, though she was not in good health most of the time. What is revealed in the diaries, much of which is reproduced in the book and which I have read from the written pages themselves, reveals that neither painted figures on glass. Some examples handed down in Emma's family reveal winter scenes in dark browns, blacks and some gray on white opalescent glass.

Mr. Barlow lectured on these finds at the Jones Museum of Glass and Ceramics in Douglas Hill, Maine several years ago. He brought examples and the diaries to convince the heavy hitters that their classification of enameled glass in the then "Mary Gregory" style should be reevaluated in light of this written evidence. Some pieces have appeared with a bird or flowers, but these were exceptions to their work, the bulk of which was winter scenes.

Waterford

During the nineteenth century, much glass was shipped here from Europe. One could write chapters on this glass alone. However, with our space limitations, we can call attention to a few facts that may be of help. In 1794, George III, still suffering from the costs of the American revolution, instituted a tax on fine glass. This was to be taxed by weight, but his collectors based the tax on the weight of the product before cutting. The makers were upset at paying tax on powdered glass that lay on the floor after cutting and appealed this, but to no avail. Several opened plants in Ireland to escape this tax. They were built in Cork, Dublin, Waterford and several other places. Managers, workmen, formulas and molds were sent across the channel.

It is next to impossible to differentiate between English and Irish glass made during the nineteenth century. This is why better informed collectors identify it merely as Anglo/Irish glass. The pros will rarely mention the name of a particular factory. One which is used very indiscriminately is

Anglo/Irish cut glass, late nineteenth century. Do not attribute any of this to Waterford; the plant was closed from 1851 to 1951.

Waterford. Few realize that this plant closed in 1851. Another was opened with this name in 1951. However, for one hundred years, no Waterford glass was made. So, if your grandmother received some as wedding gifts early in this century, it is not Waterford. None of the pre-1851 glass is known to have been marked. Glass made since 1951 does bear the Waterford name. Also, the claim that there are rare, treasured Waterford chandeliers in historic homes in this country is a myth. At a lecture on Irish antiques held at Pennsbury Manor in Morrisville, Pennsylvania in 1970, the speaker revealed that in his two years of research in Ireland and England to prepare for his talk, he found no evidence that lighting devices of any kind were made at the early Waterford plant—this includes chandeliers.

Lacy Glass

The term "lacy" is applied to clear glass which is highly decorated. It appeared about 1828 at the Boston and Sand-

Examples of early pressed "lacy" glass, so-called because of the total decoration done to hide bubbles and "straw marks," were pressed in lead glass between 1828 and 1858. After that, they were made with the cheaper lime flux glass, still being made today.

wich Glass Factory shortly after the method of pressing glass was perfected. At the time, most clear glass showed many imperfections such as bubbles and "straw marks," which are ridges resulting from this primitive manufacture. The extensive figuring on the pieces helped make these marks less evident.

During this period, practically all the companies used lead as a flux—the compound which helped turn silica into the transparent state. Early "lacy" is quite heavy and most edges, where the pieces had to be trimmed and smoothed after they were annealed, are rough. The lacy period in which this heavy metal was used extended until c. 1858. After that time, experiments with soda and lime as a flux resulted in a glass of much lesser quality. Lacy was made overseas as well, and heavily figured glass of this type is still being made today.

Art Glass

The art glass period in this country dates from between 1880 and 1900. In Victorian England, glass manufacturers began producing colored glass and our compa-

Decanter in Amberina, shading from ruby at the top to amber at the base. It is in an inverted thumbprint pattern. This is made by adding gold to the metal—the more it is heated, the redder it gets.

Covered candy dish with dolphin feet in canary yellow. This was made by Portiault in France, late in the last century. It is identified by the molded rosette at the bottom.

nies followed suit. During this period, some of the finest designed, colored, and decorated glass appeared. Some were given such exotic names as Peachblow, Burmese, Amberina, Crown Milano, Pomona, Diamond Quilted Satin and the like. Some are identified by color, such as ruby, black amethyst, cranberry and others by their finish or decoration, such as enameled or satin finished. Generally, most are referred to as art glass when there is no specific name given.

In 1917, the Libbey company issued a catalog of art glass which was made the same way it was before the company left

Ruby flashed glass. This was colored by dipping the pieces into a ruby stain while they were hot. In those made as souvenir pieces, the name of a famous resort area or a sentimental message to a loved one was scratched through the stain to reveal the clear glass beneath. Most of this work was done between about 1890 and 1910.

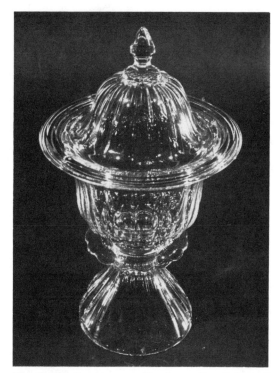

The famous Sweeney punchbowl, standing 5 feet tall and once used as a grave marker, is now in the Wheeling Museum at Ogilby Park. It is the largest cut-glass item, made in two pieces. This miniature copy was made by the Imperial Glass Company, Bellaire, Ohio, 1950. Jabe Tartar.

Massachusetts during the strike of 1888. It is difficult to separate the early from the later work. Also, from 1920 to 1940, many reproductions of the early art glass forms were made. Most of these were made by machine, so it is not difficult to separate them from the earlier hand blown examples. They can fool the newcomer, however. Libbey is still available in gift shops, today.

Cut Glass

Cut glass of the brilliant period (1890–1915) is the most desirable to collect. This was a period when the quality of the glass metal was at its best. About 25 to 28 percent of its content was lead, which gives the glass brilliance and weight and allows deep cutting to enhance its design. The advent of World War I brought with it the need for lead to be used in munitions, hence its scarcity for making glass during this period. The quality never quite recovered after the war as the new light cut glass became the fashion, with but a few holdouts in the industry continuing to stress the quality of its metal.

Over the years, the term "cut crystal" took over, signifying that this was a better metal than conventional glass, but not of the quality of the brilliant period. Today's fine glass may include no more than 10 to 12 percent lead, which accounts for its look

During the brilliant period of cut glass, makers of pressed glass competed with those who made very thick molded pieces in imitation of the more expensive glass. Look for NU-CUT, NEAR-CUT, DEEP CUT, KRYSTOL, and other names molded on the inside bottom. They are very good collectibles.

Brilliant-period cut glass, c. 1890–1915. The high lead content, 25 to 28 percent, insured quality metal which is quite brilliant after cutting. Today's lead crystal has about 10 to 12 percent content.

which cannot match that of the old. Much European crystal has found its way into this country, some of it good, and some not so good. In France, a conveyor system has been developed which makes it possible to mix the ingredients of the glass metal at the start, melting and casting it into goblets and the like and then annealing them, with the finished product cut by machine and delivered as a item ready to be packaged and sold, with no hands touching it all along the way.

Cut glass went out of favor for many years as new furniture could be scratched easily by it. It was not until the 1960s that there was a resurgence in interest in it. Remember, the signed pieces most often command much more money than those unsigned.

20th Century Glass

Carnival Glass

POOR MAN'S TIFFANY

Frank Fenton of Newark, Ohio, is credited with first turning out an inexpensive iridescent glass in fancy shapes and colors in 1907. He mixed iron oxide and iron chloride with the glass metal to give it its sheen. Other glass works picked up this development immediately, and soon such famous works as Imperial in Bellaire, Ohio; Millersburg and Westmoreland, both in Pennsylvania; and Fenton's former employer, Harry Northwood of Indiana, Pennsylvania, were turning out the poor man's Tiffany. No glass company in New England is credited with making the product. By this time, most New England glass works had closed or had moved to the mid-western area. The first new color in appearance was yellow, or marigold, but chemists soon explored the full range of colorings. Artists came up with designs ranging from the most popular grape through the tiger lily, fine cut heart, sunflower, sunken daisy, shell and jewel, fish scale and beads, open rose, scroll embossed, thistle, star, and singing birds, to name a few. Fruit bowls were popular, along with hatpin holders, powder jars, and pin trays. On the rarer side are ash trays, banks, jelly jars, paperweights, and electric lamps. Baskets and vases were popular, but most were for decorative rather than functional use. The pitcher and tumbler sets were favorite premium items and, in some cases, complete dinner sets were made.

Queen Anne highboy, tiger maple, New England, c. 1740–1760. On case pieces of this period, all four legs must be alike. Note the cabriole legs in front and the straight legs in the rear.

Gateleg table and Queen Anne spoonback chairs, c. 1700, American. The heavy baluster turnings on the front chair rounds and heavy turnings on the table legs are important to value.

Etruscan tobacco jar, Shell and Seaweed design, made by Griffin Smith and Hill, Phoenixville, Pennsylvania, c. 1880s. This is the best majolica to collect in this country.

Watercolor view of Portsmouth Harbor, New Hampshire, with Wentworth Gardner house at center. This beautiful eighteenth century house was once owned by Wallace Nutting and used as an antiques shop.

Mochaware, England, nineteenth century. Correct pattern names, left to right; Cable; Cat's Eye; Cable; next two are Seaweed; Scroddle; and Dicing. "Earthworm" is not the proper pattern name for those identified as Cable.

Porcelain tureen modeled by Jacob Kaendler, Meissen, c. 1730. Very sophisticated work only twenty-two years after the discovery of making porcelain originated there. Hermitage, St. Petersburg.

Oil on canvas, Last of the Mohicans, *American, Thomas Cole, 1801–1848. Sold May 26, 1988 for $1,540,000 at auction by Christie's, New York. This is an excellent Barbizon school landscape.*

When you see a pine chest with three graduated drawers and French-type legs (center), you are looking at
Shaker, most likely from Niskayuna, N.Y. On either
side are eldresses' desks.

French mantel clock, bronze doré, porcelain dial, and
Circassian walnut inlay. Late eighteenth century.
Most likely, it came with a pair of girandoles to be used
on a mantel.

Fire engines and related equipment are colorful and reflect the changes in our technology. Here, we see iron and painted tin engines and pumpers made in the late nineteenth and early twentieth centuries.

Flea market tables are full of toys that go back but a few years. Save those of today along with their boxes.

These are some of the best pieces of art glass to collect (c. 1880–1900). At the back of the top row are an orange and black Flambeau vase and pitcher, made at Pairpoint, and an orange Steuben vase. At the back of the bottom row is a blue and white coralene vase, in front of which is a peachblow cologne bottle. At center front and right is a grouping of various Burmese pieces.

Sampler, 1818, by Anna Maria Rovoudt. A fine example, it includes a poem, trees flowers, etc.

Contemporary folk pottery by Russell Henry, Birdsboro, Pa. Henry fashions his pieces, then decorates them with folk painting and fires them. He is famed for his forms and decoration.

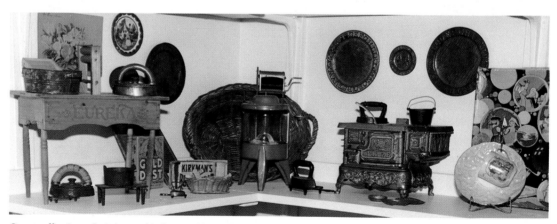

Great collection of miniature kitchen and household items. Pauline E. Glidden Toy Museum, Ashland, New Hampshire.

In later years this was called "carnival glass," as it was often given away as a prize at carnivals and fairs and was also used as a premium by cereal and tea companies. During the depression years, companies found their warehouses full, with no ready market for distribution. Loads of this glass were dumped into the market and carnival operators seized on it as an inexpensive prize for their games of chance. Long regarded as an inferior product, carnival glass was an item which had to be sold by the boxful at auctions until a few years ago. Then collectors became interested in it as there were pieces which showed definite quality, reflected by the handwork incorporated in the making. Most people think the glass was all machine made, but research has proven that up to seven or eight men spent four or five minutes making each well-moulded piece. The inexpensive pieces look inexpensive, and those of value look it, so you do not have to be an expert to evaluate most of this glass. Depth of molding, design, color, iridescence, and proportions must be judged in determining quality.

HARRY NORTHWOOD

One of the prolific makers of carnival glass was Harry Northwood who located his Northwood Glass Company in Whee-

Chrysanthemum custard glass by Harry Northwood, early 1920s. This was made to be given as premiums inside bags of flour.

ling, West Virginia. Some claim that over 1,300 patterns were created between 1909 and about 1920 when the manufacture of this type of ware began to diminish in popularity.

However, Northwood had been experimenting with other glass before this time. He worked for Hobbs and Brockunier in Wheeling as well as the La Belle Glass Company and Buckeye Glass Company in Ohio. His first factory was in Sinclaire, Pennsylvania, opening in 1896 and moved to Wheeling in 1902. He worked until 1923.

In his early years, he experimented with what is known as custard glass, an opaque variety which came in several colors—custard, blue, and green. Some light blue pieces were decorated with gilded chrysanthemums. Some say this color was produced with uranium at a time when few may have known of its radioactive qualities.

Much of this output was dedicated as giftware, some finding its way into bags of flour to be given as a premium. The smaller pieces were put into twenty-five-pound bags and the larger pieces in one hundred-pound bags. One tale has it that inspectors found weevils in flour stored near the Ohio River and ordered it destroyed. It was all dumped into the Ohio River, complete with the glass. A treasure lies down there for someone to discover.

The top favorite seems to be the Northwood pieces, which are well marked with a capital N within a circle, usually at the bottom of the piece. Fenton signed his pieces in script, and these are being reproduced today. Early Imperial glass was marked with a cross, the eight letters of its name appearing two to a section. Newer Imperial pieces are signed with a G superimposed on an I. The most popular colors in order of preference are purple, blue, green, orange, yellow, and marigold. White carnival glass is quite rare. You will find that most of this glass is rather inexpensive. Search for deep cut, well-colored quality pieces if you want to collect carnival glass.

Heisey

Augustus H. Heisey served in the War Between the States on the Union side. After the war, he had worked as a salesman for the King Glass Company of Pittsburgh. He married a daughter of one of the owners of the Duncan Glass Company, and became a partner in Duncan and Heisey. In 1893 he resigned and in 1895 he established his own glass company in Newark, Ohio.

He had three sons, George, Wilson, and Clarence all of whom worked in the business. In 1900, the diamond mark with an H inside was adopted as the trademark and appears molded in most of the Heisey pieces. Many patterns were identified with a number rather than a name. Between about 1923 and 1930, the company specialized in colored pieces. At that time, some glass was identified by name, such as Flamingo (a pink), Alexandrite (orchid), Moongleam (green), Tangerine (orange), Zircon (pale yellow), Sahara (canary yellow), and Ivorina Verde (a dark yellow opaque colored with uranium salts). The opaque and frosted glass came later.

In the 1920s, Heisey acquired some of the original Sandwich glass molds and turned out pieces which can fool the novice. In 1958, Heisey closed its doors, selling its molds to the Imperial Glass Company in Bellaire, Ohio, where they continued to make it with the H inside the diamond for several years.

The most desired Heisey glass is Verlys, which is camphor or frosted in various patterns. None is opalescent or colored. Verlys is an art glass originally made in France after 1930. Heisey obtained the rights and formula from the French factory and produced the glass for a short time. The French-produced glass can be distinguished from the American made by the signature: The French is mold marked while the American is etched script signed.

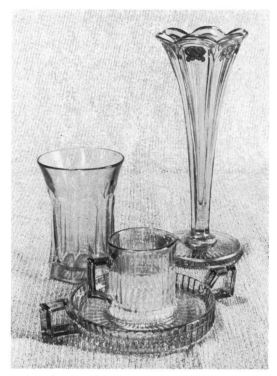

Heisey glass, made in Newark, Ohio. The product is very clear, heavy, and of fine quality. If marked, it has an H inside a diamond.

Among the rarest of pieces are the Heisey cocktail shakers of clear glass, about a foot tall, with a removable glass strainer at the top. These are unmarked.

Tiffany and Art Nouveau

The turn of the century brought with it a change in style as art nouveau motifs, made popular in France, gradually came to our shores. Some people feel that the period from 1895 to 1920 was gaudy, others say it was sterile, and some feel it was an era when the most grotesque styles were perpetrated on the public. Glass felt the design changes more than anything else. Louis Comfort Tiffany helped to popularize iridescent colored glass, and his name is attributed to many items which may or may not be the product of his factory. His stained glass windows for churches and breakfast rooms in fancy homes are over-

Blown and cameo cut-glass vase by Emile Gallé, Nancy, France, 1846–1904. Gallé is the only maker who put his name on every piece he made, or which was turned out in his factory. These pieces must be signed to be authentic.

D'Argental cameo glass landscape lamp and shade, c. 1900. Sold for $16,500 by Butterfield & Butterfield, Los Angeles. Photo courtesy of Butterfield & Butterfield.

Vase by Louis Comfort Tiffany early twentieth century. Hearts and vines decoration in pinks, browns, ivories and gold.

counterparts were very busy making and sending their iridescent and cameo-carved wares to America, where they found great favor with the wealthy.

Greentown

Whatever you call it, Greentown glass or "chocolate glass," much of it was made at the Indiana Tumbler and Goblet Company in Greentown, Indiana. Our historians tell us that Jacob Rosenthal perfected the formula for it about 1900. Prior to that time, the company was making the usual lines of dinner and decorative wares. At the Pan American Exposition in Buffalo in 1901, examples were shown to the public for the first time.

One will notice that examples found today will vary in the shading of brown to tan and even streaks of caramel white which indicates that stabalizing the colors must have been difficult just as the makers of cobalt and ruby glass experienced in their wares. Another factor in determining provenance is that some makers in the Pittsburgh area created their own versions of the colors, so one must be a student of form, design and decoration to be sure of origination.

James Measell, in his book *Greentown Glass* (Grand Rapids Public Museum), indicates such patterns as Austrian, Brazen Shield, Beaded Panel, Cord Drapery, Cupid, Dewey and others. Perhaps the most famous and valuable is the holly amber, some pieces of which have advanced into the five figures for particular sets. Chocolate glass reusable food containers were popular for mustard, peanut butter and other items. One motif used extensively was the bird with a berry in its beak (Robin with Berry). Animals and birds were subjects of decoration and one will find these on steins and mugs.

The factory burned to the ground in 1903 and the company went out of business, so this glass is not plentiful. Not all chocolate glass is Greentown, so be sure to

shadowed only by the magnificent Tiffany glass curtain at the Palace of Fine Arts in Mexico City. To see this creation, you must go there on a Sunday morning since this is the only time it is lowered. It is made up of over two million pieces of glass fused together to show the two volcanos, Popocatepetl and Ixtaccihuatl, at different seasons of the year and at different times of day as lights are changed behind it. It is one of the most artistic creations of all times by an American glassmaker. Tiffany's European

Chocolate-colored glass made by the Indiana Tumbler Company in Greentown, Indiana. Called "Greentown glass," much was made as food containers for mustard, jams and jellies, peanut butter, etc. Very desirable to collect.

read the Measell book before you start collecting.

Steuben

Various forms of glass with iridized gilt surfaces were made by the Steuben Glass works in Corning, New York. The company name, since 1903, has been associated with fine glass and still operates today. Steuben gained a great reputation for

Steuben Cluthra vase. Colors are blue to white.

its cut and engraved products, much of which has landed in fine collections both museum and private.

The plant was managed by Frederick Carder and finanaced by another great name in glass, T.G. Hawkes. Carder's art nouveau aurene and other colored glasses made Steuben famous. In the book, *Cut and Engraved Glass of Corning* (Corning Museum of Glass) we are told that Carder disliked cut glass but he made it as well as his contemporaries.

In 1918, the Corning Glass Works bought the Steuben Glass Works from Hawkes and used the factory to increase its manufacture of electric light bulbs. Very little fine glass was made there during this period. There is one interesting note: During prohibition, wine and cocktail glasses were still made in great quantity at Corning, which is a commentary on social life at the time.

In 1933 at the beginning of the depression, after many other glass works had gone out of business, Steuben embarked on an unlikely project for the future, the manufacture of the finest crystal in the world. John Monteith Gates was hired as Steuben's director of design, and sculptor Sidney Waugh designed all the glass for the first three years. Winning of World's Fair awards in 1937, 1939 and 1940 established the factory as one of the finest in the world. One may see great examples of the work at the Corning Museum of Glass in Corning, New York.

Lalique

The Art Noveau period, which dates from about 1895 to 1920, brought with it a radical change in the style and colors of glass. Louis Comfort Tiffany of New York is the acknowledged leader of this work in America, but he was merely following in the footsteps of his teachers in France. Today, one will find pieces of Lalique glass in most fine gift shops. This is the product of a company which was founded by a former jeweler, Rene Lalique of Paris. His designs in jewelry gave him international attention and his experimentation in glass accorded him additional acclaim.

He worked with rock crystal and this fired him to create his own forms in glass with his first commission coming from the noted perfumer Cote, to make bottles for the scents.

A satin finish on glass is acquired by dipping it in hydrofluoric acid. This statuary is by the famed René Lalique of France, a prolific maker of Art Nouveau and Art Deco glass. This is of Susan Au Bain, a dancer who shocked theatre patrons at the turn of the century by cavorting in the buff.

It was not until 1920 that he formed his glass company in the province of Alsace-Lorraine which was finally annexed by France after World War I, after many years of dispute concerning ownership of the territory which lies between France and Germany. He began making regular tablewares, bottles, fruit dishes, and stemware. He worked in blown and blown molded techniques and was soon creating forms of birds, people, animals, trees and flowers. Most of his statues and figures are in a satin finish, though clear glass is often used to highlight them. It would be almost safe to say that all pieces are signed.

Rene Lalique died in 1945, but his son Marc is still directing the operations of the factory. During the war years, 1939–45, the plant was demolished, but was rebuilt.

One of the finest collections of Lalique glass is at the Brighton Museum in Brighton, England. Here, one will see a full size glass table, as well as a full range of the decorative glass.

Depression Glass

A relatively new phenomenon in the collecting world is "Depression glass," so called because it was popular during the 1930s. In the past, most Depression glass ended up in the dump or at summer cottages, since no one thought it would ever be worth anything. It languished in the shadow of more exotic glass, and was being sold by auctioneers for 25 or 50 cents a boxful simply to get rid of it. The mania for collecting anything brought prominence to Depression glass, and the prices for it are now off and running. The high prices reached by the finer older glass have created the demand for Depression glass by those with limited funds. This glass was made by the Jeanette Glass Company, Indiana Glass Company, Hazel Atlas Glass Company, Imperial Glass Company, MacBeth Evans Glass Company, Anchor-Hocking Glass Company, United States Glass Company, and Federal Glass Company. Production was centered in the Pennsylva-

Table full of Depression glass, made c. 1920–1940. Values are based on color and pattern. All made in the Midwest.

nia, Ohio, and West Virginia areas, as it was with carnival glass.

Depression glass was everyday dinnerware. Pieces that were heavily used and therefore prone to breakage (butter dishes, handled pitchers, cookie jars, and even ashtrays) are not found in abundance today. American Sweetheart is the most desired pattern as more was made. Red is best, blue second, and pink least desired. Blue Madrid made by the Federal Glass Company is in short supply because they were not able to produce the exact blue wanted. Most Depression glass was made in the "mold etched" process which was unique to the period. However, some was made by the "chip mold," paste mold, or even handmade process. The latter techniques were a holdover from the carnival glass period in which some of the finer pieces of relatively inexpensive glass were produced. Many glass patterns were given names, such as Old Cafe, Lace Edge, Miss America, Queen Mary, Colonial, Coronation, Roulette, Hobnail, Oyster and Pearl, and the like. A good reference book for

this type of glass is listed in the bibliography.

Contemporary Glass

Many are concerned about the advisability of collecting contemporary glass. This is fine as long as proper documentation of artists and makers is provided. Experience has shown that most antiques change hands at far greater value if the name of the maker is known. The hours spent on research to document old unrecorded items could be spent in other pursuits, so the information should be recorded now for future generations. Some concerns do not mark their pieces, and I do not recommend collecting their output. Some companies may sign them with their name, but not with the name of the artist— again, the artist's name is most important. Several people may be involved in the making of one glass piece—be sure you get the names of all those who worked on the piece, or do not buy it. You will realize the wisdom of this if you are concerned with the future interest in and value of the piece. If value is of no concern to you, buy what you please, but realize that you have actually done the piece an injustice by not

Green glass, Art Deco vases by Bacarrat, France, 1920s. Nude modeling in the Art Deco period was a highlight of glass design.

permitting future owners to know its origin. If paper labels are provided, keep them on the piece since they are valuable for documentation. Do not put your glass in the dishwasher, just clean it with a damp rag and dry it carefully. Not long ago, a broken Tiffany bowl with the paper label intact sold for $45 at an auction. The label will undoubtedly find its way to the bottom of an unmarked bowl (which may or may not be Tiffany) in order to raise its value. As with most antiques, those items which are American made will have the most value in the future, so it is best to collect contemporary American glass. Buy rejects, samples, and closeout pieces from concerns where handwork is still in process. The oddity and small flaws which caused rejection will often command more interest and value as time goes on.

Areas of Collecting Interest

Bottles

It is recorded that the bottle made its appearance about 250 B.C. when the first blowpipes appeared in the Mediterranean area. They, along with window glass, were the main product of our early glass works, as they were a quickly made, inexpensive container which could handle the commerce of liquids and foods. They were free blown, then, early in the eighteenth century, blown into wooden and then metal molds. When the pressing of glass began in the 1820s, the hand blown bottle was still a necessity. It was not until the early twentieth century that machines took over the process of bottle making and hand work almost totally disappeared. Much philosophical glass was still made by hand, on order, such as test tubes, beakers, piping and the like which was used in laboratories. Custom glass houses still made glass items by hand, on order, to satisfy those who wanted them. This is why a bottle made by Tiffany craftsmen as late as the 1920s may be worth much more than a bottle dug from Roman ruins. The desirability of the piece sets the price.

Color in glass most often will heighten value, so one must learn which is most desired in the type of bottle you choose to collect. Cobalt blue glass was made with radioactive cobalt, but I learned at a seminar that there is no danger from handling old glass made with it. This color is much desired in most glass collecting categories.

Bottles were made as early as 1608 (when Jamestown was settled), and many interesting ones are being made today. Pre-revolutionary American-made bottles are rare. Most American bottles of that era came from overseas, primarily from England and France. During the seventeenth century, bottle and window glass houses were set up in many places in this country, but no documented pieces have been found. Some eighteenth century pieces have been located, with enough documentation to land them in museums and great collections. After the Revolutionary War,

At left is ribbed amber flask, Ohio, c. 1840s. At right is Keene, New Hampshire, water bottle, c. 1830–1840 in amber glass. The ribbed design was created by forcing a gather of glass at the end of a blowpipe into a small iron mold which bore this pattern. Then it was blown, expanding the pattern. The bottle was made by blowing directly into a wooden mold.

Most of the early square bottles can be attributed to England or the continent. These fit into special boxes which kept them separated and safe during ocean voyages. The demijohn may have been used for wine.

the American glass industry expanded quickly, and there are many examples which have survived and are available to collectors. Bottles are divided into categories—there are historical flasks, bitters, medicines, and figurals. Early flasks were free blown, but by the early part of the nineteenth century most were being blown into wooden or iron molds so that designs would appear and uniform sizes would result. The early blown mold bottles are quite plentiful which is amazing when you realize how fragile and brittle the old glass is. As the settlement of the country moved rapidly west the glassworkers went with it, and as a result there is much good glass in

bottle-form made throughout the nineteenth century. This is quite desirable today, and a directory of early glassmakers appears on pages 99 and 100.

Design, color, and condition are also important. Foreign bottles are not of great importance in American collecting, unless they are extremely old. Recent digs have uncovered seventeenth and eighteenth century English and French bottles, which have considerable value as they were used by the Indians and our first settlers. Wrecks of old ships off the coasts here and in the Caribbean have long held old bottles which are being brought up by divers every year. Bottle auctions are held throughout

the country and help set the prices by which bottles are bought and sold today.

Bottles are of great interest as a collectible, since you can dig them from the ground at no charge. Diggers will spend weekends tracking down old dumps behind farms in the country, and even hunting in old town dumps. The bottles have lain buried for years, so all you have to do is arm yourself with a shovel, pick, and hoe and you are in business. A first aid kit, gloves, and high boots are also necessary. Snakes are common around old dumps, so be sure your legs and hands are covered. Poison ivy is a hazard, so you must be protected against it. Above all, obtain permission to hunt from the landowners, as some are quite touchy about having their ground dug up. Some bottle collectors attend building wreckings and ask permission to search the foundations, cellars, and walls for hidden bottles. Many good bottles are found while a backhoe or bulldozer is digging a cellar for a new building or cleaning

up the debris from one just torn down. A cement layer and his crew, while laying a sidewalk for me, once reinforced the concrete with the many beer bottles which they emptied on a hot day and threw into the mix. These will undoubtedly be the subject of much conjecture when they are dug up someday.

BITTERS, FIGURALS, AND FLASKS

Bitters bottles are quite rare, as they were not made in quantity. Those with original labels are of most interest as they promised cures for diseases which are unheard of today. Most contained rather potent drugs such as cocaine, which lulled a person into a sense of well being. Contrary to popular opinion, America experienced its greatest drug culture in the last century when many drugs were legal. The Food and Drug Act of 1906 put an end to this and an end to the sale of bitters.

Figurals (bottles shaped in the form of

bodies, heads, animals, houses, buildings, etc.) have always been with us. Today's output is confined mostly to ceramic figurals, but since these are in the bottle category, they are collected as well as the glass. The early medicines are interesting because some were molded with identifying characteristics so the blind, or those searching for medicine at night (before the days of electric lights), could just feel the ridges, or in the case of poison, a skull and crossbones to warn them of the contents.

Perhaps the most desirable bottles are early nineteenth century historical flasks with good color. Many of the early flasks were blown into wooden molds and feature historic motifs of important people, places, and events. Early flasks, very often, were made in olive amber as much silica melted to that color, so one will find examples from many parts of the country. Beware of the Persian saddle flask. They appeared in abundance in the early 1960s when they were made by hand and aged quickly in the desert.

BOOZ BOTTLES

An interesting bottle to collect resembles a cabin and was made at the Whitney Glass Works in Glassboro, New Jersey. One will note the molded roof which reads "E.G. Booz's Old Cabin Whiskey." On the side is the address "120 Walnut Street, Philadelphia." On the reverse roof is the date 1840. Because of this, early collectors were led to believe that these bottles were made in that year during the campaign of William Henry Harrison.

However, in the book *American Glass* by George and Helen McKearin (Crown) we are told that Booz was not located at the Walnut Street address until 1860. Prior to that time he was listed as Edmund G. Booz, importer and dealer in wines, brandies and

Olive amber flasks made at the Marlborough Street Works, Keene, New Hampshire, c. 1817–1830. At left is one of 35 different Keene Masonic flasks. The differences exist because the wooden molds were hand-carved. At right is the famed Sunburst flask. A similar flask was made at Coventry, Connecticut, but the rays are much thinner and there are more of them.

Booz's Old Cabin Whiskey bottle, c. 1840s. An early example is quite desirable. These have been reproduced.

liquors, 54 South Front Street. From 1860 to 1870 he was listed at the Walnut Street Address.

About 1931, a reproduction of the bottle was made with a straight roof ridge and a period missing after the word whiskey on one end. Original colors were shades of amber and olive green, but later reproductions can be found in light blue and green. Reproductions have been made since World War II and can be found on the shelves of gift shops, so one must be alert and know what he is buying.

There were other bottles made to resemble log cabins and the term log cabin whiskey might be applied to many more. Whitney is known to have made others in this style. Also, Booz perhaps wanted to capitalize on this appelation in marketing his liquor, hence the name on this bottle which lacks the molded log sides which can be seen in others.

Rare early caster set in ribbed or fluted design. Massachusetts, c. 1830. These were popular well in to the 20th century. If one is found with colored bottles, it most likely came from overseas—England or the continent. Ray Barlow.

Booze News

One can easily see where the slang name for liquor originated as Booz was quite a famous dealer of liquors. In the book American Glass *by George and Helen McKearin we are told that the word booze actually is derived from the seventeenth-century French word bouse, and it came into common usage primarily due to this bottle.*

Caster Sets

There are still many farm tables that sport caster sets, right in the same place mother and grandmother used them. It is a handy holder of spices, condiments and sauces and is making a comeback in the contemporary home. Caster sets take up little space and can be passed around the table easily. Anything so functional was bound to be revived for use today.

Most caster sets one will find consist of a silver plated frame holding five or six bottles or shakers. One would use them for salt and pepper or other spices, and oil, vinegar, peppersauce, catsup or other dressings. They originated in the days when most families made their own sauces and grew their own spices. They did not come in the handy bottles and shaker tins one finds in the supermarket today. They

Collecting Tip

When buying a caster set, it is important that all the bottles or shakers match. Pressed design, engraving, and stoppers must all be alike. Check these carefully.

would be filled for each meal to complement whatever food was being served.

Those with colored bottles are quite desirable, but all the examples of these I have seen came from England or France. Clear bottles seem to be the choice of American makers. I have seen only one sterling frame with cut glass bottles which was made in America, though these too are common in England and France.

Most often, the glass and metal work were done by separate factories but in one case, two such manufacturers joined together to turn out the work in one building—the Mount Washington Glass Company and the Pairpoint Silver Company in New Bedford, Massachusetts.

Glass Hats

Glass hats have been made extensively from the last century into this one and have many collectors. One will find glass hats in many colors, designs and sizes. They were made in New England as well as in the midwest region around Pittsburgh. There is much conjecture as to their original use. Years ago, most identified them as toothpick holders. Some felt they were for after dinner candies or nuts. Years ago, one found them holding stick matches alongside ashtrays.

However, some years ago at a seminar, Kenneth Wilson, former curator at the Corning Museum of Glass and director of collections at the Henry Ford Museum, stated that they originated as master salts. This caused a minor stir in the crowd. In discussion, some have argued that if they were made as master salts, where were the individual salts to match them? All the glass books I have do not even mention glass hats. None is pictured in Mr. Wilson's book, *New England Glass and Glassmaking*, nor in *Pittsburgh Glass* by Lowell Innes, or the 1874 reprint of the Boston and Sandwich Company's catalog, by Ruth Webb Lee. One opinion is that they were mere whimsies originally, then mass manufac-

tured to take care of those who found specific uses for them, such as toothpick holders.

Many are found pressed in the popular daisy and button pattern. After World War II, the glass houses in Murano shipped thousands in millifiori, opalescent, burmese and other exotic glasses to capitalize on the American craze of collecting them. Whatever your opinion, they are functional and inexpensive to collect. Do not invest heavily in them—there is no shortage, nor does it seem there will be one to stimulate higher prices. Just have fun with them.

Oddities

Many whimsies were made from glass, since this was an easily worked material and colors could be used at little extra cost. Canes, penny banks, pipes, toys, candy holders, darning balls, animals, birds, floral displays, and the like poured from the factories. Some say this was the result of extra glass being used up at the close of the day by workmen who made such trinkets as gifts for families and friends. You must judge these items on their interest and workmanship, and on whether they are pleasing and desirable. It is not necessary to spend huge sums of money for them— you should enjoy them for the artistic artifacts they are.

Paperweights

Paperweights are an important facet of glass collecting, since they represent an art form which demands good workmanship and are usually pretty and functional. Many fine weights were made overseas, especially at Bacarrat, Clichy, and St. Cloud in France, but some weights on a par with these were made in America. Most of the large glass factories employed paperweight makers, but this effort must have been concentrated in New England. Both the Boston and Sandwich Glass Company and the New England Glass Company were well

At left is a type of paperweight which is coming into the country today from China. In the center is the end-of-day type, most likely New England from the last quarter of the nineteenth century. At right is a rare French sulphide with classic figures.

known for this work. The Pairpoint works in New Bedford and some works in New Jersey (such as the works at Millville) contributed some elegant pieces.

Many private makers have been at work, and some of the contemporary pieces are commanding more money than the old ones. Domenick Labino of Grand Rapids, Ohio; Charles Kaziun of Brockton, Massachusetts; Ronald Hansen of Mackinac City, Michigan; and Johnny Gentile of Star City, Morgantown, West Virginia are among the contemporary makers whose works are being studiously collected at this time. There are a lot of handmade weights coming to America from the Orient and Europe—some quite good, but all must be judged on the quality of the design and workmanship.

Some weights are referred to as having sulphide interior decoration. This is merely a porcelain design or figure of some sort imbedded in the glass. The difficulty of molding the decoration into hot glass without destroying it is what gives these weights interest and value.

One of America's greatest glass craftsmen, the late Dominic Labino of Grand Rapids, Ohio. Here, he is seen decorating a paperweight. Many of his great works are in Toledo in public buildings, and in the Toledo Museum of Art.

98 *Glass*

Early Glass Manufactories

Amelung, John Frederick—See New Bremen Glass Manufactory.

Bakewell & Ensell—Pittsburgh, Pennsylvania, 1808–1882; operated under various partnership names; *Bakewell & Pages; Bakewell, Pears & Bakewell; Bakewell, Pears & Co.*, etc.; glass of all kinds including art and pressed.

Boston and Sandwich Glass Company—Sandwich, Massachusetts, 1825–1888; Deming Jarves; all types of glass, including early pressed glass.

Boston Crown Glass Company—Boston, Massachusetts, 1793–1829; Robert Hewes and others; window glass, bottles.

Boston Porcelain & Glass Manufacturing Company—Cambridge, Massachusetts, 1814–1888; George Blake, Thomas Curtis, and Jesse Putnam; glass, stoneware, porcelain. In 1817, became the *New England Glass Company*. Originated amberina, pomona. Prolific in the art glass period. Moved by final owner, Edward Libbey, to Toledo, Ohio, in 1888.

Brooklyn Glass Works—Brooklyn, New York, 1823–1868; full range of glass items. John Gilliland. Moved in 1868 to Corning, New York, to become the Corning Glass Company.

Cape Cod Glass Company—Sandwich, Massachusetts, 1858–1869; under direction of Deming Jarves. Operated 1869–1881 by a Dr. Flowers. Cut, pressed, and decorative glass.

Chelmsford Glass Works—Chelmsford, Massachusetts, 1802–1839; Jonathan Hunnewell and Samuel Gore. Window glass and bottles. Moved to Suncook, New Hampshire, in 1839 and operated there until 1850.

Cincinnati Glass Manufacturing Company—Cincinnati, Ohio, 1814–1822; Isaac Craig. Bottles, window glass.

Dorflinger Glass Works—Greenpoint, Long Island, New York, 1858–1865; Christian and Christopher Dorflinger. Also, White Mills, Pennsylvania, 1865–1918. Cut and colored glass; table and decorative wares.

Glassboro—New Jersey, 1781–1824; started by members of the Stanger family.

Granite Glass Works—Stoddard, New Hampshire, 1846–1872; bottles and flasks.

Hewes, Robert—Temple, New Hampshire, 1780–1782; window glass and bottles.

Jersey Glass Company—Jersey City, New Jersey, 1824–1860; established by George Dummer. All types of glass.

Kensington Glass Works—Philadelphia, Pennsylvania, 1771; advertised with the name of Thomas Dyott after 1824. Changed to *Dyottville Glass Works* in 1833. Operated under various ownerships into the twentieth century. Noted for historical flasks and bottles under Dyott's ownership.

LaBelle Glass Works—Bridgeport, Ohio, 1872–1900; pressed and flint glass.

Mantua Glass Works—Mantua, Ohio, 1821–1829; bottles, flint glassware.

Marlboro Street Works—Keene, New Hampshire, 1815–1850; Henry Rowe Schoolcraft and Timothy Twitchell. Historical flasks, bottles, tableware.

McKee & Brothers—East Birmingham, Pennsylvania, 1850–1890; J. & F. McKee; all types of glass.

Millville, New Jersey, Glass Works—founded 1806 and still in business. Originated by James Lee. Originally produced window glass and bottles. Acquired by Whitall Brothers in 1844 and became *Whitall-Tatum Company.*

Mount Vernon Glass Company—Mount Vernon, New York, 1810–1844; bottles, flasks, flint glass, historical flasks, etc.

Mount Washington Glass Company—South Boston, Massachusetts, 1837–1869. Moved in 1869 to New Bedford, joined with Pairpoint Silver Company. Closed in 1958. Reopened by Robert Bryden as *Pairpoint Glass Company,* 1970, Sagamore, Massachusetts. Glass of all kinds. Originated burmese, peachblow, rose amber.

New Bremen Glass Manufactory—Frederick, Maryland, 1784–1795; started by John Frederick Amelung. Noted for engraved glass.

New Geneva Glass Works—New Geneva, Pennsylvania, 1797–1807; Albert Gallatin and others. Window glass, bottles, tableware. Later moved to Greensboro.

New Hampshire Glass Factory—Keene, New Hampshire (North Works), 1814–1855; window glass.

Pitkin Glass Works—Manchester, Connecticut, 1783–1830; Elisha Pitkin and Samuel Bishop. Originators of Pitkin type flask; also made bottles and tableware.

Pittsburgh Glassworks—Pittsburgh, Pennsylvania, 1797–1886; James O'Hara and Isaac Craig. Window glass, bottles, holloware.

Portland Glass Works—Portland, Maine, 1863–1873; lamps, tableware, colored glass.

South Stoddard Glass Works—South Stoddard, New Hampshire, 1850–1873; bottles and historical flasks.

South Wheeling Glass Works—Wheeling, West Virginia, 1835–1880; flint and colored glass.

Stiegel, Henry William—Manheim, Pennsylvania, 1764–1774; noted for enameled, decorated, and colored wares.

Stoddard Glass Works—South Stoddard, New Hampshire, 1842–1850; Joseph Foster. Mostly bottles and flasks.

Suncook Glass Works—Suncook, New Hampshire, 1839–1850; moved from Chelmsford. Window glass, tableware.

Vermont Glass Factory—Salisbury, Vermont, 1813–1842; in 1842, became the *Lake Dunmore Glass Company.* Bottles, flasks, and holloware.

Willington Glass Company—West Willington, Connecticut, 1815–1872; bottles, flasks, and holloware.

Wistar, Caspar—Salem County, New Jersey, 1739–1780; window glass, bottles, and holloware.

Zanesville Glass Manufacturing Company—Zanesville, Ohio, 1815–1851; holloware, bottles, and historical flasks.

Glossary

Agata—A mottled effect obtained by spraying alcohol or other chemicals onto the bodies of colored glass.

Amber—Amber colored, very popular during the last part of the nineteenth century into the twentieth.

Amber (Rose)—Basically an amberina made by the Mount Washington Glass Company.

Amberina—An art glass, most popular during the last part of the nineteenth century, believed to have originated at the New England Glass Company. Shaded from ruby to amber by including gold in the glass metal, which would turn amber first and then to varying hues of red as more heat was applied.

Amberina (Cased or Plated)—An inner core of glass which is most often fiery opalescent creamy white, covered with an amberina exterior. Most glass in this style is ribbed.

Art—A general term used to describe the many various colored fancy glasswares of the late nineteenth century.

Art Deco—The period between 1920 and 1940. Artistic work was done as well as the inexpensive work now called carnival and Depression glass.

Art Noveau—The period between about 1895 and 1915, characterized by the iridescent colorings and Oriental shapes. Leading makers were Tiffany, Lalique, Galle, etc.

Aurene—A product of the Corning Glass Works, attributed to Frederick Carder, most often in a blue shade with gold iridescence. Twentieth century.

Baccarat—High quality French glass manufacturer, still in business since early in the nineteenth century. Well known for its paperweights.

Blown Three Mold—Glass hand blown into a tri-divided mold, found in vertical ribbed patterns; diamond quilting, gothic, sunburst, and fluted. Some geometric. Early nineteenth century.

Bryden—Robert Bryden, last manager of the original Mount Washington-Pairpoint Glass Works in New Bedford, closed in 1958. Reopened the Pairpoint Glass Works at Sagamore, Massachusetts, 1970.

Burmese—Shaded pink to a lemon yellow. First made in the 1880s at the Mount Washington Glass Works, New Bedford, by Frederick Shirley. Most often found in a satin finish.

Cameo—Glass which has been dipped into another colored glass (or "flashed") then cut in cameo relief.

Carnival—An inexpensive iridescent glass first produced by Frank Fenton in Newark, Ohio in 1907. None was made in New England. It received its name as a result of being used as prizes at carnivals and fairs.

Clichy—A French glassworks at Clichy, dating from the early nineteenth century. A maker of fine paperweights.

Coralene—Art glass with frosted crystal decoration.

Crown Milano—Made by Frederick Shirley at Mount Washington Glass works. A satin finish ecru colored glass, decorated with flowers and gilding. 1880s.

Cut Glass—Usually heavy lead crystal with designs cut into it by a spinning abrasive wheel. The Mount Washington Glass Company is considered by many to have made the best in the world. The most brilliant period for this product is 1890–1915, when it was the height of fashion.

Daum—During the last half of the nineteenth century, Antonin and Auguste Daum worked at Nancy, France, with Emile Galle. Their pieces are usually signed "Daum-Nancy."

Depression—A name given to the inexpensive colorful glass made during the Depression, and often given away at theaters as an incentive to go to the movies on slow nights. It was used as premiums, and also sold at the five and dime stores.

Durand—Victor Durand worked 1925–1932 in Vineland, New Jersey, and produced colorful glass in both art noveau and art deco styles.

Etched—A reference to inexpensive glass which was decorated by lightly etching it with a spinning copper wheel.

Favrile—Made by Louis Comfort Tiffany in the first quarter of this century. The word is taken from the German word "faber," which means color. It can be any color, with iridescent tints and highlights.

Flashed—Flashed glass is made by dipping a clear body of glass into a liquid mixture of colored glass. This is bonded by heat to create a coating which may be cut or etched to reveal the clear glass beneath.

Galle—The master French glassmaker of Nancy, France, Emile Galle is noted for his art noveau glass and cameo glass.

Gunderson—Robert Gunderson was plant manager of the Pairpoint Works in New Bedford from 1939–1952. Glass made there during this period is often referred to as Gunderson glass.

Iridescent—A name applied to any glass which has an iridescent shine which is created by chemical processes. It was made in imitation of early Roman glass which had absorbed minerals from the soil while lying buried for hundreds of years.

Kew Blas—Gold iridescent glass made at the Union Glass Company in Somerville, Massachusetts. Late nineteenth century.

Lalique—Rene Lalique, France, first quarter of this century. Worked in art noveau styles; with pressing, cutting, frosting, cameo, etc.

Lutz—Best known for his threaded glass and other art glass work at the Boston and Sandwich Glass Company. Worked also for Dorflinger and the Mount Washington Glass Works, mostly during the third quarter of the nineteenth century.

Mother of Pearl—A satin finish glass with design worked into it, created by Joseph Webb in 1885 in Beaver Falls, Pennsylvania.

Mount Washington—The Mount Washington Glass Company was formed by Deming Jarves in 1837 for his son. It was later moved to New Bedford. The name has been synonymous with the name Pairpoint since 1894 when the two companies merged, the latter originally being the Pairpoint Silver Company.

Pattern—Glass which is pressed mechanically into a mold is called pattern glass. This was first done by Benjamin Bakewell in Pittsburgh in 1825, and was improved at the Boston and Sandwich Glass Company in 1827.

Peachblow—That made by Hobbs and Brockunier in Wheeling shades from rose to yellow. That made at the New England Glass Works shades from a rose-red at the top to white at the base. The latter is also called "Wild Rose" and was first made in the 1880s.

Pigeonblood—Known to have been made by Hobbs and Brockunier. It looks ruby in color until it is held to the light, which causes the color to change to an orange-yellow.

Pomona—Made by Joseph Locke at the New England Glass Company. It is a clear glass with etched pattern, having amber staining and often blue cornflowers for decoration.

Portiault—A noted concern of the nineteenth century at Portiault, France. Identified by imprint of name and later by a rosette design, generally at the base of the piece.

Quezal—Named after the exotic Quetzal bird of South America whose brilliant plumage it resembles. Made in 1916–1918 by the Quezal Art Glass and Decorating Company in Brooklyn. It features deep colorings and iridescence, much in the manner of Tiffany. Most is art noveau in style.

Rubena Crystal—First made by Hobbs and Brockunier. A ware which shades from red to clear.

Rubena Verde—A ware which shades from red to yellow.

Sandwich—Common name given to items made at the Boston and Sandwich Glass Company, Sandwich, Massachusetts, 1825–1888.

Satin—Glass which has been bathed in hydrofluoric acid to give it a soft, satin finish.

Spangled—Generally, a cased glass which has been colored with design and fragments of metals such as gold to make it sparkle.

Spatter—Made by rolling hot glass over broken bits of colored glass to incorporate them into the body of the piece.

St. Louis—A firm which had its beginnings in the seventeenth century in France. Noted for its pressed glass and paperweights.

Stained—Glass is often colored by staining it while hot. Much pressed glass is colored this way.

Steuben—The famous works still operating at Corning, New York. Well known for its handmade clear glass.

Threaded—The best known artisan of this style is Nicholas Lutz, who worked at the Boston and Sandwich Glass Factory. The glass is threaded and striped in the Venetian style.

Tiffany—Louis Comfort Tiffany was an American pioneer of art noveau designs and iridescent glass. He worked beginning in 1878, and his plant continued working until 1933, the year of his death.

Vasa Murrhina—The Vasa Murrhina Art Glass Company operated in Hartford, Connecticut, during the art glass period. This glass sparkled with imbedded mica colored with gold.

Venetian—A term given to the delicate styled glass which has been made in that region of Italy since the fourteenth century.

Waterford—Originally operated at Waterford, Ireland, between 1794 and 1851. It was reopened in 1951 as the Waterford Glassworks.

CHAPTER THREE

Ceramics

Introduction

Historical Overview

Surely the earliest collectibles—as notable for their artistic merit as for their functional value—are ceramic objects. The art of fashioning clay into usable vessels is as old as civilization. In ancient times, people learned to shape readily available clay into useful objects, and then harden them in the sun. They learned to make them hard enough to withstand heat, and also that such heat hardened them even more. They learned later that with the addition of crushed flint or other stone they could make a very strong body that would withstand rough usage. The final step in early ceramics was the discovery that after glazing, the clay vessels would no longer soak up water and that liquids could then be stored in them for indefinite periods.

The simplest glaze was that of a clay with a lower firing temperature than the body clay. This would be mixed with water and then slipped (or poured) over the vessel and fired, leaving a clear, hard coating that was bonded to the surface by the intense heat. In the late eighteenth century metal glazes were perfected, with lead being the most preferred and the most dangerous. Lead was mixed with a liquid clay mixture, and after firing provided a very luminescent surface, though dangerous if food or edible liquids were stored against it for any length of time. The lives of our ancestors were undoubtedly shortened immeasurably by the amount of lead used in household ceramics, plates, and other cooking utensils. Tin was often used in glazes, as were iron filings, zinc, copper, and other minerals and metals that would contribute a hard surface or color to the piece.

A later technique involved the use of common table salt, which was thrown into a kiln during the last minutes of firing. As it vaporized, it was deposited on the clay bodies, providing a hard sheen, rough with imperfections.

The art of ceramic making in Europe was confined to the most basic work in earthenware when the Pilgrims settled this country. The secret of porcelain making lay locked in the Orient, and it was not until the later seventeenth century in France that porcelain was made with much success. The first porcelains that bore any resemblance to those from China were turned out at Rouen and St. Cloud in France. However, it was not until 1708 that Johann Freiderich Bottger perfected a

Amphora, Attica, c. 530–510 B.C.; black figures, lidded neck. This shows early sophistication in the decoration of ceramics. (Butterfield & Butterfield.)

Fine and rare monumental glazed pottery floor vase, executed by Gates Pottery as Teco, c. 1910. Sold for $22,000 by Butterfield & Butterfield, Los Angeles. (Butterfield & Butterfield.)

true porcelain body by the use of kaolin and the petuntse clays which had been an oriental secret for so many centuries. It was not long before potteries copying Bottger's formula and techniques were set up both on the continent and in England, and the vast ceramics industry was born. To attempt to discuss the industry before that time would hardly be worthwhile as little of that production can be found today, either here or overseas. It is enough of a project to concentrate on what can be found and collected today.

There are actually many more fine types of ceramics from all over the world in America today than there were at the turn of the century. The importation of such antique ceramic pieces did not reach great heights until after World War I, when American affluence climbed. Before then,

most homes were equipped with relatively inexpensive dinnerware made by some concern in this country and little interest in these wares was noted in antiques collecting. Lucky was the bride who received a complete service of French, English, or German dinnerware, as this was the ultimate gift. Much of this dinnerware has survived, but hardly enough to satisfy the demand on the part of collectors who want something old and of good quality. We were fortunate that the makers continued to turn out the same patterns in open stock for many years so that replacements were easy to obtain. Today, you must most often scrounge about in antiques shops and shows looking for needed items to fill out a set, since many patterns have been discontinued in favor of more contemporary designs.

Types of Ceramic Ware

The most desirable ware to collect is *porcelain*—a fine, thin-bodied ceramic which is translucent and beautiful when decorated. Next in importance is *bone china*, which originated in England. Instead of the expensive kaolin clay used for porcelain, it is made from ground calcined bone ash, which gives a good thin body, but is opaque.

The term *earthenware* is used to de-

Collection of stoneware at the Folk Art Museum, Witmer, Pennsylvania.

Stoneware From Vermont

John Norton established a pottery at Bennington, Vermont, to make jugs in which he could sell his cider. His stoneware business soon outdid his cider business and he expanded to take care of the demand for his wares. The pottery continued to operate in the hands of his family through most of the century, turning out a variety of functional and decorative pieces. His son-in-law, Christopher Weber Fenton, opened the United States Pottery Company in 1847 and continued in business until 1858. Fenton hired the great English modeler Daniel Greatback, who turned out designs for many animal figures and other decorative pieces which were made in both the brown colored Rockinghamware and the pure white parian. Rockinghamware is reputed to have originated at the estates of the Earl of Rockingham in England, and found much favor in England and America. Many American concerns turned it out, but that from Bennington seems to be the most desired.

Daniel Greatback modeled this hound-handled pitcher while at the Trenton Pottery in the early 1840s. The hound is resting his muzzle upon his paws.

Rockinghamware dog with basket made at the United States Pottery Company in Bennington. Dogs from this pottery must be standing, not sitting or lying down.

Two hound-handled pitchers modeled by Daniel Greatback while at the United States Pottery Company in Bennington, Vermont, in the late 1840s. You will note that these vary from that done in Trenton (there is space under the hound's muzzle).

scribe most pieces found as common china in the home. Earthenware is also opaque. Just hold any piece to the light. If you can see light through it, it is porcelain. If not, it is earthenware.

Another type of china is *vitreous ware.* This is quite hard, most often very thick, and is used extensively for commercial chinas for hotels, trains, ships, etc. It has better quality and is stronger than earthenware, but does not possess the fragility or beauty of porcelain.

Beneath earthenware is *stoneware,* made from various colored clays. Stoneware clay pieces must be made with thick walls to prevent its collapse in the kiln. This is why stoneware crocks, butter pots, jugs, etc., are so thick and heavy. There is no stoneware clay in New England; all of it had to be hauled in by wagon or ship until the railroads were in operation. One potter, Jeremiah Burpee (c. 1805) died with his secret of making stoneware pieces with

Decorated Pennsylvania redware, nineteenth century.

thin bodies. Whatever he added to the clay is not known. Where he obtained his clay is not known either, as he was a native of Boscawen, New Hampshire, and there is no stoneware clay in the area.

At the bottom is *redware,* made from common red clay out of which bricks, tiles, flower pots, etc., are made.

Americans are inclined to collect simple redware and stoneware, which is most often made of light colored clays reinforced with flint or other hardening material. Both products are still made today, some by kilns operating in the same way they did in the nineteenth century, and some by craft potters working in both traditional and contemporary motifs.

Manufacturing Techniques

It is interesting to note the technique of making simple stoneware. The following recipe is from *Mackezies 5,000 Receipts* (sic) published in 1828:

Tobacco-pipe clay is beaten much in water; by this process, the finer parts of the clay remain suspended in the water, while the coarser sand and other impurities fall to the bottom. The thick liquid consisting of water and finer parts of the clay is further purified by passing it through hair and lawn sieves of different degrees of fineness. After this, the liquor is mixed in various proportions for various ware with another liquor of the same density, and consisting of flints calcined, ground and suspended in water. The mixture is then dried in a kiln and afterwards beaten to a proper temper, it becomes fit for being formed at the wheel into dishes, plates, bowls, etc. When this ware is to be put into the furnace to be baked, the several pieces of it are placed in the cases made of clay, called saggars, which are piled one upon another, in the dome of the furnace. A fire is lighted; when the ware is brought to a proper temper, which happens in about 48 hours, it is glazed by common salt. The salt is thrown into the furnace through holes in the upper part of it, by the heat of which it is instantly converted into a thick vapour; which, circulating through the furnace, enters the saggar through the holes made in its side (the top being covered to prevent the salt from falling on the ware) and attaching itself to the surface of the ware, it forms that vitreous coat upon the surface, which is called its glaze.

The formulas for the more sophisticated wares, such as porcelain, bone china, soft and hard paste, Queensware, and the like, are much more complicated, but all ceramics begin with the basics noted above. A once-popular glaze was a shining black which was made up of 100 parts of lead, 18 parts of crushed flint, and 40 parts of manganese. With such ingredients, the glaze must have helped spoil the food. Most manufacturers today use fritted, body sheen, or soft glazes which are made up of basic clays with nothing to affect any food stored next to them. You must be careful in purchasing clay artifacts from underdeveloped nations as some may be coated with the dangerous lead glaze. It was not until the 1820s that experimentation resulted in glazes made with no lead, but they were expensive at the time and did not come into general use on stoneware until a decade or two later.

Determining Age and Authenticity

There are no set rules for determining the age and authenticity of early ceramics, but the following pointers are offered as an aid. No one rule can guarantee authenticity—you must inspect many features before attribution can be made. A simple clue is the wear on the bottom of any piece that must rest on a table or shelf. If the piece is old, this wear will show as roughness, wear of the glaze, or small chips and cracks. Many early ceramics become crazed with age, and this crazing is difficult to reproduce. Items fired in kilns before the middle of the nineteenth century often show the marks of the tripod on which they rested in

the saggar so that the heat could flow evenly around them. These are called tripod marks, and there are usually three which pierce the glaze on the underside of the dish out toward the rim. They will show up as three dots. There may be a triple dot at each point—this is almost always a guarantee of age. Contemporary pieces are still being fired on tripods, so this clue is not always constant. I have seen tripod marks on Doulton pieces whose other markings put them as being made after 1892. However, a piece without tripod marks should not be evaluated as being made before 1850.

Painting designs on the clay bodies, then glazing and firing was the most popular technique used in all countries back to the eighteenth century. However, some pottery was painted over the first glaze, and then reglazed and fired. A good general rule to early handmade pottery value is that the more colors used, the higher the value. In the early days, each color had to be painted on, glazed, and then fired, which was a time-consuming process. Some plants used the technique of painting with colored glazes which would then be fired, doing away with the extra steps color usually demanded. Such glazes used at the Fenton works in Bennington are still brilliant today.

Some people feel that a piece must look old to be old, but on the surface many Chinese porcelains several hundred years old look as if they were made just a few days ago. This is a tribute to the superior formulas and ingenuity used by the Chinese artisans. However, most ceramics will show their age up to a point; it is up to you to evaluate how old a piece is if there are no markings or other identification to help you. If you are concerned about age, and are not satisfied with the determination of age either from the person from whom you are buying or from your own analysis, leave the item alone. A "lost" treasure can sometimes be a headache you really don't need.

Some American potteries capitalized on famous European names when marking their lines. In 1900, the Sèvres China Company opened its doors in East Liverpool, Ohio. Their mark is "SÈVRES" beneath a fleur-de-lis. Some are marked "Geneva." Some pieces made at the Potters Cooperative in East Liverpool after 1876 are marked "Dresden."

Originally, the American Limoges Company of Sebring, Ohio, marked its pieces "LIMOGES." It was first called the Limoges China Company, but in 1949 as a result of a dispute with the Limoges China Company of France, changed its name to include the word "American."

Many marks look extremely English— lion's heads, crowns, the word "ironstone," and the like, were stamped on pieces to fool buyers. There was no law requiring identification of country of origin to sell these pieces here; companies made the most of it. Today, buyers may think they have something from England when it is really a poor-quality earthenware with a similar name.

America

Early Ceramics

An American experiment in porcelain making took place in the 1740s, when a clay called "unaker" was found in Virginia. Without sufficient moneyed clientele to support it, the project went out of business, but not until it had established a unique link with the mother country. The clay was so pure and perfect that all through that century it was shipped to England; thus much of the desired ceramics there was made of American raw material.

Inventories of estates in eighteenth-century America reveal little or no fine china, except in the homes of the wealthy. Tea drinking was not really popular until the time of Queen Anne, although tea is known to have been imported as early as the 1660s. Ceramic tea sets were in demand after her time, and most wealthy homes were equipped with at least one. The poorer people were still eating from wooden or pewter plates and vessels. Perhaps our first recognized potter was John Pride of Salem, Massachusetts, who was registered as early as 1641. A brickworks was established in nearby Danvers as early as 1629, but there is no evidence that eating vessels or plates were made. I could provide a relatively good list of seventeenth- and eighteenth-century potters, but it would do little good to collectors, as little or none of the production can be documented today. Fortunately, some stoneware bears the imprint of makers' names and often bears the name of a commercial concern for whom they might have made it. Most noted among these are the Remmy and Crolius families of New York City, who imprinted their names, as well as that of Manhattan Wells, which was near the site where they worked. The wells were the water supply for the city. If you find marked stoneware, you can document it from books listed in the bibliography, as space does not permit a complete listing here. Needless to say, any eighteenth-century work is very desirable. Of course, the best area in which to look would be the thirteen original colonies. However, the area that includes New Jersey, Pennsylvania, New York, and New England is the prime place to look, as their output was the greatest during those times. Unmarked redware and stoneware has value if the shapes and workmanship are good. The decorated slipware made of red clay and then hand-painted throughout the northern colonies has now become highly collectible. Some of these pieces have reached the high three figure price range and have no place to go but up.

Types of Ceramics

DELFT-TYPE WARE

There is evidence that a delft-type ware was made in this country in the latter part of the seventeenth century and well into the eighteenth, but none has survived. Inventories of the period tell of the blue and white ware copied after the fashion of its European counterpart. This type of decorated earthenware originated in Ireland. Dutch traders hauled clay from there for the makers in their own country and brought with them some gaily decorated tin glazed ware that caught the fancy of those on the continent. The Dutch copied the style and are generally credited with originating it due to the large output from Delft, whose name was eventually attached to it. Delft was made in other countries, including the Lowlands, Germany, France, and England.

REDWARE

The first American redware was unmarked, but as the eighteenth century progressed, the Pennsylvania Germans began coloring their pieces with designs and sayings and some were well-signed by their makers. Added to this was the technique of sgraffito—the scratch carving believed to have originated in the Commonwealth of Pennsylvania. Artisans created these designs by carving the original clay body before firing, filling the indentations with a coloring agent, and then glazing and firing it. The carving might also be done after the glaze was applied, with the coloring added using a colored glaze. For protection, painting was done under a glaze which was later fired. Tin glazes were popular at the time since they could be colored themselves, lending a better look to the piece. Though most of this work seems to have turned up in Pennsylvania, it is known that this technique was copied throughout the colonies. Perhaps you can trace the origins of such pieces through design, as the Pennsylvania motifs are quite regional in their look.

However, you must be careful in your attribution, since much simple ware was shipped in from other countries, notably England, during these years. Fragments have been found at many historic sites in this country and their documentation has led back across the ocean, even though most people would think that such simple wares were most likely made in the colonies.

As clay-refining methods improved, potters grew more sophisticated in their work, and much thinner and very functional wares appeared including shaving mugs, drinking mugs, milk pitchers, and batter jugs. The bean pot made its appearance early in the nineteenth century in both redware and stoneware. This type of work is being reproduced today. With the knowledge of old recipes and methods of firing, all of us are exposed to the possibility of buying a recently made piece which has been aged quite quickly through the use of chemicals. There is no known easy way to tell the old from the new, but science can prove the age of an item if a fragment is examined. Most of you will not want to go through the expense of this, so you must familiarize yourself with the "look" of old redware by searching it out in museums and collections and doing a lot of studying. There is no formula that I can put into print to help you. So far as collecting is concerned, you should look for pieces documented with dates and makers' names. Next in importance are those pieces with good folk art decoration, with animals, birds, and people being the most popular. Color must be good and condition is very important. Many a cat, dog, or chicken has been fed from old redware as it fell from popularity, and many pieces have suffered as a result.

STONEWARE

The American stoneware industry did not take hold until after the Revolutionary

War. Eighteenth century production is noted and some of it is cataloged, but there is not much chance of finding examples today, except in the better shops which specialize in ferreting out such pieces for discriminating customers. Most pieces are preserved in museums or historical societies, as well they should be. After the turn of the century, production was increased to the point that much ware was exported to other countries. Accounts of American manufacturing in 1828 reveal that stoneware was one of our greatest exports. Rarely would a piece be discarded if it were still usable, so if you are a traveler, you may look for it in antiques shops in Europe as well as South America.

Designs were created by sgraffito (scratch carving) and by direct painting under the glaze. You can easily determine the most valuable pieces by following simple rules, which, of course, must have their exceptions. *Shapes and forms* are important as well as good workmanship. *Decorations* are graded for importance, as follows: at the top of the list are buildings, most often farmhouses and the like; next in rarity are those of animals and fish, followed by birds, floral designs, and finally those with unidentifable designs or no decoration at all. Some feature the names of concerns who marketed them, drawn in cobalt blue or stamped in various colors. Age is helpful, regardless of decoration, but most collect these pieces only as examples of early folk art.

Rare pieces such as large water coolers, footwarmers, batter and switchel jugs, and funerary urns command much interest regardless of decoration, since they are difficult forms to find. (One used a switchel jug to carry a rugged rum drink out into the fields. Hung from a horse's harness, the potion was well mixed in time for enjoyment at the noontime meal.)

You must realize that stoneware items were made well into this century and that as recently as the 1920s, concerns were still using them in marketing products such as molasses, vinegar, tea, jams and jellies, and

Stoneware is graded more by its decoration than its maker or location of manufacture. Most desirable is the home or farm (left). Pieces with animals are next in importance, such as this deer on the butter pot made by L&E Norton of Bennington, Vermont (right). Next in desirability is a bird decoration, notably the eagle; next is floral (center). Least valuable are those marked with names of businesses which used them in commerce.

Stoneware made in Bennington, Vermont, nineteenth-century. The decoration of the "Bennington" deer in cobalt is among the most prized by collectors.

chemicals and other liquid products. By today's standards, they look quite old and most acquire a good patina after lying unused in cellars and barns for many years.

The kiln needed to mass produce such items had to be quite large and this limited the number that were set up in America. If a kiln was used for salt glazing, no other glaze could be fired in it, as the residue of salt from past firings would make it impossible for other glazes to stick to the bodies. Fuel for the kilns and availability of clay were important and often dictated the location of a business. Richard Carter Barret relates that farmers from the Bennington area traveling to sell their produce in Troy or Albany were encouraged to return loaded with clay from any cellar hole being dug along the way, since they could sell the clay to the potteries in Bennington. The clays of New Jersey are world famous, and were shipped just about everywhere—at first by boat and ox cart, and later by rail and ferry. Colored clays will not necessarily

Two-handled jug made by Chapman, Upson and Wright, Middlebury, Connecticut. Note the unusual eagle and flag decoration.

Spongeware

Spongeware is one of the hottest collectibles today. It is stoneware on which a mottled decoration has been applied by use of a sponge. Artisans dip the flat edge of a sponge in cobalt blue and apply the design. The earliest examples of spongeware date from about 1840 in this country. It can be found on most forms of stoneware and was made practically all over the country where suitable clays could be found.

There are some who question whether sponges were really used on some pieces we call spongeware. But contemporary artisans are still using this method, not only demonstrating that it is possible, but also proving without doubt that it was the manner in which the cobalt was applied. One of the most noted contemporary potters who make spongeware is Nancy Sampson of Westminster, Massachusetts. She has demonstrated the technique and her work is a true reproduction of the old we collect. She feels there is no other way it could have been done as conveniently and quickly.

Only twenty years ago, simple milk pitchers with spongeware decoration were selling at but a dollar or two as they were considered country pieces and the demand was not great. However, the rising interest in folk art has prompted a reexamination of tech-

Covered butter jar, stoneware with sponge decoration in cobalt blue.

niques used and the product has risen so that some pieces are in the three figures today.

A companion to spongeware is greenware, which is a green mottled decoration on a buff or beige body of clay. This is rarer than the blue, so commands better prices in equivalent form. Spongeware can be found all over the country, though the best place to locate it is at farm auctions out in the country.

remain the same hue after firing. Some blue clays are known to turn red and some green clays turn black. Tobacco-pipe clay was favored for delicate pieces and was much in demand.

Naturally, the first fuel was wood. Coal was adapted for this purpose after the Revolutionary War. As early as 1827, a railroad was built in Carbon County, Pennsylvania, to haul coal down to the ferryboats which plied the Delaware River to Philadelphia. After the discovery of oil wells in Pennsylvania at mid-century, oil was successfully used as a fuel for kilns. Mary Chase Perry Stratton first used electricity for firing during the late 1800s at her Pewabic Pottery in Detroit. Gas was employed where available, and to this day natural gas is very much accepted.

Ceramic makers are still experimenting with glazes in an effort to come up with something new. One potter frequents a local junk yard to retrieve ashes after the dealers have burned the tarred coatings from old electric and telephone wire. Mixed with a clear glaze, these ashes create an unusual effect on his pottery. Other potters use manganese and manganese oxide, and still others work with tin, zinc, copper, and other minerals which create an illuminating effect. The greatest artisans are those who combine a talent for design with skill in painting on their pieces. Perhaps the most noted craftsman in this field is left-handed Russell Henry of Birdsboro, Pennsylvania, whose artwork is as compelling as the shapes and forms he spins on his wheel.

PORCELAIN

America was quite late in developing good porcelain for sale to the public in any quantity. The first firm on record is that of Bonnin and Morris of Philadelphia. Some of their output has survived, but there was very little made, which accounts for the fact that it is not regarded as collectible. The next successful effort was that of Dr. Daniel Mead in New York City about 1812. His work was on a par with that of the Euro-peans, but again little was made. The first really successful porcelain maker was William Ellis Tucker, who produced ware as early as 1825, and though perhaps not on a par with its European counterparts, Tucker's work survives today as the most collectible of the early work in this area. The plant survived under various partnerships until 1838, and produced much ware that has survived. Tucker imported workers from France; hence the French look to his work. You might mistake his pieces for the contemporary Sèvres in color, shape, and decoration. Not much Tucker china has turned up on the open market in recent years. The Hammerslough collection of Tucker china at the William Penn Memorial Museum in Harrisburg was acquired piece by piece in Pennsylvania, New Jersey, and Delaware years ago. Very little of it was marked, as many companies dur-

Porcelain made by William Ellis Tucker, Philadelphia, 1826–1838. Note the French styled vase (front center). *On Tucker pieces, the square pedestal base must be white on top; there can be slight decoration, but only white background.*

ing that era were willing to let the public think they might be buying a foreign-made product, since most buyers felt that the best work was not done in America. For identification: Tucker bodies have a greenish tint to the white; the gilding has a purplish tint; the pedestals on vases and urns are never fully painted and often turn up at the corners, and the top surface of the pedestal is always white, but some decoration or gilding may be on it. Some of the Tucker workers also signed their pieces with their initials. Edwin Attlee Barber's book *Marks of American Potters* (listed in the bibliography) will provide you with the complete listing, as well as that of other potters and potteries in this country.

Another maker of porcelain was Smith, Fife & Co. of Philadelphia, who were in business about 1830. Some pieces bear a marked resemblance to Tucker's work, and it has been learned that one moulding concern supplied both potteries. It is also known that professional modelers sold their designs to more than one company. Other modelers might have worked for several different concerns, causing a great similarity in the work produced.

David Henderson was involved in the creation of the Jersey City Pottery Company in 1829 and the American Pottery Company in 1833. The American Pottery Company was operated under different ownerships until 1892. It created a prodigious amount of good pottery and porcelain which is prized by collectors today.

Lotus Ware

If you have any ceramics with the initials K. T. & K. stamped on the bottom, you will know that this is the mark of Knowles, Taylor, and Knowles which was incorporated in 1854 in East Liverpool, Ohio. In its early years, the pottery specialized in making ceramic food-canning jars. Also under production were brown Rockinghamware, creamware, and eventually whitewares. By 1891, it was the country's largest pottery, with twenty-nine kilns in operation.

In the 1880s the company hired Joshua Poole, a former manager of the Belleek Factory in Ireland, and brought him to this country to supervise the making of a similar translucent porcelain. Production continued until the plant burned. After the plant was rebuilt, the company introduced its now famous Lotus Ware in 1890, which was made until about 1897. Lotus Ware rivaled the best of fine porcelains made anywhere in the world. Paper thin, its survival rate was very low— hence the scarcity today. It was decorated with underglazed painting as well as applied figures in flowers, leaves, lacy patterns, and filigree. All the decoration was done by hand and is perhaps as fine as any found on American

porcelain. However, the cost of production exceeded what the public could pay, and it went off the market.

Little Lotus Ware is found in the East. Perhaps it was too fragile to ship any great distance. One can see excellent examples of Lotus at the Museum of Ceramics in East Liverpool, which is administered by the Ohio Historical Society.

Examples of Lotus Ware made by Knowles, Taylor and Knowles, East Liverpool, Ohio between 1890 and 1896. It is considered by many to be the finest Belleek porcelain in the world. Mark is of blue leaves with the name Lotus Ware above the initials K.T. & K. Jabe Tartar

The company pioneered the use of transfer printing in America and did much commemorative work.

It was not until the 1880s, when Lenox set up shop in New Jersey and Castleton went into business just above Pittsburgh, that America enjoyed any long-lived production of fine porcelains. Most collectors will agree their output is on a par with that of the rest of the world as far as quality is concerned. Both concerns are still in business and are engaged to do many custom presentation pieces by the White House, as well as making dinner services for the president's home. However, collectors have not yet taken to collecting these porcelains as antiques, perhaps because most of the patterns are still being made and do not possess any aura of age and early workmanship.

There are many other American potteries that made their mark with very good production, most of which is well marked, which makes identification easy. You must approach ceramic collecting with a definite set of rules to follow. Since much of the collectible American production was made during the period of industrial growth, you are faced with the problem of determining if you will be content with machine-made items, or if you will zero in on only those items that were handmade or custom modeled and hand-decorated.

Imports—Europe and the Orient represent the other sources for most of the ceramics to be found here. Though America lagged in porcelain manufacture, we were not hesitant in importing it from countries that made it well. The Winterthur Conference Report of 1972 reveals how limited such trade was before the Revolutionary War, in that very little china appears in the inventory of estates through the seventeenth and eighteenth centuries. Archaeological digs along the coast from Virginia to Massachusetts have unearthed fragments of all kinds of pottery and porcelain which reveal a great deal about their origins. As

Very rare English combware that could date from the late 17th to the early 18th centuries. It is easier to find it in this country, as collectors and museums in England bought what was available there, years ago.

would be expected, china from England predominates, but it was limited to those who were wealthy. Researchers have been able to pinpoint the area in England from which some sherds came. In one dig at Plymouth, Massachusetts (which reflected the period between 1760 and 1835), they uncovered eight plates, eight chamber pots, and three bowls in delftware; three mugs, a bowl, a teacup, teapot lid, saucer, and plate in white salt-glazed stoneware; an agateware bowl; a slip-decorated redware pitcher; four slip-decorated redware chamber pots; three redware crocks; five smaller redware bowls; and one Whieldon-type teapot. The predominance of chamber pots is puzzling, but they must have been considered more essential than dinnerware through those years.

In the September, 1891 edition of *Scribners* magazine, Alice Morse Earle wrote of her experiences as a "China Hunter in New England." She bemoaned the fact that there was little early work to be found. She stated that Bow, Chelsea, and Derby wares were seldom seen in old New England homes, "nor have we found specimens of the better class of Wedgwood's manufactures in any great numbers." The demand for the better Wedgwood ware was great in England, so little of it was sent to America.

Ceramics **117**

PICKARD CHINA

The information about Pickard china comes from a booklet called "Secrets of Correct Table Service," which was published by the Pickard Studios in Chicago in 1911. This concern imported porcelain and china blanks from foreign manufacturers in Japan and Europe, decorating them and marking them with the Pickard name. Skilled decorators from Germany, France, England, Russia, Italy, and America worked their own ideas into the decorations, most of them including applied gold, and then signed their work. They created some of the most beautiful pottery ever to be sold in this country; there is great interest in collecting it today. The Pickard China Company was formed in 1898 and continues working to this day making commemorative and limited-edition items.

Hyacinthus

THE Hyacinthus decoration shows conventionalized white hyacinths arranged in panels against a soft gray background. The bottom of the design shows the white florets against a dull dark blue background. This composition, though extremely elaborate, best illustrates the restful character of a low-toned color harmony.

From an early catalog of the Pickard Studios of Chicago, dated 1911. The company specialized in decorating the finest porcelains. Hyacinthus is but one of their designs.

The booklet "Secrets of Correct Table Service" is priceless in its instructions, which include the following: "A "silence" cloth should always be used under a tablecloth to protect the surface of the table and to lessen noise. Twenty-five to thirty inches should be allowed from plate to plate. The advantage of passing a dish first to the hostess is that it enables her to see if it is properly prepared and provided with the necessary fork and spoon. Before dessert is brought in, everything not pertaining directly to it should be removed and the table crumbed." There is much more.

Designs pictured in the booklet are the Hyacinthus Bordure Antique, Dahlia Rubra, Lily Ornatum, Orange Tree Decoration, Enamel Chrysanthemums, and the Modern Conventional. The value of a complete set of any of these would be astronomical today. The work is elegant, the gold is real, the beauty unsurpassed. Collect your Pickard before it is totally gone. Many of the gilt pieces still appear on the market.

Art Pottery

The art pottery era began shortly after the Civil War. Located mostly in Pennsylvania, Ohio, Indiana, and West Virginia, the art pottery concerns developed lines of specialty and decorative pieces, glazing them in many colors. Flowers and fruits were popular, with most designs molded in relief. Much of the production was good and much was shoddy, yet this type of production continues to this day, with many lesser quality pieces commanding attention as collectibles. Most of these items were made in earthenware, but some of the better companies turned out porcelains.

BUFFALO

Deldare Ware—Deldare ware, made by the Buffalo Pottery in Buffalo, New York, early in this century, was given as premiums for the purchase of Larkin Soap. This is an earthenware that is decorated with decals or by means of transfer print-

Deldare Ware, Buffalo Pottery, c. 1920s. Transfer prints illustrate the travels of Dr. Syntax, taken from an eighteenth-century English book. Given as premiums for sale of Larkin Soap.

ing. The scenes are taken from an eighteenth-century English book on the travels of fictitious Dr. Syntax. The book was lavishly illustrated with hand-tinted prints. In the nineteenth century, Royal Doulton made a series of Dr. Syntax plates in England, and these are good collectibles as well. Sensing this great interest in the Doulton plates, Larkin decided to capitalize on the popularity of them as well. Because they started out literally worth nothing, people who owned them often relegated them to summer cottages or just threw them away outright, as they did carnival and Depression glass.

There are some variations in Deldare ware design, but the most wanted pieces involve Dr. Syntax. Unusual forms command a premium. The body of the pieces is olive drab with white, black, and various colors creating the scene. Deldare just seems to keep going up in price. Copies of the Dr. Syntax book have appeared at auction, as well.

DEDHAM

Perhaps the most innovative artist in American pottery was Hugh Cornwall Robertson of Chelsea, Massachusetts. In

1868, he and his brother, James, opened the famed Chelsea Keramic Art Works, specializing in making terra-cotta and redware pieces. From this, they branched out into decorative art pottery and some of the forms and colors they created met with instant appreciation. At the Philadelphia Centennial Exhibition, their wares won prizes and attention. In 1880, James Robertson died, and Hugh took over control of the company, which continued production until 1948, when it closed its doors.

Perhaps his greatest achievement was making crackleware, which looks like it sounds, with a spiderweb appearance over the surface. In a contest for a trademark, a local teacher submitted a design featuring a rabbit, and this was chosen as the identifying mark. The company moved to Dedham, Massachusetts, in 1895, and the words "Dedham Pottery" appeared with the rabbit. Perhaps the most collected Dedham pottery today is in the crackle glaze with a blue border, hand painted with designs of flowers, animals, and other forms of nature. The rabbit border was most popular and featured the bunnies heading in a clockwise direction. Some plates were made with them facing counterclockwise, however. These are rarities and are called "reverse rabbit" plates and are worth much more than the clockwise facing bunnies.

Robertson uncovered the secret of the oxblood color, which until late in the last century was known only in the Orient. He made but three hundred pieces in stoneware with the oxblood glaze. Two fine examples of these, the Twin Stars of Chelsea, are at the Museum of Fine Arts in Boston. Much Dedham pottery goes unnoticed in many homes. It is quite valuable today. Look for the rabbit mark with the words "Dedham Pottery," or the CKAC mark, or, in some rare instances, the initials HR for Hugh Robertson.

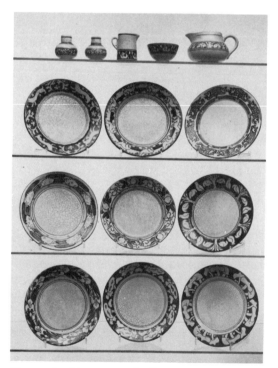

Blue and white pottery, Dedham Pottery, Dedham, Massachusetts. Borders are decorated with various animals and flowers. Dedham pottery features a rabbit trademark, with the name of the pottery on the base. The company went out of business in 1948.

DORCHESTER

The Dorchester Pottery, located just off the Southeast Expressway, south of the center of Boston, was founded by George Henderson in 1894. All the pottery was made and decorated by hand. Much work was done for business clients, such as Mug and Muffin who uses their wares at their tables. Many footwarmers were made and these are well-marked. The company made a wide range of table and decorative wares, much of which is still used in homes.

Practically all the late output in the 1960s and 1970s was cobalt blue decoration on white stoneware. Floral patterns such as dahlia, chrysanthemum and lilies were featured. The blueberry and scroll patterns were popular as well. In 1967, regular drinking mugs were selling for $3.85 at the pottery. Today, most fetch between fifty and a hundred dollars. Dinner plates were eight to ten dollars—today most are over fifty dollars.

Pitchers from the Dorchester Pottery, Dorchester, Massachusetts. The pottery worked from 1894–1979. Top, left to right: *scroll; fantasy; blueberry.* Bottom, left to right: *striped, pine cone, clematis. Decorations in blue by Charles A. Hill. Well-marked with pottery name, "CAH," and often "NR" for Nando Ricci, who potted the pieces.*

Some pieces are initialed with NR, indicating Nando Ricci as the potter. CAH are the initials of Charles A. Hill, who did the decorating in the later years. Ethel Henderson, the daughter-in-law of the founder, ran the pottery with the help of her sister, Lily Yeaton, and Charles Hill, her brother. She passed on in the 1970s and a few years later, the pottery closed.

MAJOLICA

Majolica was and still is quite popular. Majorcan potters are generally credited with making the first majolica ware. This is an earthenware that has been highly decorated and is most often quite colorful. Colored tin glazes were used as early as the twelfth century. They were applied over a white glaze which gave good background to the decoration. In 1743, the Majolika Geschirrfabrik went into business at Holitsch to serve the nobility in Austria and Hungary. Some pieces from this factory are marked with an HF, or often an H alone. During this period there were many makers in practically every European country, but such wares do not seem to have been made in this country until after the Civil War, when there was a boom in art pottery.

The best known is that made by Griffen, Smith and Hill in Phoenixville, Pennsylvania. This company began making it in 1878. The native clay and glazes gave it color and beauty that is unmatched either in this country or abroad. Pieces were hand decorated by local girls and women and the pastel shades they used make this majolica the most desired in this country today. GSH entered two vases and a jug in an exhibition in New Orleans in 1884 and won

Majolica pitcher made by Griffen, Smith and Hill, Phoenixville, Pennsylvania, c. 1880s. It may be marked with "Etruscan" and/or "GSH" superimposed on the base.

the gold medal, its highest honor. A colorful catalog was prepared and soon the product, named Etruscan Majolica, spread all over the country. Most pieces bear this name as well as the initials G, S, and H, superimposed on one another. Many pieces are identified only by number and decoration, so a pottery marking book must be employed to authenticate them.

Decorations were drawn from nature, and among the most popular are shell and seaweed, begonia, lily, fern, bamboo, and even cauliflower. There may be variations in color on identical pieces as each painter decorated as she saw fit. An original catalog with color illustrations and number code was printed by Brooke Weidner in Phoenixville.

NILOAK

Niloak pottery is native to Benton, Arkansas, which is the only area that contains the special clay that make it up. C. D. Hyten discovered the unique clay as far back as 1868 and began making the distinctive ware, which is characterized by the wavy graining of various colored clays. Between 1868 and 1898 there were as many as a dozen potteries in Benton turning out Niloak, which is a clay name, kaolin, spelled backwards. At the turn of the century, however, Hyten's was the sole operating concern and was pretty much out of

business by 1950. Niloak features a satiny unglazed finish with colors of blue, tan, red, white, and cream. Potters today, attempting to imitate the original, are having little luck, as it seems the secret in blending the colors came in the firing.

Some experimental pieces of Niloak were glazed; these would be quite valuable today if located. The product most collected today was perfected about 1912. An additive had to be used to keep the blue a true color, and other chemicals were present to assure color and even shrinkage of the clays in firing. Vases and bowls should be sought in this color.

Though most Niloak was sold in the Arkansas area, it was nationally advertised. Hyten toured the country putting on demonstrations with his pottery wheel. Buyers are collecting it today, as no more is being made, and it is unlikely that anyone will unlock the secret of reproducing it. Niloak is most likely unmarked.

OHIO CERAMICS

James Bennet, who was born in Newhall, South Derbyshire, England, opened the first pottery in East Liverpool, Ohio, in 1839. Early in the 1840s, three bothers joined him. At first, they made yellowware, then the popular Rockinghamware, often miscalled Bennington by the unknowing. Though much was made in Bennington, the greatest production was in Ohio and nearby West Virginia. During the late nineteenth century, East Liverpool earned the title of "Crockery City." In 1877, twenty-three potteries were listed as being in business in the town, with their output going all over the country.

Naturally, much of the work showed the influence of potters who emigrated there from Europe. One has but to visit the Museum of Ceramics in East Liverpool to see the wide range of forms and designs, much of which could be mistaken for European production. One wonders if this were some intent to suggest foreign manufacture at a time when most felt the best goods came from overseas. In 1887, the Laughlin

Semi-porcelain bluebird china made for mail-order houses from 1880 to 1915 in Sebring, Ohio. Jabe Tartar

Brothers Pottery declared its superiority over English ceramics by introducing a mark showing the American Eagle standing over a prostrate British lion.

By 1930, East Liverpool was at its zenith, with about seven thousand employed in its area potteries. However, the Depression took its toll, and some firms also moved to new locations. Collectors are learning now that at East Liverpool ceramicware was made as well as anywhere in the world.

Rookwood—The Rookwood Pottery was founded in 1880 by Mrs. Maria Longworth Storer, who named it after her father's country estate near Cincinnati, Ohio. In 1883, Mr. W. W. Taylor became a partner and director of the works. In 1890 Mr. Taylor acquired the interests of Mrs. Storer when she retired. He enlarged the facility in 1892 and again in 1899 and 1904. The pottery closed in 1960. The site now houses a fine restaurant overlooking the city.

Rookwood is best known for its Art Nouveau and Deco forms with underglazed painted decoration. However the pottery made tiles, mantels, architectural faience, and garden pottery as well. All pieces can be identified by the marks shown on page 124, which comes from a page in a promotional booklet put out by

Fine and large Rookwood jardiniere painted by Maria Storer, 1882. Sold for $11,000 by Butterfield & Butterfield, Los Angeles. Photo courtesy of Butterfield & Butterfield.

Rookwood Marks

Impressed in the clay. The regular mark from 1882, the date changing each year until 1886. **ROOKWOOD 1882**

 This mark was adopted in 1886.

The flame at the top indicates 1887, thus—and a flame is added for every year thereafter, so that the mark for 1900 shows fourteen.

For the next century the mark of 1900 is continued with the Roman numerals to designate the year. The mark for 1901 is given in the margin.

It is also customary for purposes of record, to stamp on the bottom of each piece a shape number with a letter indicating size, and another letter referring to the color of the clay used in the body of the piece, W for white, etc.

Marks found on Rookwood pottery help identify the year in which a piece was made. From an original catalog.

the pottery early in this century. The top mark, Rookwood 1882, was used until 1886, when the R in reverse and P were conjoined. A flame added above this RP mark indicates 1887. A flame mark was added for every year thereafter, which makes the pieces quite easy to date. On the bottom of each is a shape number with a letter indicating size and another referring to the color of clay used in the body. It was customary, but not necessary, for the decorators to cut their initials on the bottoms of pieces they decorated. Quite often, owners of such pieces do not realize what they have as no name is mentioned.

Roseville—As interest in American art pottery grew, so did interest in pieces made by the Roseville Pottery Company in Zanesville, Ohio. Years ago it was a common gift to newlyweds, most of whom could not wait

Pieces from the brilliant period of Weller (Sicardo from c. 1905–1907). Jabe Tartar

Roseville vase, late 1940s.

to dispose of it as many considered it gaudy and not of very good quality. New appreciation has grown for work of this type, however, and today the name "Roseville" guarantees an immediate sale as the collectors are numerous all over the country.

The factory was begun in 1890 in Roseville, Ohio, in a plant once owned by the Owens Pottery. In 1898, the owners bought the Midland Pottery in Roseville and then the Mosaic Tile Company. In 1910, all production was at Zanesville, which had become an important pottery center in Ohio.

In addition to the mass-produced wares, the pottery made some art pieces, which sell for much money today. Patterns such as Rozanne, Mara, Egypto, Wood-

Early Weller ware of the classical period, c. 1885. Zanesville, Ohio. Jabe Tartar

land, Crystallis, Azurean, and Woodland made their appearance. The competition with other potteries was keen, and the best designers and decoraters that could be found were employed. Fortunately, the pieces were well marked, often with the artist's signature or initials. Many of the production pieces came only with a paper label, but in later years the name "Roseville" was molded on the bottom.

Weller—Zanesville, Ohio was the location of several fine potteries. Among them was one owned by Samuel A. Weller, who founded it in 1872. He made pottery with such strange names as Lowelsa, Eocean and Sicardo. The company continued in business until 1948.

In the manner of other Ohio potters, flowers were a mainstay of decoration at Weller. He used metallic tints to highlight his work. In 1901, a French potter, Jacques Sicard, joined the firm and gave his name to one of his creations. Dickensware featured characters from the famous writer's books. Since the pottery operated during the period when both Art Nouveau and Art Deco styles were in vogue, one may collect a wide range of forms.

VAN BRIGGLE

The Van Briggle Pottery is located in Colorado Springs, Colorado. Artus Van Briggle worked both for the Avon Pottery and Rockwood in Cincinnati before heading west because of his health. He went to Colorado Springs in 1899 and by 1901 was in business turning out work that won him awards and immediate fame. His wife,

Rosary vase and Louwelsa pitcher by Weller, Zanesville, Ohio, in the 1920–1940 period. The name was created by Weller from the first name of his daughter, Louise and initials from his name. Jabe Tartar

Anne, was his model for some of the Art Deco-type nudes which appeared on his decorative wares. The mark, two A's joined together, was derived from their names. Mr. Van Briggle died in 1904, leaving his wife president of the firm.

In the early 1970s, the company moved to larger quarters where it continues to make fine pottery. The company achieved fame with its unusual glazes, some applied by means of a spray unit. Much decorative art ware was made as well as flower holders, tiles, and garden ornaments. The company continues today, turning out well-molded handmade items, which are being collected by those who know that such items will be much in demand if production ever ceases. This *can* happen—witness the demise of the Pennsbury Pottery in Morrisville, Pennsylvania, which closed its doors in 1971 after having been in business about twenty years. Its story is typical of the many small enterprises which are set up to provide an interesting quality product but which surrender slowly to competition from within this country as well as from overseas. Since Pennsbury is a current collectible which has not yet entirely disappeared, and one about which little is known, I feel it is of enough importance to devote space to it. (See page 149.)

England and the Continent

Problems in Attribution

Even pieces that are well marked are subject to suspicion because of imitators and fakers of the nineteenth century. Quite notable in this respect was the firm of Mssrs. Samson and Company of Paris, which went into business in 1845 and worked late into the century. The company usually produced wares in the style of the eighteenth century and marked them with original marks, and this can confuse the average student of ceramics today. In the eighteenth century most potters in England were still working with soft paste bodies, using a mixture of powdered glass and clays. Samson reproduced porcelain, and this might have been made from the oriental formula of china clay and kaolin, or from the Spode formula, which included bone ash and good china clay. You must arm yourself with information on how to tell the two apart. Hard paste does not warm quickly to the touch. If there is a chip on a soft paste piece, its open surface will appear glassy. A glaze on soft paste can wear away, whereas a glaze on hard paste will survive almost intact over many years. An enameled decoration on soft paste will sink into the ceramic, but it will remain on the surface of hard paste.

Nicholas Sprimont, a French silversmith, brought the Chelsea Works to the attention of the ceramics world in the 1740s by copying the oriental porcelains. You will have to do your homework to learn to differentiate the Bow, Meissen, St. Cloud, and Chantilly blanc de chine from that made in the Orient in the eighteenth century as they all look alike to the untrained eye. Samson's work in the nine-

Chelsea porcelain Cupid and the Lamb, England, eighteenth century. There were many forms of Cupid with various animals in various poses.

teenth century just adds more confusion. Fortunately, by the nineteenth century most firms in England were well established, and were contemporary enough so that others did not attempt to imitate them or copy them in later years. By the middle of the century, each company's work and markings were so distinctive that we have little trouble in accurate attribution.

During the eighteenth century, English makers copied the best Chinese designs, as these were popular, and also copied the Chinese porcelain bodies. Thus determining the country of origin can be quite difficult even for experienced students. Some of the early Bow, Worcester, Newhall, and Caughley pieces are easily mistaken for Chinese work. A concern at Lowestoft gave its name to a great deal of what must have been Chinese export porcelain. History records that some potteries acted as importers and exporters as well as makers, and sold both native and export chinas. It seems likely that Lowestoft was one of these, attaching its name to both, and this has helped to cause this confusion.

The ceramics factory at Bow is considered to be the oldest in England. It was located in the eastern section of London. Some of its product was stamped "New Canton" because the buildings were in the Chinese style. Bow is thought to have been founded as early as 1730, but its first patents for making porcelain using Virginia unaker clay were taken out in 1744. Bow led in the production of the first bone china, made with the addition of powdered bone ash, and is also credited with turning out the first china with transfer prints done under the glaze.

A factory was established in Chelsea about 1742 and made fine porcelain, which was the counterpart of the best from Europe. A Huguenot refugee brought his knowledge to this plant thus enabling it to copy the best French work. William Duesbury (owner of the Derby Works, also in London) purchased the Chelsea enterprise, and at one time owned the Bow Works as well. This creates a real problem in identifying the output from these plants,

Charity, by Ralph Wood, Burslem, England, c. 1775–1780. Wood is called the "Father of English Potters." This soft paste porcelain piece is one of many figures he made.

as molds were interchanged and workers might work in one or more of the plants, taking their designs with them. You must rely on the markings of these pieces to aid in identification. The bibliography lists books that will help.

China was made to order in both the Orient and England, and it is likely that much was made for the wealthy in America. Alice Morse Earle tells the story of a Miss Leslie, the sister of a great painter, who ordered a dinner service made and decorated for her in China. She directed that a coat of arms be placed in the center of each plate, and made a drawing which she pasted in the center of a specimen she had drawn. She wrote "Put this in the middle" under the coat of arms. When the service arrived, she found on every piece

Prior to 1842, most English chinas were marked with the pattern name and the name or initials of the maker. Naturally, there are variations, but they are few.

The English "diamond" mark was used between 1842 and 1884. The letters and numerals indicate month, day, and year the item was made, as well as the type of ceramic. There was a variation of the position of the letters and numerals in 1867. A good marking book will help you interpret these.

not only the coat of arms, but also, carefully written and fired in, the words "Put this in the middle." I wonder at the whereabouts of this set today.

Collectors are fortunate the English provided a good marking system for their nineteenth-century ceramics. Until 1842, pieces were often identified by the name of the pattern or design, and either the name or initials of the maker, and, at times, the location of the factory. Between 1842 and 1883, the "diamond" mark, which enables us to pinpoint the day the piece was made, came into use. In the corners of the diamond are numbers or letters, which, according to established charts, reveal the day, month, and year, as well as the class of ceramic, and the lot number from which it came. In 1867, this was modified with a clue that can be helpful. If one sees a letter of the alphabet at the top point of the diamond, he knows the piece was made before 1867; if there is a number at the point, it came after 1867. Beginning in 1884, a numerical marking system was used, with a combination of numerals following the prefix (Rd. or Rd. No.). The number is the clue to the year the item was made, up to 1892. In that year, a U.S. law was passed which required the country of origin to be stamped on items imported here. However, one must examine each piece for other clues as to age. Between 1892 and 1908 one might find England and the Rd. or registry number. The number disappeared about 1908, leaving only "England" until about 1920, when items for export were marked "Made in England." Much has been brought here by immigrants or imported by dealers which does not have the country of origin marked because this was not required for sale in Great Britain.

England

BLUE WILLOW CHINA

One type of china that seems to hold its value despite changing tastes is Blue Willow. Made in great quantities years ago, it was used not only in the home but in restaurants and hotels as well. Most people are familiar with the pattern: willow trees, a pagoda, bridge, and fences—all in oriental motif. Though the subject matter is from the Far East and was used in porcelains made there, the Blue Willow as we know it originated in England about 1780.

The design is credited to Thomas Minton, who worked at the Caughley Works owned by Thomas Turner. Turner is best known for his Salopian ware, which was the first really successful transfer printed china made in complete sets. The Willow ware was but another pattern he popularized. Soon it was being made by other potters in Staffordshire County, so unless a piece is marked, it is difficult to attribute it to any particular pottery. Other names one might find on a piece are Standard Willow, Old Willow, Real Willow, Caughley Willow, and English Willow.

Blue Willow was made in the United States by several concerns, the most noted being the Buffalo Pottery Company in Buffalo, New York. This company was created by the Larkin Soap Company to make premiums, which were given away for soap wrappers. Most of the Buffalo output was commercial, for hotels and restaurants, and examples of this china keep turning up at auctions and marketplaces. Willow ware was also made in Germany, France, and Holland.

There is a legend that the design depicts an event of unrequited love between a mandarin's daughter and one of his accountants. According to this sad story, both met an untimely death and turned into doves, which are depicted on the china.

COMMEMORATIVE AND
HISTORICAL WARE

After the Revolutionary War, English potters were quick to forgive political differences in return for American business, and a lively trade was begun, with commemorative and historical wares shipped here in great quantities. The art of transfer printing had been perfected in the 1770s

by Thomas Turner, who was the first to turn out complete dinner services in this manner. Artists were sent to America to paint or sketch scenes of prominent buildings, landmarks, or landscapes. These scenes were immediately transformed into transfer prints for china. Famous military and naval engagements were also portrayed, along with portraits of famous men and ships that did the British in during the war. These rose in popularity until the War of 1812. Interest was renewed in them after this war, and between 1820 and 1840 a great amount of historic china entered the country. Blue was the most popular color, but much was also done in other colors. Items with a lot of detail, such as ships and rigging, were most often done in black against a cream or off-white background. Most of the black and white transfers are referred to as "Liverpool transfers," as they came from this port. The blue pieces are commonly referred to as "historical blues" since most portray a place, event, or person of American historical importance. Another series of the blues was done as a revival during the 1890s, but these blues are

Liverpool transfer pitcher in black and white. It reads, "Success To the Commerce in Newburyport." These were made for export to the U.S., and many came through the port of Liverpool.

Staffordshire blue transfer printed ware, called Historic Blues, c. 1820–1940, England. Those made for the American trade featured scenes, buildings, and people of America.

clearly marked to document their age. Even these later blues are assuming some importance now. You might do well to collect the blues being made today by such firms as Wedgwood for historic homes, churches, and the like, as these will be among the collectibles someday. Some that sold as souvenirs as recently as fifteen years ago for $2 or $3 are commanding up to $50 now, because they were made in limited edition.

CREAMWARE AND PEARLWARE

Creamware (or Queensware, as it was called later in the eighteenth century) is simply a yellow lead glazed ware popular from about 1750 to 1820. Wedgwood is commonly referred to as the originator, but this is an uncertain attribution because

Creamware pitcher made by the Jersey City Pottery Co., Jersey City, N.J., originally called the American Pottery Company. This was made during the 1840 presidential campaign of William Henry Harrison.

others were making it at the same time. Ivor Noel Hume tells us that nine out of ten creamware pieces were unmarked and probably no more than one out of a thousand was dated. Pearlware is a whiter composition that came into favor at the turn of the century, and is often decorated in oriental motifs.

LUSTERED CHINA

Applying metallic oxides to decorate china is a practice that has been with us a long time. The technique of lustering pieces seems to have originated in Mesopotamia, then spread to Syria, Egypt, and Spain. It is the art of applying a metallic overglaze to clay, sometimes lustrous and sometimes almost iridescent. Though this was done in about the ninth century, it was not until the latter part of the eighteenth century that it became a popular decorating technique. The reincarnation is attributed to Josiah Wedgwood in the 1790s, and it was not long before many potteries in England were turning out the same product.

We are most familiar with the copper luster as this was the least expensive to make then and the least expensive now. There are lusters in silver, gold, platinum, bronze, and even brass. The production prior to 1842 is not marked, so it is difficult to know which pottery made particular pieces. The pottery at Sunderland is known to have employed this luster in the decoration of the transfer printed bowls and pitchers, which are often called "Liverpool transfer ware." The luster would be in addition to a picture of some scene, perhaps patriotic or historic.

The silver resist pieces of the early nineteenth century are much desired and quite rare in good condition, as they can tarnish. However, the production of the copper lusters has never stopped, and the reproductions coming in from overseas are hurting the values of the older pieces. Those not skilled in distinguishing new from the old can make mistakes in buy-ing—hence the declining interest. Also, it is almost impossible to tell old from new at an auction because of the distance from the auctioneer. There are better ceramics in which to invest as the future of the value of copper luster items is in doubt.

MOCHA WARE

Growing in popularity is mocha ware, which is a brittle pottery with various colorful decorations. Most of it was made in England between the 1820s and 1925. I have never seen a piece that is marked, but it was made by potteries located in Staffordshire County. It has also been made in East Liverpool, Ohio, at the Bennet Brothers Pottery.

The most common decorative pattern on mocha ware is called seaweed, because of its resemblance to it. This pattern is created by placing on the wet clay a drop of steroid, which spreads naturally to create the abstract design. Other designs on mocha ware are marbled agate, scroddle, banded, cat's eye, and oyster. C. John Smith, from the Stourbridge College of Technology, lectured on mocha at the Shelburne Museum some years ago. He indicated that the pattern called "worm" rightfully should be called "cable." Also those with geometric design should be called "dicing."

The bodies shade from white to cream. Much that we find with simple

Mocha handled pot with cat's eye and wave pattern, England, nineteenth century.

bands for decoration may have been made in Ohio, particularly mixing bowls and mugs.

One can recognize mocha ware by its weight; it is quite light and is fragile to the touch. It is best not to invest in chipped or cracked pieces as repair is expensive. The best place to buy it is in England, where it is regarded as only a country ceramic.

PARIAN

In 1842 at the Copeland Spode works at Stoke-on-Trent, England, a new porcelain—white and unglazed—was developed. It was named Parian because it resembled the Parian marble which was used extensively for busts and classic figures on the islands of Crete and Paros. By 1843, it was a well-accepted product on both sides of the Atlantic. It was made that same year in Bennington, Vermont, at the Norton Works which employed the services of an English modeler, John Harrison. It is only natural that porcelain was eventually made in Vermont as the state has some of the finest kaolin clay available in the country. This, mixed with other clays, gives the body a hard, translucent quality. The pieces were glazed on the interior, leaving the outer surface with a marble-like, satin finish.

Much was made at the United States Pottery, which was run by Christopher Webber Fenton along with various associates, between 1847 and 1858. I have never seen a marked piece. Richard Carter Barret gives us clues on how to identify the Vermont parian. There was much iron pyrite in the soil and clay, which made screening the particles quite difficult, so one will find black specks in the Bennington pieces, whereas those from England or other potteries will be clear white. Parian was made in the heart of the Victorian period, in which grapes were a popular decorative motif. Look for large, crude grapes in the Bennington pieces and smaller, refined examples in the English. Some parian from England and America is decorated with a cobalt blue glaze. Some pieces have pictures fired on them, as well.

ROYAL DOULTON, MINTON AND ROYAL CROWN DERBY

Space does not permit an examination of all the English concerns that contributed so much to the development of the industry. However, I will examine the history of one concern that is still operating in order to show the numerous changes it has undergone. Sir Henry Doulton was the second son of John, founder of Doulton and Company in the late eighteenth century. Sir Henry was a creative Victorian potter, and during his lifetime outstripped his competitors in the production of such industrial wares as airtight jars for storing food and tobacco; Screw-topped food warmers and bottles; and architectural terra-cotta statuary and tiles used by many London architects. An example of this work is the lion outside Waterloo Station. Doulton concentrated on industrial ware until 1862, with the exception of some stoneware Toby jugs and mugs which were shown at the International Exhibition of 1862. Following this was an association with the Lambeth School of Art, which designed salt-glazed vases and jars with simple incised and colored decorations along with terra-cotta statues, portrait heads, and medallions. In 1877, Sir Henry purchased a works at Burslem, Staffordshire, and began to manufacture decorated earthenware and bone china. Most of the china collected today stems from this late nineteenth-century production.

Another important potter was Thomas Minton, who began his career as an engraver apprenticed to Thomas Turner. Minton supplied Josiah Spode with printed designs for his wares for a short time, and then opened his own plant in 1796. It was not until 1824 that he made his reputation in the field by turning his production to forms influenced by the then popular Sèvres factory in France. One of the most important techniques developed

Garniture of pedestal vases by Doulton, England. Handpainted scenes on mazarine blue background.

by Minton was the Pate-sur-pate, brought from France by Marc Louis Solon, acknowledged master of this art form. Pate-sur-pate, meaning body on body, is an expensive and frustrating method of decoration developed from the original Chinese technique. Solon went to work for Minton in 1870, and, though it was imitated, this art product was turned out only by Minton. Spectacular models were produced showing the prevailing influence of interest in Sèvres china of the Louis XV style, Grecian influence parian figures, chinoiserie designs, and an overriding opulence of decoration. The Minton concern was later purchased by Doulton as the second member of the triumvirate that makes up Doulton today.

The third member of the Doulton triumvirate is the oldest. Royal Crown Derby has been in continuous operation since 1756, when an agreement between André

Planche, William Duesbury, and John Hatch made them partners. Duesbury insisted on thinner potting than was prevalent at the time. This work, along with the finer enameling used, attracted the attention of George III, who conferred the right to use the crown as a factory mark. The ware then became known as Crown Derby, and by the end of the eighteenth century, Crown Derby was the leader in the English fine china industry. Early in the nineteenth century the factory passed into the hands of Robert Bloor, a former clerk. He introduced the highly colored Japanese or Imari decorations for which Crown Derby became famous. Much of the production of this period was actually of inferior quality and could be listed as seconds.

By 1877 a new company was formed, and the management of the Derby Crown Porcelain Company set about recovering its reputation. By 1890 the excellence of

Imari covered box, Japan, nineteenth century. The blue/purple, orange and often gilt decoration on these pieces was imitated in England early in the nineteenth century where it was called Japanware. Over thirty potters made it and Royal Crown Derby still utilizes these colors and Oriental decoration.

the wares and the favored Japanese decorations had come to the attention of Queen Victoria, who permitted the pottery to change its name to the Royal Crown Derby Porcelain Company. It was the only pottery permitted the honor of using the Royal and Crown designations in its name. Also in 1890, a decorator by the name of Desire Leroy left Minton. His raised gilding, white enamel painting on colored grounds, and delicate floral and bird studies are uniquely beautiful.

The three great potteries, Royal Doulton, Minton, and Royal Crown Derby are now all part of Doulton and Company. It is currently engaged in producing a collector's series of many types of modeled human and animal figures, some of which are selling in the four-figure price range. Fine modeling and fine coloring are featured in these collectibles for tomorrow. The tradition of great work done by three separate concerns is obviously still very much alive in the consolidated company of today.

SPATTERWARE

Spatterware looks like it sounds. The colors in the border are applied in spotted fashion to form a design much finer than that of spongeware. It was most popular during the first half of the nineteenth century, with much supposedly made for the Pennsylvania German trade. Those pieces that picture the peafowl are among the most desired and most valuable today. Some came with various floral designs such as the Adams rose pattern. Others feature what is thought to be a schoolhouse.

Various colors were used in the borders, the most common being blue. Green and yellow were used, but the latter is so scarce one might never find one for sale. Plates and platters are the forms that seem to have survived best. One can occasionally find a sugar bowl and creamer, but the larger hollowware pieces such as teapots and chocolate pots are rare. Cups and saucers were made in abundance in sets, so these are more readily available. Spatterware cup plates are not common; one might judge that few were made as the less expensive glass plates were heavily in production after 1827.

Not all spatterware was made by Staffordshire in England; some was made in Ohio. Though not the same weight and quality as the English, it is being collected because of its lower prices, which collectors feel will eventually rise. There are more recent reproductions, but anyone who can judge old china will have no difficulty in identifying it. Excellent spatterware can be seen in the permanent collections at the William Penn Memorial Museum in Harrisburg.

WEDGWOOD

Josiah Wedgwood, who lived from 1730 to 1795, started his pottery business with only twenty English pounds in the 1750s. An apprentice of Thomas Whieldon, he founded a concern that is still quite active in making ceramics at Barlaston, Staffordshire County, England. During tours of the factory, I have always been told, "If the name Wedgwood is not on a piece of ceramic, it is not one of ours." Thus one should not be enticed into buying "unmarked" Wedgwood, for, according to those in the factory, it does not exist.

Many examples of Wedgwood jasperware made in the nineteenth century.

They even mark their seconds, which are sold from a shop there, and have always done so. This may disturb some dealers and collectors, but I can only repeat what I have always been told at the factory, as I have taken tour groups through there on six occasions.

Most noted of the Wedgwood wares are those identified as jasperware, which is made of basalt. Made in many colors, the most common are those in dark and light blue and green featuring figures in white relief. I have watched them make the figures by hand-pressing the white clay into a continuous mold. It is elastic enough that they can pick up the entire piece which will surround a plate or pot, and by moistening the clay, make it stick to the piece being decorated. The potters have time to arrange the figures perfectly, then they are fired on permanently.

Remember, there is no middle E in the name Wedgwood. This is a much imitated form of decorative ware.

Wedgwood and Spode—Names like Wedgwood and Spode are known even to the casual observer, as a lot has been written about these two famous concerns, both of which are still operating. The Wedgwoods were involved in pottery making by the end of the seventeenth century, but it was not until Josiah took command in the mid–eighteenth century that Wedgwood developed into a respected manufacturer responsible for much of the best ceramics available. Both Josiah Wedgwood and Josiah Spode served as apprentices to Thomas Whieldon, who is credited with making the popular tortoiseshell ware. Spode is located at Stoke-on-Trent. Both are in Staffordshire County, which had 150 potteries at work within its borders after 1800. Today, Wedgwood and Spode are one and the same concern, joining other pottery firms who have found that consolidation is necessary for survival in this competitive business. Staffordshire was occupied by the Romans at the time of Christ

Portland vase made in ceramic by Wedgwood, late eighteenth century.

as there was abundant clay and plenty of firewood available. Also, the fog and dampness that plague southern England are not as evident in Staffordshire. This is quite important in manufacturing ceramics because humidity affects glazing and firing. The term "Staffordshire" is generic when referring to chinas made in that county—it could have been used by any or all of the potters. The term is now used by collectors and dealers as a quick reference to the area of origin of the china in question.

France

Another country that competed for American business was France, whose famous factories at Rouen and St. Cloud date back into the seventeenth century. Very little of the Rouen production has survived, although it is known that a reasonably good European porcelain was first made at Rouen. This porcelain was soft paste, and most was decorated in blue. The St. Cloud production is documented by pieces marked as early as 1697, decorated in Japanese and other oriental styles, with gilding featured. Another factory, founded at Chantilly in 1725, produced wares that imitated currently favored oriental designs.

SÈVRES

One of the most prominent works—Sèvres—had its humble beginnings in Vincennes. It was in operation there from 1738 to 1756, when King Louis XV took it under his patronage. He allowed the formation of a new company, which was moved to Sèvres to make soft paste porcelain. Most of the Sèvres production from 1753 to 1756 carries the same markings as that of Vincennes. In 1761, the formula for making hard paste porcelain was acquired, and this made up the bulk of the company's production thereafter. The concern used the double L as a mark from 1740 on. From 1753 to the time of the revolution (1789) a date letter was inserted. After 1802, the Sèvres markings were done in red, with a date abbreviation used between 1818 and 1834. After 1834, the full date was used. On the orders of the Nazis, a special edition of eighty small plates was turned out in 1943 to commemorate the reuniting of the French and German lands

Unusual French porcelain tea warmer, second quarter of the nineteenth century. The lower unit holds hot water to keep pots at proper temperature.

Faience

About 2,000 B.C., potters learned they must glaze works of clay so that liquids put in a piece would not be absorbed. Early glazes were made of a clay that would fire at a lower temperature than the pottery. Later, the use of minerals and even metals was introduced into glaze mixtures. Among them was tin, which is traced back to a Babylonian pottery dating about 1000 B.C. It seems to have disappeared between about 500 B.C. and the eighth century, when Persian potters used the mixture. The Moors carried the formula to the Mediterranean, where it was used on the island of Majorca, which is usually credited as the location where majolica originated. In France, majolica pieces, made at that time, highly decorated and given a tin oxide glaze, were called faience.

The term "faience" is still used to describe very early pottery that has been hand-decorated and glazed with tin. Pieces turn up from time to time, but most are chipped as it is brittle.

One of the best known contemporary makers of similar ware is Quimper, which is in Brittany, France, and was founded in 1690. Scenes on the pottery are of peasant life. Many people collect the new as well as the old; one must learn the marks and colors to tell them apart. I have seen it used as everyday china in homes in New England.

by Hitler. I wonder about the location of these today. Sèvres was one of the most imitated potteries, and it trained some fine craftsmen who later joined other concerns, bringing with them skills unsurpassed anywhere.

LIMOGES

Another famous name in French porcelain is Limoges. A pottery was formed in this town as early as 1771, and as many as thirty-five concerns were eventually located there. You will see such markings as Elite, JP or J. Pouyat, Guerin, JPL, Aron and Valin, Pierre Tharaud, and, perhaps the most famous of all, Haviland. David Haviland, an importer from New York, established a plant at Limoges in the 1840s and provided his own outlet for the product in America. This high-quality porcelain caught the fancy of the American public, so much so that Haviland Limoges was once considered a necessary wedding gift for the well-to-do bride.

Two sons of David Haviland became owners of separate porcelain works at Limoges. They were Charles Field Haviland, identified by name or by CFH underlined with an L below to denote the town. Theodore Haviland identified his pieces by

name or by TH with an L beneath. In 1908, the two companies became Haviland and Company, identified by H & Co with an L beneath.

Germany

Americans have always held ceramics from the Germanic regions of Europe in high esteem. After Bottger perfected the porcelain body recipe in Dresden and the famed Meissen works opened there, the secret for making porcelain soon spread throughout the area, so that by 1718 it was quite well known. The names Meissen and Dresden are synonymous with respect to ceramics and both are similarly marked. The work was greatly imitated by other concerns in Germany in the nineteenth century, and Samson imitated it in Paris. Although he was required to mark his pieces to show they were reproductions, he got around this nicely by stamping the original marks beneath the glaze, and putting his mark on the glaze where it could be rubbed off at will, in the same manner that paper labels used today to identify country of origin fall off so easily. There were many other great porcelain manufactories in Germany, but none captured the fancy of

Two vases painted by the German artist Lux, depicting Col. George Custer and his wife Libby. Sold for $46,750 at auction by Butterfield and Butterfield, San Francisco, on Nov. 20, 1989. (Butterfield & Butterfield.)

the American buyer as much as Dresden. As a result, little of their production is found in America.

Although very good work was done, the production from potteries elsewhere in Europe had little impact in America. People have a fetish for collecting not only good work but good names as well, and if the supply of an item is not sufficient, they will lose interest in trying to locate it. Scarcity can hurt collecting by lowering the price, quite contrary to the idea that if something is rare it is more valuable.

MEISSEN FIGURES

Since the earliest days of ceramics, figures, both human and animal, have been subjects of the potters' art. At first, simple clay was used, but when porcelain was perfected in the Orient, this became the favored material.

One of the early great modelers of the famed Meissen works was Johann Kaendler, who worked between 1731 and 1775. A former court sculptor, he brought new vigor to the art and became the source of inspiration for all the European porcelain artists. One series of figures of musicians has been attributed to him. They are whimsical and charming at the same time and date back to the second quarter of the eighteenth century. He is known for his crinoline figures, shepherdesses, and ladies and gentlemen of most walks of life. He was a student of mythology and created many allegorical groups.

Many other fine modelers were at work as well at this famous plant, among them Horoldt, Meyer, and Acier. From about 1774 to 1814, Kaendler was dominated by Count Marcolini, who introduced an academic, classical taste into the figures made.

The famed crossed swords as a factory mark were used early in the century. This mark was changed to swords with a point added from 1763 to 1774, and this was referred to as the point period. Not all crossed swords are Meissen, however. It is one of the most copied symbols, used in England, France, and the Orient as well. The true student can identify the Meissen work easily; generally the work was much superior to that from other potteries. Early Meissen figures are quite rare. Most fine museums have good collections.

ROYAL BAYREUTH

Sunbonnet Babies—There has always been a pottery in Bayreuth, Germany, since the sixteenth century. The pieces made late in the last century and into this one are the most available and collectible. One type, labeled "Royal Bayreuth," is generally a fine porcelain, often made into forms of people and animals, colored and decorated. Among the most desirable Royal Bayreuth to collect are the pieces with decorations of the Sunbonnet Babies. Bertha L. Corbett is known as the mother of the Sunbonnet Babies. She studied art in Philadelphia and later moved to Chicago, where she was employed to design picture postcards. A fellow employee once told her that no figure could show expression if the face was not shown, but Bertha managed to

Queen Louise

Louise Augusta Wilhelmina was born March 10, 1776, in Hanover, Germany. Her mother died when she was six, and she went to live with her grandmother. To escape advancing French troops a few years later, she sought refuge with her eldest sister, the Duchess of Hildburghausen. While there, she was presented to the king and was seen by Crown Prince Frederich Wilhelm III, who fell madly in love with her. On Christmas Eve, 1793, they were married, going eventually to Potsdam to live.

Being of royalty, it is natural that Queen Louise was painted many times. A story has been told that she had a goiter on her neck and always wore a scarf to conceal it. The interest in collecting Queen Louise decorated objects today centers around the scarf. One will find portraits of beautiful women on dishes, cups and saucers, framed porcelains, miniatures, jewelry, and the like, and it is customary to refer to all of them as Queen Louise if the scarf is there to hide the real or imaginary goiter. I have a painted ivory Queen Louise, framed, about 4 by 6 inches; the star on her hairband is jeweled, and her hair is done in long curls. The value of it is considerably higher than it would be if the scarf were missing, as then it would not be as easy to identify as Queen Louise. Those who grade these pieces suggest that the scarf must always be white; hair in long curls; dress white trimmed in gold; and cloak, if worn, scarlet, trimmed with brown-tailed white ermine. As best we know, Queen Louise died in 1810 from heart spasms.

She left us a legend of beauty—one that inspired porcelain makers to extol her face and form so that she might be seen and appreciated around the world. Most of the porcelains were made in the Germanic countries such as Austria, Bavaria, and Germany. They represent fine collectibles, and investments for the future, as it is unlikely they will ever be duplicated.

achieve immortality by creating such figures with their faces hidden by large white bonnets.

The days of the week series, which portrays the Sunbonnet Babies in various household chores, were done on postcards made of paper and leather, as well as china by Royal Bayreuth, who purchased the rights to Bertha's designs. This series was quite popular as gifts for children because they taught the Puritan ethic of keeping gainfully employed every day of the week. Some pieces, however, portray the babies visiting a circus, taking a balloon ride, or even having parties as rewards for their work.

The porcelain Bayreuth pieces have not yet been reproduced, so they have maintained high value. Collecting these Sunbonnet Babies on both the porcelain and the postcards is a rewarding challenge.

VILLEROY AND BOCH

The Abbey of Mettlach was built in the second half of the sixteenth century on the banks of the Saar River. More buildings were added in the eighteenth century, only to fall prey to the architects of the French Revolution, who plundered religious or-

Royal Bayreuth Sunbonnet Baby plate. This depicts Monday, which is washday.

ders and laid waste to many buildings. The French laid claim to the Saar region at this time and stole all the wealth from it, with no respect for churches and monasteries. Jean François Boch bought the ravaged premises in 1809 and turned it into a pottery. Part of his deal with the state was that he would have to burn the plentiful coal in the area to fire his kilns. Since wood firing was the order of the day, he had to devise a way to make coal heat compatible to the process. He succeeded. The old abbey is represented by the castle, a trademark of Mettlach, which is imprinted on the steins. Later, Boch joined forces with Nicholas Villeroy, who ran a pottery near Saarlouis, and the firm became known as Villeroy and Boch.

The concern studied methods of old stoneware construction and decoration and turned out the many items we like to collect today, as perhaps the best examples of that period. The chromolith method of ornamentation—a process of inlaying various colored clays to create beautiful designs, in much the same manner as enameling—reached new heights at the hands of Mettlach workers. This method won the concern new fame and established it as one of the outstanding potteries in the world—hence the interest from collectors everywhere.

Perhaps the artistry was inspired by management–worker relations which were second to none. Workers were given retirement pay at a time when it was unheard of elsewhere. If they lived outside the town, they were given free transportation via rail. At noon, specially heated wagons came to the homes of the workers and brought their noontime meals back to them, straight from their own kitchens. There were amusement parks and recreational plans that made it quite bearable to work for this concern. The attrition rate of workers was low.

Along with inlaid and decorated stoneware, Mettlach produced dinner sets, jardinières and pedestals, steins, tea sets, toilet sets, and the like. Like the steins, these pieces are marked with the castle imprint, most often with an interlocked VB in a circle. Numerals were used to indicate the year a piece was made, for instance 07 for 1907. Roman numerals indicate that the piece comes in more than one size. If you see a combination of numerals, such as 1077/880, the first refers to the shape, and the second, the style of decoration. A later mark, which appeared in 1874, was the winged head of Mercury, most often printed in green under the glaze. Those with Mercury which read "Reg. U.S. Pat. Off." are products of post-1900, when the pieces were imported for sale in this country.

There are several other less common marks, including the initials VB or V&B, which were used mostly at the end of the last century.

German regimental stein, early twentieth century. Figure at the top indicates the branch of service in which the soldier served—in this case the infantry.

Steins—The lids on steins were designed primarily for health reasons, to keep away flies and other insects attracted to the lip of mugs at outdoor beer gardens. Some steins have lithophane bottoms which held to the light, show damsels in various stages of undress, to encourage the imbiber to down his drink hurriedly so he could enjoy the sights.

The Mettlach stein is the most desired. There are steins made by other manufacturers, some of which are of good quality, but one must judge them on this quality before buying. There are regimental steins, popular at the turn of the century, which list the officers and men who belonged to a particular military group. Atop the lid is a metal figure that signifies the branch of the service in which they served. There were several makers of regimental steins.

Mettlach pitcher stein, stoneware, used in beer halls to fill smaller steins.

Many production steins were brought to this country by servicemen after both world wars and by tourists as well. This is the type made for beer halls, which used them as advertising pieces. These are not very good in quality, so are not bought by the serious collector. As with other items, quality is the most important factor—the Mettlach will not let you down. The unique designs, inscriptions and hand work in their creation, decoration and coloring set them apart from all others.

Central and Eastern Europe

Porcelain making began in Germany, where many potteries operated in the eighteenth and nineteenth centuries. Notable is the first, the Meissen works at Dresden. At a visit to the art museum in Hamburg, I noted many potteries not heard of in this century—so many, in fact, it would take a book just to list them. The work of these potteries is very similar—fine, fragile porcelain with all types of floral and gilt decoration. This tradition spilled over into all the adjoining countries. The ready availability of kaolin clay, which is a necessary ingredient to porcelain, was the key to the development of these industries.

There is a tradition of porcelain manufacture in Russia, as well, with potteries at St. Petersburg, Moscow, and Minsk. Today several are operating to make the collector plates of Russian scenery, which are marketed around the world. Some years ago, we noted in the commission shops in Moscow and St. Petersburg lots of small porcelain items that had been consigned to them for sale. Many pieces came from continental Europe as well as the Orient. There were makers' names I've never seen in books in this country and that have not appeared in any markets or shops I have visited.

There is a problem in buying dinnerware services made in countries other than England—there is practically no available open stock for replacement of broken items.

CASTLE AUGARTEN PORCELAIN

The Vienna Porcelain Manufactory was founded by a Dutchman, Claudius Du Parquier, in 1717. A few years before, in 1708, Johann Bottger of Germany uncovered the oriental secret of making porcelain. Two professional potters hired away from Meissen destroyed many of the Meissen models made for future manufacture. Du Parquier learned the location of a good supply of kaolin clay, which is necessary to the making of porcelain, near Passau, Germany, which insured that the finest work could be accomplished. Between 1744 and 1781 under the reign of Maria Theresa, the pottery prospered. Its work was acknowledged as the best in the world at that time. In 1749, a better clay was found at Schmolnitz in Hungary. Products made with this clay are marked with a blue shield under the glaze. Workers came from Dresden to create new forms, which were gilded and hand-decorated. The factory prospered under Baron Sorgenthal between 1781 and 1805 in a period described as

The Vienna Porcelain Manufactory at Castle Augarten makes the finest of porcelains. They are noted for the classic forms of the Lippizaner horses at the Spanish Riding School located there.

Modeler at Castle Augarten assembling a porcelain rendition of Guilliame Cousteau's Marly Horses.

classical. Other influences on style were Joseph Niedermeyer (took over the factory at the time of Napoleon) and Franz Joseph I (1848 to the closing of the pottery in 1864). Wahliss in Karlsbad tried to copy the original shapes and forms.

In 1922, the pottery was revived as the Vienna Porcelain Manufactory Augarten. It is best known today for the figures of the Lippizaners, the horses that perform at the Spanish Court Riding School in Vienna and around the world. Fine porcelain dinnerware as well as decorative wares are made in the tradition of the original factories. Located in a wing of an old castle, its original site (which I visited in 1971), continues to produce as fine a porcelain as there is.

China

There has been much speculation as to the feasibility of collecting Chinese porcelains. This country closed its doors to the

Worker at Castle Augarten, putting finishing touches on a soup bowl, shaping it while the clay is still "green."

western world for over twenty years, during which time the interest in oriental artifacts steadily increased. There has been some feeling that the market would be flooded with shipments of all kinds of antiques, as such a large country must surely have antiques going back to its earliest civilization. Since the Chinese worker, under communism, is unable to amass the wealth needed to indulge in collecting, it would be logical to assume that many artifacts would find their way to western countries in search of dollars and other hard currency. If the markets were flooded with such merchandise, it would again be logical to assume that the law of supply and demand would drive down the prices of existing treasures outside China and provide an unsettling effect on collecting them. However, in the opinion of those who deal in

Blanc de chine porcelain figure, Kuan Yin, c. 1675–1750, with the "all nations" mark. This work is being reproduced today.

such antiquities, this is not going to happen. Years ago, the great capitals at Anyang and Loyang were stripped of their antiquities, most of which found their way into western museums, providing the basis for some of the world's finest collections of this art. When the railway system was expanded in China in the early part of the century, many lines were run through old cemeteries. When the graves were dug up for relocation, all sorts of worldly possessions were found with the bodies, having evidently been buried with them for their trip to the unknown. The easy sale of such items led to grave robbing everywhere, which has provided many antiques for the western world.

China developed the earliest porcelain industry, and until its wares were duplicated in Europe, much fine porcelain was sent there in trade. This trade continued throughout the rise of the porcelain industry elsewhere. Chinese trade with Europe began in earnest early in the seventeenth century, but it was not common in America until after the Revolutionary War. America began sending clipper ships directly to the Orient, bypassing the necessity of transshipment through England. You can assume that most of the oriental ware collected today came to America after 1800. This is the period when Canton blue earthenware and porcelains from Nanking, Fukien, and Canton first made their presence felt. The popular five-color Chinese export porcelain, often called Rose Medallion, arrived in America as early as the 1790s, yet the bulk of it appears to have arrived after 1850 during the height of the Chinese-American trade. Little or no green-colored celadon arrived in America until after the War of 1812. You must be careful in purchasing the pure white blanc de chine figures (whose history goes back many centuries) as they are being reproduced quite well today. Imari ware (first made in Japan in blue and orange with gilding) is now being reproduced in China with remarkable fidelity. It is still being handmade and hand-decorated, which

Porcelain bowl, 15", Chinese five color, nineteenth century, commonly called rose medallion. *The hand decoration, color and condition are important to value.*

guarantees that quality pieces will rank high as collectibles in some future generation.

When Chiang Kai-shek left the mainland to occupy Taiwan, he took with him the palace treasures from Peking. Since then the People's Republic has been trying to replace them with similar items to restore the old palaces to their original dignity. There are agents from the People's Republic buying items all over the world for return to China, and their buying offers keen competition to anyone interested in oriental artifacts. There is no indication that markets throughout the world will be flooded with Chinese antiques, since there really is little of fine quality or value left to export. No one looks for a drop in prices for such items. Some of the best will undoubtedly continue to rise in price despite the "open door."

BLANC DE CHINE

Perhaps some of the purest white in porcelain is blanc de chine (which means "white china"). Not much has been learned of the history and origination of blanc de chine in China. What we know about it today has been learned from records kept in Europe by collectors. Some feel that blanc de chine originated as early as the sixteenth century. This was a time when the royal kilns at Chintechen were not operating. Most of the early production came from Té-hua in Fukien Province. Much was exported to Europe in the late seventeenth and eighteenth centuries. Historians tell us that the pieces were fired only once, giving them a quality that cannot be matched by any other porcelain. The quality of the porcelain was never duplicated in Europe.

Most of the figures are Buddhist-inspired, but there are decorative wares as well. The beauty of the early modeling in China lies in the delicate work done on the fingers, hair, and facial expressions.

Reproductions of these white porcelain figures can be found in import shops today, so it is necessary to learn how to tell the old from the new, which is not easy for the novice collector. Potteries in Germany, England, and France attempted to duplicate the wares in the eighteenth century, but without much success. Some of the best early examples can be seen at Blenheim Palace at Woodstock, England, as well as at the Victoria and Albert Museum in London. The Danish Royal Cabinet of Curiosities began acquiring the figures in about 1690. I have seen the collection at Rosenberg Palace in Copenhagen as well as that at Hampton Court in England. Only three dated pieces have turned up. There is a challenge in collecting good blanc de chine. The work is beautiful.

Areas of Collecting Interest

China Dogs

A favorite among collectors in America are the pairs of china dogs most often called Staffordshire dogs. They hail from Staffordshire County in England, and most were made in the last century.

There were more than 130 potters in that region, many of whom made such whimsies. I have never seen one marked by its maker, which makes attribution difficult. The quality of the pottery and its decoration and glaze help identify it.

In this country, for years these figures were called Staffordshire dogs. In England, they are called Sitting Spaniels, as tradition tells us that this breed was a favorite of Charles II in the seventeenth century. I am told Staffordshire dogs were popular gifts for newlyweds, who put them on either side of the fireplace to ward off the evil spirits who might descend there.

Early potters such as Thomas Whieldon, Ralph Woods, Astbury, and Walton called them pot dogs. More than 200 models have been identified, varying in height from 5 to 18 inches. Early forms had incised decorations, which make them more desirable than those simply molded. Dalmatians seem the first favored as models, but gradually the spaniel took over. Fancy models have molded chains, which are then gilded.

Actually, most of the work on these dogs is quite crude. They were made to appeal to people with lower incomes. Very little has been written about them as most people do not consider them art objects. I might mention that some artisans are reproducing them, making them look very

The English call these "Sitting Spaniels" or "King Charles Spaniels" as they were the favorite dog of the seventeenth century monarch. In this country they are called "Staffordshire Dogs."

old. In 1972 I bought a 16-inch pair in England for $29, including delivery here. I couldn't tell them from the old ones.

Fish and Game Services

Since the advent of mass production of dinnerware, potters have created many forms just to make business good. Just as the silvermakers created various spoons, forks, and knives for serving and eating different foods, so did the potters. Special dishes were created for serving all types of food, and they were promoted to create a complete service.

The French popularized this idea by making separate sets of twelve dishes to be used for dignified eating. For example, there were bowls with two handles for cream soups and fish platters for the fish course. The better sets, in porcelain, many made at Limoges, were hand-painted with different fish on them. This painting was done before glazing, and most pieces were signed by the artists. Later, transfer printing was used for decoration, so these are of less value. The next course was the meat, so a meat platter with twelve dishes decorated with various animals was a must.

Similar services were made in this country, notably in Ohio. The Pennsbury Pottery Company in Pennsylvania made platters, shaped like fish with scales. These are quite rare and are a good addition to any collection.

Game bird platter, porcelain, Guerin Limoges.

Home-Painted China

Late in the nineteenth century, nights were long and many looked for ways to busy themselves with crafts or other work. One of the favorite pastimes was painting china. White blanks of porcelain and earthenware were turned out by many of the major factories in Europe. Some of the finest in Limoges and Austrian porcelains were shipped here to be sold to enterprising home painters who did the work for the love of it and to occupy themselves in the days when there were few diversions to take one's mind off the chores of the day.

I have seen one hardcover book with instructions on how to paint china. It appeared at an auction and sold for well over $100.

Why such great interest? Though the painting is over the glaze and will not stand up well under washing, some of the artwork is quite good. Patterns were copied from books or other china pieces, and each artisan tried to put some of herself or himself into the piece.

If you wish to collect this home-painted china, here are a few guidelines: Porcelain blanks are preferable to earthenware. The quality of work, design, and colors must be good. Look for pieces signed or initialed by the artisan. This is quite important as the signed pieces generally command much more attention and price. You may see a factory stamp on the bottom, along with a name or initials in gilt or paint. Keep the pieces out of the dishwasher because the painting is not protected by the glaze. They are subject to wear for the same reason, so handle them as little as possible.

Occupied Japan

Items from Japan with the mark "Made in Occupied Japan" were made there during the occupation by American forces between 1945 and 1952. The *New York Times* reported that the first merchandise with this mark reached our shores in 1948.

Our country always enjoyed a big trade with Japan before the war, though the quality of much that was shipped here could be in question. Ceramics were perhaps the greatest export, but most items were channeled through our five-and-ten-cent stores during the Depression. Figurines, lamps, animals, birds, vases and planters, wall plaques, and the like continually turn up at auctions and flea markets. Unless they are of the paper thin, hand-painted porcelain, there is little demand, even today. After the war, however, greater attention was given to quality, as reviving the postwar economy in that country was of prime concern.

Much was shipped here in ceramics, metals, papier mâché, dolls, toys, and the like, stamped "Made in Occupied Japan." Collectors like ready identification as well as interesting objects to acquire, so it is natural that interest grew in this area. Books have been written on marks, makers, and what to collect. There are very few auctions where prices are not many times more today than they were when the items came here a scant 40 years ago.

Pennsbury Pottery

Pennsbury Pottery was started by Ernest Below, who had been a ceramics engineer at the Stangl Pottery in New Jersey. His mother served as the designer and was responsible for the Pennsylvania "Dutch" motifs which were so successful. His father worked creating shapes in ceramics. Most of his work was cast in a brown-tone background, which made the hand-painted artwork stand out. Local housewives and schoolgirls were trained to decorate the ceramics. The plant started with eight people and grew to employ between forty and fifty at the time of its demise. Clay came from Tennessee and Georgia and was mixed with flint and other ingredients. The plant originally used six different clays, and then narrowed it to two or three. Glazes were

Pennsbury pottery, c. 1950–1971, Morrisville, Pennsylvania, decorated by hand with Pennsylvania Dutch motifs. Most are browntone in color and marked with the pottery name on the base.

fritted, body sheen, and soft. Complete dinnerware sets and gift items were popular. The pottery started with sculptured birds but found these hard to sell in the face of competition from Japan.

Pennsbury Pottery will be remembered best for its commemorative work. The pottery made ashtrays for Electrolux, dishes for railroads, plates for fraternal organizations and churches, mugs and ashtrays for nearby Washington Crossing State Park, and just about anything demanded by clubs or organizations for presentation at annual meetings and the like. The rarest item of all is a single plate made for presentation to Walt Disney when he attended the opening of the Walt Disney School in nearby Tullytown. It has never turned up, and its whereabouts are unknown even to the Disney Archives in California. There are mugs for Historic Fallsington and another great rarity—scenic plates made for the last steam engine run on the Reading Railroad. The tray for this set had the engine pictured on it, and only 3,500 plates were made to be given to the passengers. The rooster was a popular design as it symbolized happiness. Pennsylvania hex symbols and designs with Amish figures were popular with the tourists. The pottery burned down shortly after an auction was held to dispose of the remaining ceramic pieces. All the machinery and dies were destroyed.

There has been some reproduction of Pennsbury Pottery done at a kiln in the Pocono Mountains. However, the coloring is different and can easily be noted by those who collect the original.

Phoenix Bird and Flying Turkey China

The phoenix was a fabled bird in Greek mythology. It was supposed to have a life span of thousands of years. No one is sure when it first appeared on pottery made in Japan. Collectors feel most was made in this century judging from the marks of "Nippon," which would date it after 1892, and the mark "Made in Japan," which came after 1920. The flying turkey pattern is very similar and some collectors feel there is no problem in mixing phoenix and flying turkey pieces in a collection.

The wings of the phoenix are always spread wide; it almost always has spots on its chest and its head is facing in the opposite direction from its body. Traditionally, the head is facing to the right, or back over its left wing, in what is called the "sinister" stance. With the head facing left and the body right, it is in the "dexter" stance. Some pieces feature both stances. The better grade designs depict the head perpendicular to the body with the head feathers pointing upward and carries mark #17 or #18, an indication of the fine quality. The majority of heads are horizontal with the hint of a slant. There are four to eight spots on the chest. Some chrysanthemum's (a standard design motif) centers are blue and some are white, perhaps at the discretion of the decorator. Very rare is a green and white piece of phoenix and rarer still is a fluted piece.

Phoenix bird china was advertised as "HOWO ware," from the Japanese word for phoenix. Early in this century it was used as a premium to boost sales of other items, and even to boost attendance at Radio City Music Hall.

Rebekah at the Well

If you have a Rockinghamware teapot with a molded figure of a lady at a well with the words "REBEKAH AT THE WELL" beneath, do not identify it as Bennington. Richard Carter Barret tells us that as many as thirty-five potteries could have made it late in the last century.

In his book *Early American Pottery and China* (Tuttle, 1926), John Spargo informs us that Charles Coxon, chief modeler at E & W Bennet in Baltimore, is the person who created Rebekah in this country. He copied the design from S. Alcock & Company in England, which featured the figure of Rebekah in white relief on a blue background. Potteries in New Jersey and Ohio made them as well, but in the brown ceramic. Some are modeled without the wording at the bottom. While director-curator at the Bennington (VT) Museum, Richard Carter Barret wrote the book, *How*

Rockinghamware teapot, "Rebekah at the Well."

to *Identify Bennington Pottery* in which he indicates that Rebekah was not made at Bennington.

Shaving Mugs

The development of the shaving mug follows closely the changing hairstyles of men throughout the world. Before the middle of the last century, the barber's basin was the common holder for soap and water used for shaving. During the time of the Civil War, beards became popular, so much so that even President Lincoln grew one. Shortly after this time the shaving mug became popular as men suddenly decided it was time to rebel against the prevailing styles and be clean shaven again.

Mugs were made to hold water and shaving cream, which was worked into a lather. Many shaving mugs were made in this country, but most of the better ones came from overseas. The latter are hand-painted and made of porcelain. It was not unusual for men to have their names painted or gilded on their shaving mugs. Each barbershop had a line of shelves to hold their customers' mugs, and each would be used only by its owner. Most mugs look like drinking vessels with built-in holders for the brush. The scuttle-type mugs seem to have been made only overseas; they do not appear in catalogs from this country. Some were made in silver-plate and sterling; most of these were listed in the silver company catalogs and not in the barber books. Mail-order concerns such as Sears sold shaving mugs as well. The Lenox Company in New Jersey listed their mugs only in their own catalogs and sold them in fine china shops as well. Country of origin had to be marked after 1892, but many have no such mark as the mugs were quite popular before that time.

Shaving mugs were still quite common on shelves in barber shops into the 1930s. The collapsible tube for creams and the electric shaver helped bring on their demise. They are interesting, colorful collectibles, today.

Glossary

Basalt—A black stoneware made by mixing iron ore byproducts with basic clay.

Belleek—A delicate porcelain that originated in Ireland, characterized by its sheen and fragility.

Biscuit—A molded clay item fired only once.

Bone china—A clay mixture that includes powdered, calcined bone powder to strengthen it and give it a porcelain-hard quality.

Caffette—A clay container that holds unfired bodies in a kiln.

Calcine—A technique for baking metals, stone, bone, or other materials to reduce them to powder before mixing with clay or a glaze.

Ceramic—A generic term for items made from clay and fired to hardness.

China—A generic term used to describe tablewares and decorative items made from clay and other ingredients.

Chinese export—The ceramic wares that arrived in Europe and America from the Orient in the eighteenth and nineteenth centuries.

Clay—Fine grained earth made up of hydrated silicates of aluminum, which forms a paste with water and can be molded and fired to hardness.

Creamware—A cream or ivory colored pottery which originated in England in the eighteenth century.

Delft—Originated in Ireland as a tin-glazed blue and white decorated earthenware. Received its name from the city in Holland where it was made and popularized. Made also in England, Germany, and other countries.

Dresden—The home of the original porcelain in Germany, discovered by Johann Freiderich Bottger.

Earthenware—Simple opaque ware made of clay and requiring glazing to offset its porosity.

Enameling—Decoration of ceramic bodies before firing with paints made from various substances.

Flint enamel—A pottery enamel made by calcining flint stone into powder, then mixing it with liquid glaze.

Glaze—A transparent or colored coating put on ceramics before firing to offset their porosity.

Graniteware—A very hard earthenware toughened with calcined flint stone.

Greenware—Clay products in their unfired state.

Ironstone—Patented by Mason in England in 1813. Usually a thicker, very tough earthenware; mostly in pure white with impressed or raised decoration.

Jasperware—Barium sulphate is added to clay to produce a nonporous hard body akin to porcelain. It is easily colored. Wedgwood is best known for working with it.

Kaolin—A fine clay used in making porcelain.

Kiln—An oven in which clay products are baked to hardness.

Lowestoft—A name often applied to Chinese export porcelains of the eighteenth and nineteenth centuries as late as the 1890s. It is believed that Lowestoft originally imported wares from China and reshipped them under its name from East Anglia, England.

Lusterware—Any ceramic body glazed with a metallic compound which will give it luster and shine.

Majolica—Originally an Majorcan redware which was colorfully fired with tin glazes. It became a product of practically every country with minor variations.

Meissen—Synonymous with Dresden, as the wares were made at the Meissen plant in Dresden, Germany.

Parian—An unglazed porcelain originated early in the nineteenth century as a poor man's imitation of Parian marble.

Petuntse—A form of feldspar which was mixed with clay to make various ceramics, including stoneware and porcelain.

Porcelain—A hard, translucent ceramic that originated in China.

Potter's wheel—A whirling device on which clay objects are formed by hand.

Queensware—Another name for creamware.

Redware—Made of red clay and glazed when needed to cancel its porosity.

Rockinghamware—A name given to the brown and mottled colored wares reputedly originating at the estate of the Earl of Rockingham in England in the eighteenth century. Much is referred to mistakenly as Benningtonware, a reference to the community in Vermont where a lot was made.

Salt glaze—An inexpensive quick glazing achieved by throwing salt into the kiln during the final moments of firing—the vapors then depositing on the bodies.

Saggar—Clay holder inside a kiln which holds the green clay for firing and protects it from direct heat.

Slip—A simple glaze made by mixing clay with water and slipping or trailing it on the piece to be protected.

Stoneware—A very strong earthenware which has the strength of porcelain and does not require an inside glaze to make it impervious to water.

Transferwares—Ceramic bodies with transfer printing done by the use of paper decals or transfers.

Underglaze—A reference to the painting or other decorating done on ceramics before glazing and firing.

Vitreous china—A strong earthenware body with an almost glasslike shiny glaze.

CHAPTER FOUR

Metalwork

Silver

Historical Overview

Silversmiths and metalworkers have always had a place in history, from the Egyptians of more than 3,000 years ago to the armorers of the Middle Ages, from Paul Revere to the present. Silversmithing, the cold working of metal, is both an art and a craft. The natural beauty of silver lends itself to the design of artists and craftsmen. It has been mined and worked into an endless variety of useful and decorative items that are highly sought after today.

Silversmithing in America goes back to the early seventeenth century. Silversmiths working in Boston were trained in England. Because of this, we owe much of our silver heritage to the British. Noted English craftsmen of the late eighteenth century include Matthew Boulton (1728–1809); Paul Storr, who began his work in 1792; and members of the Batemen family, including two women, Hester and Anne. Names like Philip Syng, Joseph Richardson, Johannis Nys, Ceasar Ghiselin, and William Vilant attest to the influence of European artisans on American silver.

The great silvermaking centers of the eighteenth century were Boston, New York, and Philadelphia. The craft then spread into the smaller cities and towns and some very sophisticated country work

has turned up to rival the urban centers.

Much of the early work by these and other makers is scarce, for several reasons. First, there was a limited output of eighteenth century American work because of a shortage of metal. The English withheld supplies of silver from the colonies in order to keep their own craftsmen busy, which held down production here. There was much melting down of coins and surreptitious buying of stolen metal from prize ships captured by pirates and others. A great deal of Spanish silver from the mines in Mexico and South America found its way into the hands of American silversmiths as booty from battles at sea. Pieces were made to order and in most cases the buyer would bring his own metal to the silversmith who would be paid for his efforts by retaining a percentage of it.

Second, at the time of the Revolution, many Tories still loyal to the Crown returned to England taking whatever they could, and if they owned silver it was the first thing they took. Much silver was donated to be melted down to help pay for the war effort. In the course of the war, the English also beseiged many cities along the American coast. When they received no cooperation from the colonists in supplying them with food or other needs, they would stand their battleships offshore and

153

Sterling tea set, c. 1855. This could be American or Continental. Generally, footed silver is more striking in design and more valuable.

Sterling wine goblets by Nathaniel Hayden and William Gregg, Charleston, South Carolina, 1838–1863. Hammerslough Collection.

demolish the community. This resulted in the wholesale destruction of many of our native decorative arts. When the British captured a town, the first thing the soldiers stole was the silver, since it was wealth that could be picked up and carried away.

Third, in 1793 and 1798, Philadelphia was scourged with serious epidemics of yellow fever, and silversmiths either died along with everyone else or quickly relocated, draining the city of its talents. The capital was moved to Washington and the demand for fine silver in Philadelphia lessened. Naturally, after the turn of the century, as machines arrived to do the work, the quality of silver declined and gradually disappeared—hence the importance of early Philadelphia silver.

It was not until the twentieth century that much attention was paid to American handmade silver. Those who owned old silver thought most of it was made in England, since not much research had been done on early makers in this country, and names and touchmarks gave no apparent clues. Late in the nineteenth century Professor Woolsey of Yale suggested that more research should be done, and this was followed at the turn of the century by a book prepared by N. W. Elwell which had forty pages of photography of both American and English silver. In 1906, The Museum of Fine Arts in Boston mounted the first exhibition of American silver, featuring silver which had been identified as to maker. The Museum of Fine Arts held another display in 1911, at which over a thousand pieces were shown. Since then, many books have been written and much information has been assembled, and several large museums keep permanent collections on display.

Collecting Guidelines

AMERICA

The great interest in American silver has all but depleted the available supply for the common collector. Today, you must wait for the liquidation of an estate where there are no heirs, or where money is more desired than old silver. Until recently, nineteenth-century silver was not much in demand, but as the rarity of early work increased, so did the interest in later work. Actually, there were many silversmiths doing handwork until the Civil War, as this industry was not affected by the industrial revolution until the 1840's when the method for electroplating was discovered.

Today, much nineteenth-century sterling is purchased for its scrap value. You will find it difficult to match pieces in a flatware set, and very few people wish to set a table unless the service is complete. There are some dealers who specialize in selling odd silver pieces, so if you have patience and get around to shows you may be able to select items you need.

The thin coin silver spoons which obviously were made in abundance during the early nineteenth century are still quite plentiful. Most are well marked, and a

Coin silver teapot on stand, with warmer. American, c. 1850. Its decoration heightens value.

book such as Seymour Wyler's *Old Silver, English, American, Foreign* (Crown Publishers) is quite helpful in identifying makers. Collect spoons of native or regional interest to you. Spoon racks are handy for display. After polishing coin silver pieces, rub them with ordinary flour to remove the excess polish and to give them a sheen which will not tarnish quickly.

Commemorative and souvenir spoons in sterling are quite common and represent an interesting facet of collecting. Friends touring foreign countries can acquire some for you, and you can begin a collection on your own by purchasing them new or old from dealers. When such a collection comes up for sale it will reward the collector well for his efforts, as long as the pieces are varied and difficult to acquire unless one travels a lot.

Silversmiths were known to have done a great deal of work other than turning out pieces of church or tableware. Some smiths engraved the plates from which money was printed. Others turned out sword handles, belt buckles, coins, buttons, card boxes, and other necessities of the day. Fortunately, since most American silversmiths

Silver teapot by Nathaniel Vernon of Charleston, South Carolina, 1777–1843. Hammerslough Collection.

were of English birth or descent, they marked their pieces well and because of this we know the origin of the pieces and can note regional differences in style and workmanship.

Silver knives were used during the seventeenth century, but spoons did not make their appearance until the 1800s. Forks are rare, even in the eighteenth century, since the soft silver did not lend itself

Early American Silversmiths

Many silversmiths worked in the seventeenth and eighteenth centuries, and to attempt to list them all would require a separate volume. However, it is well worth mentioning a few of the more notable.

Robert Sanderson (1608–1693) of Hampton, New Hampshire is credited with being the first American silversmith. With his partner, John Hull, he turned out work on a par with that made in England. Sanderson moved to Watertown, Massachusetts, in 1642 where he and Hull made the famous pine tree shillings, which became coin of the commonwealth at the time. Sanderson's three sons (Joseph, Benjamin, and Robert) all followed their father's trade, and all worked in the making of church plate, much of which has survived.

Samuel Casey (1723–1773) of Kingston, Rhode Island, lived an interesting life. He was caught making counterfeit coins and was sentenced by the crown to hang. However, friends spirited him away from his jail cell and he was never seen again. Needless to say, his silver is a very premium collectible.

Philip Syng had a shop in Philadelphia on Front Street amid the docks and other busy shops. He made the beautiful inkstand which was used to hold the pen at the signing of the Declaration of Independence and the Constitution.

Unusually large bureau set in sterling by Gorham, c. 1920s. Twenty-one pieces include three brushes, mirror, clothing brush, nail buffer, nail file, two manicure tools, button hook, hair curler, two toothbrushes, two scissors, comb, shoe horn, and four cutglass jars with sterling covers.

to rough usage. The English made Sheffield forks, but few or none of these were manufactured in America.

In the early part of the eighteenth century, American silversmiths did not copy the style of the tall English teapots, preferring the lower ones in the pigeon-breasted Queen Anne style. Even these went out of fashion during the third quarter of the eighteenth century, when tea urns became the standard. Most of these urns were built with warmers underneath, and some had a place where a piece of hot iron could be inserted to maintain the heat. The basic style was low pots for tea and tall pots for coffee and chocolate. Ceramics makers later evolved a pattern for the latter which had the spout at the top for easier pouring. It is not known why the silver makers retained the spout emerging from the center of the pot, as chocolate is a heavy liquid and can clog the spout. Chocolate arrived in England in the mid-seventeenth century, about the same time as tea and coffee. You can easily tell a chocolate pot from the early period, as most were made with a removable piece at the top where a stirring rod could be inserted. The English pots may have this device, but it does not appear in American colonial work.

Tea caddies were popular—the name

coming from the Malaysian word meaning pound, with reference to the amount packed in a container of this size. Tobacco was another product which came into favor in the mid-seventeenth century, and boxes were made to hold it. Snuff became quite popular during the time of Queen Anne and snuff boxes became fashionable. Silver spice boxes (or nutmeg boxes as they were often called) came into vogue in the eighteenth century, so one might season his food properly while traveling. Sugar was a very expensive luxury in England until the end of the seventeenth century, when the demand for it to sweeten hot drinks resulted in greater imports. It came in loaf or chunk form, so sugar boxes were made to house it with proper decorum for the fancy table. Tongs and cutters were added to the inventory of silver wares to handle the chunk sugar. One of the American colonial makers of sugar boxes was John Coney of

Sterling tankard by Myer Myers, eighteenth century, New York. Myers was the only maker of Jewish descent who worked during this period in America. Hammerslough Collection.

Pair of American sterling six-light candelabra, Tiffany & Co., date mark 1891–1902. Height 17", spread 13", 228 troy ounces. Sold for $25,300 by Grogan & Company, Auctioneers, Boston, March 9, 1991.

Boston (1655–1722), who trained a very important Huguenot apprentice, Appolos Rivoire, the father of the noted Paul Revere. The Revere silver is cataloged *Revere I* and *Revere II* for identification.

Dish crosses, which served as trivets to raise heated dishes from the table, are rare in American made silver. Marrow spoons were common in England, but not here. Chafing stands are rare in both countries; they were generally quite small in order to accommodate small silver pots. Ladles, wine siphons, andirons, chandeliers, sconces, and frames for looking glasses were not common products by American silversmiths.

There is much contemporary silver being collected for investment purposes, and there is no doubt that most of it will increase in value. The price of the raw metal will rise with the economy and if the work is good, of artistic quality, or in a limited edition to make it rare, contempo-

rary silver can represent a good investment. Many mints are turning out plates, coins, statues, and the like with a published assurance that only a limited number will be made. However, you must remember that any machine-made item can be reproduced at any time in the future and there can be no guarantee to protect you against reproductions. The best investment is in old handmade work which cannot be duplicated. Buy the contemporary silver if you like it, but remember that there is only a chance that it will acquire some importance in the future, and do not depend on it.

Plated Silver—The manufacture of less expensive silverware in America began when the electroplating technique was developed about 1840. A body of lesser metal such as copper, brass, Britannia or white metal was dipped into a silver solution. When electricity was short-circuited within the solution, it deposited the silver on the body. To provide the necessary thickness for wear, each piece was dipped several times and marked "triple plate" for three dippings or "quadruple plate" for four. This process continued until the 1890s when the method of dipping was improved to the point where only one submersion was required to deposit the necessary coating on the base metal. The public had been conditioned to the designation "quadruple plate" as a term for the best in plated ware and rather than risk loss of sales with reference to a single plate, the old designation was used up until World War I. In the 1920s, the term "silver on copper" was introduced and most plated ware is so marked today. If the letters EP appear, this indicates electroplate. NS is nickel silver plate; EPNS, electroplated nickel silver; EPBM, electroplated britannia metal.

After the Civil War, plated silver came into its own. The war industries were geared to making items out of metal and when peace came they turned their efforts to everyday items. Victorian styling was still very much in vogue, and highly decorated

Silver-plated punch pot with bear finial atop the handle, c. 1850s. Simpson Hall & Miller, Wallingford, Connecticut. The pot is double-walled, providing insulation for cold or hot beverages.

work began to appear since machines made mass production possible. In the hand era (before 1840) decoration was applied by chasing or engraving the outside of the piece, or by repousse (hammering it from the inside against a mold). The highly figured pieces were stamped out in sections and then soldered together and plated. This type of work is popular to this day, although the designs have changed. Some experts feel that when these pieces are replated they do not have the look of the originals of years ago, but this is quite easily explained. After dipping, the early makers would have each piece polished ready for the trade, usually with a substance that would turn black with use. This was allowed to remain in the cracks and crevices in order to highlight the raised shiny surfaces. A man who had worked at a silver factory before the turn of the century gave me this information. It is unlikely this technique would be duplicated today, especially if the public knew how it was done.

There is a fad today for collecting old silver pieces and having them stripped to reveal the base metal, which can be copper, brass, white metal, or even steel. The pieces were often made of combinations of different metals, with copper forming the places where there is less stress, and other metals used for feet, handles, finials, and spouts. This rule also applies to those pieces which were plated in nickel and, later, chromium. You should look for interesting forms, as this is most important in determining the value of such items.

Englander

As mentioned, America owes its heritage in silvermaking to England. The early craftsmen who came from there were trained in the most progressive techniques. Silversmiths were regulated by the crown as early as the thirteenth century with stiff penalties levied on those who attempted to defraud the public. Until then, most work had been done in gold, primarily for royalty and the church. A goldsmith's guild had been formed to police its members and upgrade the quality of work by providing for an apprentice system in order to train craftsmen properly. Some of the great early work was done in monasteries since ecclesiastical gold and silver were in great demand for communion services, salvers, crosses, and candleholders.

A marking system instituted in 1477 required that a leopard's head, with or without crown, had to be stamped on every piece that met the weight of 22 shillings to the pound. Two years later, the date letter was required on every piece and this makes it possible to document the year it was smithed. Silversmiths began stamping their pieces with touchmarks for identification about 1479. Most people were illiterate, so these marks were important for identifying the maker. The mark might be a flower, horse head, star, moon, or some other recognizable object which was registered as the maker's mark. Silver had to be sent to the guild hall where it was tested for purity and marked—hence the term "hall-marked."

In 1560, the sterling standard 1000 indicated pure metal (sterling was 925 parts silver and 75 parts alloy). Coin, metal from which coins of the realm were made, had 875 parts silver and 125 parts of alloy. Some continental silver will be marked 800, which indicates 800 parts of silver to 200 parts of alloy. This is frequently found on metal from Germany, Italy, and Holland.

In 1794, a new system of marking appeared in England which consisted of five cartouches impressed on the back sides of tableware and on the bottom of serving and decorative pieces. Most often, the first cartouche contains the initials of the maker or makers. The next will hold the touch-mark, with the head of the reigning monarch beneath it, stamped to signify that the tax has been paid. The third is the lion passant (which holds the sterling mark), and the final cartouche bears the date letter indicating the year the piece was made. Marking books help interpret these. A

The height of the coin silver period extended from about 1790 to the 1850s. Coin spoons seem to have been made in abundance between about 1820 and 1840. These are quite thin. Though many think this is because of the high silver content, it is not. There is less silver in these than in their sterling counterparts.

The Origin of "Sterling"

The term "sterling" was adopted from the name of a group of German craftsmen known as the "Easterlings" who migrated to England early in the fourteenth century. Their work in refining silver to its pure standards prompted a royal edict which set forth their formula as the law of the realm. However, it was not until after the Civil War that the term was much in use in America, so if you see the word "sterling" stamped on a piece, you will know that it was most likely made after that time.

Set of four Victorian silver-gilt figural salts; Walter, John, Michael & Stanley Barnard, London, 1898. Sold for $6,050 by Butterfield & Butterfield, Los Angeles and San Francisco. Photo courtesy of Butterfield & Butterfield.

span of years is indicated quickly by noting the head of the reigning monarch. Male profiles will appear from 1794 until Queen Victoria's ascension to the throne in 1837. In 1892 this marking system was discontinued, so one can figure approximate dates quickly.

In America, we followed the English standards. After the War Between the States a law was passed requiring that all items of sterling be so marked to guarantee its metal content. One will find the word sterling spelled out or a mark of 925, which indicates the silver content. Some concerns, such as Tiffany, used 925/1000. If a piece is not marked in this manner, one should not assume it is sterling.

Coin silver was used in the manufacture of many items in both America and England. The height of the period was between about 1790 and 1850. Most of the teaspoons and tablespoons—those which are very thin and bend easily—were made between about 1820 and 1840. Most are well-marked, which helps in identification.

Sheffield Plate and Electroplating—It was not until the eighteenth century that much

silver was made for those whose station was below that of royalty. As England's trade with the world increased, so did the affluency of her traders and they soon became patrons of the arts and crafts. At first, production was limited to functional items such as tankards, mugs, pieces for tea and coffee sets, and tableware. A later development in production that was to have a far-reaching effect was the creation of Sheffield plate. Two centers for its production were the cities of Sheffield and Birmingham. The process was discovered about 1743 by a Sheffield metal worker, Thomas Boulsover. Originally a sheet of silver was bonded to one side of a copper ingot by rolling or hammering. After 1765, the silver was introduced to both sides of the copper. These were rolled and pounded to remove any air between them. Then, the metals were heated until the silver began to melt and the unit was rolled into a thin sheet with the copper sandwiched between the silver layers. Pieces could then be fashioned from this plated metal. Silver solder was used at the seams which were hidden by burnishing and polishing.

Sheffield plate became very popular in

English, Sheffield figural cow cover on Waterford glass jam dish, early nineteenth century.

both Europe and America, but there is no evidence that this type of plate was actually made in this country. One will find many examples here in the Georgian style, but since it is not sterling, none of it is marked. When Sheffield plate wears, the copper will shine through the edges of the repousse decoration. One should not electroplate Sheffield to hide this, as this destroys its value.

CHINA

The Chinese-American trade brought with it a Chinese export silver of very good quality. A great deal of this silver came into America during the nineteenth century; yet it has been only recently that sufficient research has been done to make identification possible.

For some time, collectors and appraisers came upon pieces of "English" Georgian silver with marks that could not be found in marking books, hence the designation of "unrecorded maker." It was not until 1975 that this mystery was solved.

The former Museum of the American China Trade, which was located in Milton, Massachusetts, published the book *Chinese Export Silver*, written by the director, Dr. H.A. Crosby Forbes, John Devereux, and Ruth S. Wilkins. In it, the authors document Georgian style silver made in nineteenth-century China and stamped with phony British hallmarks. A coffeepot marked "SS" within a cartouche had been identified by a museum as being made by Silas Sawin, an eighteenth-century New York silvermaker. The mark proved to be that of Sunshing, who worked in the middle of the last century in Shanghai.

The collections of the Museum of the American China Trade are now at the Peabody Institute in Salem, Massachusetts. A copy of the book on Chinese silver is available there or you may order it (see the Bibliography).

DENMARK

When one discusses Danish silver, the name Georg Jensen heads the list of those

Danish silver, four-piece tea and coffee service with tray in the blossom pattern, bone handles. Georg Jensen, Copenhagen. Sold by Butterfield & Butterfield at auction, September 17, 1990, for $17,600.

who are known to have been great craftsmen in that country. Jensen (1866–1935) opened his shop in Copenhagen in 1904. Originally a sculptor, he turned his talents toward designing and making silver items now considered to be some of the greatest examples of Art Nouveau and Art Deco styles. The Georg Jensen Company carries on the tradition of excellent design and production. From 1909, the majority of production was exported and sold in Jensen's own shops in Berlin, Stockholm, Paris, London, New York, and other major cities.

Other early twentieth-century designers include Johan Rohde, Harold Nielsen, Sigvard Bernadotte, and Henning Koppel. Kay Bojesen was apprenticed to Jensen in 1907 and went on to establish his own company in 1958. His silver is much like Jensen's in style—undecorated and very functional. Great makers include Evald Nielsen (1879–1958), Frantz Hingelberg (who worked in Aarhus as early as 1897), Holger Kyster who worked c. 1898–1944, Hans Hansen (1884–1940), Mogins Ballin (1871–1914), and Peter Hertz (1811–1885). Some were appointed to the Royal Court.

Before World War II, much fine Danish silver was sent to a museum in the United States for safekeeping. Much of it is still here, the former owners having disappeared during the war. Makers' marks appear on all Danish silver made between 1490 and 1893. Since then, retailers have added their names to the makers' marks as well.

FRANCE

There is a new interest in early French silver today, but very little is available here. Actually, many of the styles popularized in England in the late seventeenth and early eighteenth centuries were created by Huguenot craftsmen who left their country after the Edict of Nantes was revoked in 1685, again denying them freedom from religious persecution. Among those who fled to England were the forebears of Paul Lamerie, who was destined to become England's most noted silversmith. Other Huguenots who had a great influence were Peter Platel and Anthony Nelme. The workmen who were not affected by the Edict of Nantes continued to work in France, turning out the same quality of work as that made in England.

Pair of french silver five light candelabra, Veyrat, late nineteenth century. Sold for $12,100 by Butterfield & Butterfield, Los Angeles and San Francisco. Photo courtesy of Butterfield & Butterfield.

Collectors are well aware of a wide range of antique and contemporary works from Japan, including porcelains, paintings, prints, furniture and the like. However, not much attention is being given to handmade silver by Dresser and Tiffany which is being sought today.

Christopher Dresser was born in Scotland. He was a silversmith who believed that items made of this metal should be functional. He travelled to Japan to seek new ideas in design and this resulted in a book, *Japan: Its Architecture, Art and Art Manufactures*, which was published in 1882. This set off a round of imitation of these designs by craftsmen throughout the world which some feel gave birth to the Art Nouveau movement. Dresser's work at his plants in Sheffield and Birmingham resulted in pieces which often are mistaken for work in this century as it reflected the Art Nouveau influence which prevailed into the 1920s.

Louis Comfort Tiffany must have been inspired by Dresser's book, as he was a leader in the movement. One will note the resemblance to decorative ideas seen in the porcelains, paintings, prints, etc., in the form of animals, birds, fish, flowers and other inspirations taken from nature. Look

Important Japanese movement silver nautical punch bowl, Tiffany & Company. Sold by Butterfield & Butterfield at auction, April 30, 1990, for $67,500. San Francisco.

for marks to determine provenance and quality of the silver. The few pieces I have seen at the Tokyo Museum do not seem to enjoy the quality of our sterling at 925/1000, but, not being able to see the marks underneath, this is only an observation. If you travel to Japan, the elegant native silver work is something you should seek.

Identifying Reproductions

Most buyers of silver realize that any sort of marking system is not without its hazards, as fakers have been at work to turn it to their advantage. It is not too difficult to cast a die in the exact mold of an early touchmark, and then impress it on a later piece whose style and workmanship will not give it away. Another trick is to cut an authentic hallmark from a lesser piece and insert it in a more important one to increase its value. The marks from a spoon can be imbedded in the bottom of a teapot, as silver is quite malleable and this work can be done well enough to fool the naked eye. However, such fakery can be detected by the use of lights and close examination. Another method is to breathe on the piece—the moisture will reveal any reconstruction work. Experts who study shapes and forms can readily tell if there has been any tampering. Not long ago, a fine pair of candlesticks with marks of a mid-eighteenth century maker were sold as his work. However, he worked in a period when the style they represented could not have been made. Needless to say, the smarter dealers offered no bids at the auction. You would not expect to find Federal period styling done by a maker quite prominent in the rococo period which preceded it, especially when none of his known work reflects such design.

Design and Style

Decorating silver is an exacting art, and there are several ways in which it was done. Perhaps the first technique was en-

Victorian silver figural epergne, Robert Garrard, London, 1826. Sold for $11,000 by Butterfield & Butterfield, Los Angeles and San Francisco. Photo courtesy of Butterfield & Butterfield.

Two pairs of covered entree dishes from the Mackay Service, Tiffany & Co., c. 1878. In March 1992, the large pair sold for $35,000 and the small pair for $25,000. Photo courtesy of Butterfield & Butterfield.

graving, which is done with a sharp tool to remove the metal where it is cut. The term "bright cut" is used to define cutting which is deep and often undercut so that there will be more brilliance as it reflects light. Chasing resembles engraved work, but it is done with a tool which impresses the design, thus removing no metal. Repousse is done by hammering a body of silver from the inside to produce a raised surface with a shaped decoration. A gadroon or fluted decoration around rims was very popular. Some pieces, such as feet, handles, spouts, and finials, were cast and then joined by silver soldering to the main body. Polishing with a jeweler's rouge erases the markings of such joined work.

You can trace the design of silver easily, as it followed the tastes in furniture. Pieces were made to compliment room settings of furniture, and with such a clue you can reasonably ascribe the period of its manufacture. In the eighteenth century,

silversmiths worked in pure forms, with little thought to fancy design or decoration. The Queen Anne period brought with it grace and elegance in curves and a delicate style which was reflected in all the decorative arts. The mid-century styles of Chippendale influenced the arts with their rococo decoration. This became especially

George IV silver-gilt sideboard dish depicting the Battle of Agincourt, applied royal arms of H.R.H. Adolphus Frederick, 1st Duke of Cambridge. William Elliott, London, 1826. Sold for $27,500 by Butterfield & Butterfield, Los Angeles and San Francisco. Photo courtesy of Butterfield & Butterfield.

popular after the excavations in Greece and Italy, which created a revival of interest in classical decorative forms. After the Revolutionary War, the austerity of Hepplewhite brought a return to dignity, expressed through straight lines and less embellishment. What is known now as the Federal style was quite popular well into the 1830s, after which machines began to erode the quality of silver work. The gaudy productions of the Empire and Victorian periods were in keeping with the furniture of the day and like the furniture of that time, have only recently been accepted on a wide scale for collecting. Until now, no silver collector would have allowed any nineteenth century silver made after 1830 into his collection. Recent studies into the decorative arts have revealed that much silver was still handmade after 1830, and regardless of style, it represents the craftsmanship of the times. Rather than being made by individual small shops as in the past, large factories were set up to take care of the growing demand for the product at the time of America's great industrial growth.

Pewter

Historical Overview

Pewter is made by casting, hammering, or lathe spinning on a mold. Generally, ornamentation is simple, consisting mostly of rims, molding, or engraving. However, some continental pewter (especially that of the Renaissance period in France and Germany) has intricate ornamentation.

Early on, pewter was used in the Far East, and Roman pieces are known to exist. England was a major center of production from the Middle Ages, and, until china replaced it, pewter was the chief tableware. America imported much English pewter in colonial times and, starting in 1700, began producing its own in large quantities.

Pewter is composed primarily of tin, with the basic formula being 90% tin plus 10% antimony, copper, or other alloys. Lead can be added to give it weight and this is a good clue to Continental pewter since American and English pewter are lighter in comparison. It is felt that the lead content helped to promote the poisoning of food and caused illness in many of its users. Fortunately, American makers used little or no lead in their production.

Since pewter is soft the pieces would not survive, and they would be taken to the local pewterer, who melted them down in order to recast the metal into new pieces. As payment for his services he would retain part of the metal, using it for his own new production. This practice helped diminish the available supply of eighteenth-century pewter, since so much of it was melted down. The Revolutionary War also helped to create this shortage, as much plate was melted down for bullets. Pewter cannot withstand high temperatures, and any piece coming in contact with excessive heat will be damaged or destroyed instantly. A lot of the early production must have been lost in this manner.

Following the lead of the silversmiths, the pewterers were conscientious in marking their handmade pieces. Those pieces

Set of Irish haystack pewter measures, so named because of the similarity in shape. This set is nineteenth century, but they have been reproduced extensively in the last twenty years.

Pewter communion set by Thomas Danforth and Samuel Boardman, Middletown, Connecticut. Correct terminology for pieces is salver, communion cups, and flagon.

which were cast in molds were less likely to be marked. Other makers would not mark pieces, hoping to mislead the public into thinking that they were buying imported pewter which was considered to be of finer quality.

In the eighteenth century, a shortage of tin plagued American pewter makers. They were entirely dependent on exports as there was no established source in America at the time. Plenty of English pewter was shipped in to take care of the demand and this in effect helped provide the material for some American production.

AMERICAN PEWTERERS

Almost every community had its resident pewterer. The pewterer might have been no more than a reworker of metal who had equipped himself with molds into which melted down scrap could be poured. Craftsmen who worked with the hammer and primitive lathes were in the minority, and it is this handwork which brings top dollar today.

Roswell Gleason—Roswell Gleason worked as a pewterer from 1822 to 1871 in Dorchester, Massachusetts. His plant used both the old pewter metal as well as the newer Britannia metal in turning out many pieces which are high on collecting lists today. He is regarded as a top craftsman in the field as his designs were pure in form and the execution of them was impeccable.

Early in his career, he utilized the popular eagle mark as a touch on his work, but later used "R. Gleason," impressed on the bottom. Any piece with both the eagle mark and his name is worth more than the name alone. Also, he used the Massachusetts coat of arms on some pieces and these are highly desired. Some pieces have his first name spelled out in full but there is no premium for this.

Gleason is known to have made coffee and tea pots and related items: candleholders, communion sets, coffee urns, water pitchers with covers, mugs, syrup jugs, and even cuspidors. The latter, though very rare, will not command much money because of the lack of desirability for such a piece. In his book *American Pewter* (Bonanza), J.B. Kerfoot illustrates an unusual tankard that boasts a top which screws on instead of being hinged. Kerfoot opines that it may have been a communion piece in which a priest might carry consecrated wine safely to the home of an ill person. If one were to begin collecting pewter (Brittania) of the nineteenth century, he would be well advised to begin with the quality pieces of Gleason.

Zachariah Stevens and His Apprentices— About 1820, Zachariah Stevens moved from England to Maine where he set up shop as a tin knocker in the small town of Stevens Plains, which was eventually named after him. This is just north of Portland and the name has since been changed to Westbrook.

From his shop came some of the finest and most desired pieces of painted tin (his wife and daughters did the decorating). Stevens trained Freeman and Allen Porter, both of whom became pewterers who went out on their own and worked together. Freeman (1835–1860s) and Allen (1830– 1840) made some of the most collectible examples of pewter in all forms. The pieces are well-marked. (If one finds F. Porter on silver, this is the mark of Franklin Porter who worked in New York City c. 1820s.) Another apprentice to Stevens was Rufus Dunham (1837–1861) of Westbrook who founded R. Dunham and Sons of Portland

Cupboard full of pewter and Brittania ware. At top, far right *is a coffeepot by Rufus Dunham.*

(1861–1882). Dunham pieces are also well marked.

Another to seek is Israel Trask (1807–1856) of Beverly, Massachusetts. (All of the above worked in Britannia metal.) It would take an entire book to write about the early pewter workers like the Will family in Philadelphia, the Boardmans and Danforths in Connecticut, etc. One should study books on them if interested in collecting eighteenth century pieces.

Collecting Guidelines

The availability of eighteenth-century American pewter is quite limited. Serious collectors have been buying it for years and, along with museums and historical societies, they have locked up most of it from the general trade channels. An estate will occasionally come up for sale with such early pieces and prices seem to skyrocket every year as the demand exceeds the supply. There are books providing identification of makers by name and touchmark listed in the bibliography, so there is no great mystery in identifying pewter. You must be careful of fake touches as these will crop up from time to time, but they are the great minority, so do not worry too much

Pewter whale oil lamp, Thomas Wildes, c. 1829–1840, Philadelphia and New York City.

about it. Pewter has not been considered a valuable commodity until recently, so there has been little reason to doctor it. Until now, most pewter has gone to serious buyers who would recognize any alteration and there has been little incentive for fakery. Now that public acceptance has broadened for the product, it is only natural to assume that some unscrupulous people will attempt to take advantage of those with limited knowledge, so the danger is now more present than ever. You should only rely on competent dealers for advice. When an estate is settled, you may also buy with relative safety, as the collector put his stamp of approval on the piece just by owning it. If an auctioneer suspects that later work has been done on an item, he will gladly give you the benefit of this advice if you ask him during the pre-sale inspection.

Woodenware in kitchens gave way to pewter early in the eighteenth century, both in America and abroad, but a century later pewter suffered a decline in the face of competition from the expanding ceramics and glass industries. Its final ignominy came after the 1850s at the hands of the silver platers who used Britannia bodies for their wares, covering up the metal which was once so important to the well-being and economy of the world. Collectors who recognize the forms are having these pieces stripped of their blackened and fading silverplate, restoring them to greater interest and value. Much of the early Reed and Barton silverware made in Taunton, Massachusetts, during this period could be plated Britannia.

HANDMADE PEWTER

Casting pewter in a mold would often leave pits and hollows in the metal. These would be filled with a soldering iron using scrap pewter metal or solder. The piece would then be placed in a lathe and "skimmed" by holding a sharp tool against it, shaving off any rough spots and raised imperfections. A spiral mark would quite often be left from this process and it will still be visible. Pieces which were completely hand hammered are most desired and this work can usually be noted at the

Pewter porringer, Thomas Danforth and Sherman Boardman, Hartford, Connecticut, c. 1810–1830. Their initials are imprinted on the handle.

booge, where the hammer marks will be most visible.

An early porringer can often be identified by the method in which the handle has been attached. The body would be formed and then a mold for the handle would be held against it in proper position. The body would be hung over an anvil or other support during this process, and a wet rag or burlap would be used to prevent contact between the piece and the support. When the hot pewter was poured into the handle mold, it would melt and fuse with the body, but the body would also soften enough to absorb an imprint from the cloth on the inside at the point where the handle was attached. This "crosshatching," as it is called, indicates the manner in which a piece was made.

MACHINE-MADE PEWTER

Mechanization began creeping slowly into industry in the mid-1790s, when Josiah Wedgwood introduced machinery which speeded up his production in ceramics. But it was until after the War of 1812 that such progress made any great impact in America. The approximate date used for the beginning of the industrial age is 1830, which coincides with the deterioration of all the decorative arts, pewter being no exception. By this time a harder metal called Brittania was in general use. Developed in England during the eighteenth century, the Brittania formula does not seem to have come into general use in America until after 1820. By 1830, most work was in Britannia, and by 1840, most was machine-made. Some work was done by molding and other work was turned out individually on lathes powered by steam or water. Wooden forms were created in the sizes of dishes or bowls, and these would be fastened in a lathe with a sheet of Brittania held against them. As the mold and metal were spun, the artisan would hold a steel tool against the metal, molding it to the wooden shape. The piece would then be removed and finished at the workbench,

where rims could be worked, and feet, handles, spouts, and the like could be added by soldering. Some very collectible work was done during this period and though not as valuable as the earlier production, it has found great favor with collectors who must settle for second best. Actually, much desirable production was done as late as the 1880s, especially in the newer parts of the country, where artisans worked with less sophisticated tools for a longer period.

MARKS

In the British Isles, it was a requirement that all pewter be marked by the maker. The letter X could be added to signify a superior metal. So long as the mark is visible, the marking books help in identifying provenance, maker and age. Since American pewter of the eighteenth century has ascended to such high prices, there is growing interest for that made overseas. Fortunately, American and British pieces do not contain lead, much of which was used in Continental and Scandinavian pewter, making it heavier. Some feel it is not advisable to eat from dishes with lead content. One good clue in collecting is that if the word pewter appears stamped on the bottom of a piece, it

Unusual touchmark in pewter which was used by some eighteenth-century workmen to suggest the piece was done in London. The first O was stamped as a Q, so it would not be an outright forgery. Bush and Perkins of Bristol, England, are known to have used this mark.

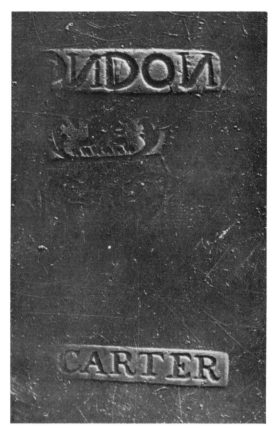

Another unusual pewter touchmark with the reverse N. No explanation is known for this, although the piece is known to be English, eighteenth century. William Penn Memorial Museum, Harrisburg.

is not considered collectible. This stamp indicates a factory mark used from the late nineteenth century to the present. It is the handmade product which has value.

There is much unmarked pewter which could be American and it is being bought by those who hope for a magic formula which will someday unlock the secret of its origin. Some appears with an eagle touch, which would seem American, but is yet unidentified as to maker.

DESIGN AND STYLE

Some collectors feel that the rolled edge of a plate or dish could signify country of origin—if it is rolled on the top, it's English; if rolled on the underside, Ameri-

can. There is little to support this theory as it is generally accepted that most American pewterers were trained in England and practiced those techniques here. Tom Williams, perhaps the best known dealer/collector in the country, told me that if a dish has a hammered booge (a curved raised wall at the bottom of plates and dishes), this is an indication of English work.

Measurements are not much of a clue to country of origin, though no one can authenticate an American charger which measures more than sixteen inches in diameter (known English pieces are larger). You should refer to any flat piece less than nine inches in diameter as a plate, and any nine inches or greater in diameter as a dish. The latter may also be referred to as trenchers or chargers, as these are old English names for serving dishes.

Little engraving or chasing was done on pewter in this country. Some European work was decorated in this manner. It is noticeably absent on church communion services, as most of these must have been presentation pieces. However, unlike silver, pewter presentation pieces were rarely marked.

Oriental pewter has been imported for a long time, but it is of poor quality with a heavy lead content. Some work which is mistaken for pewter might even be made of a white metal which colors to resemble it greatly. The weight of the piece is a clue to its contents—you must learn to "feel" pewter as well as look at it.

Forms in pewter are important. Items with interesting shapes make ideal shelf and decorative pieces and are most in demand. Tankards, chargers, whale oil lamps, porringers, sets of measures, posset cups, salts, tea caddies, tea and coffee pots, candle holders, and tureens are ideal items. Rare items like wine funnels and pumps, brandy warmers, barber's basins, chamber pots, and medical items may be in short supply, but are also in short demand. Some enthusiasts like to collect church pewter, such as the beakers, salvers, and flagons used for communion, but these are rare

Hexagonal teapot with Oriental designs, c. 1700.

since most churches have disposed of theirs by now.

Pewter should be more decorative than functional, so it is those pieces with beauty of design and great handcraftsmanship which command the highest interest and prices. Proportions and workmanship are vital, but the most important feature is identification with a maker. Some experts feel that Americans pursue this too much as a prerequisite to collecting, and that the piece should stand on its own merit, regardless of maker. This is high idealism and the collecting fraternity is not yet ready for it, so unless you have money to burn, do not get too involved with unmarked pewter.

Cleaning

If pewter is black and scaly with age, do not attempt to clean it yourself. This work should be done by those equipped for it. Good cleaning requires dipping or scouring with such materials as hydrochloric acid, and this can be dangerous work. It must be done under ideal conditions in a well-ventilated area. The acid must be neutralized at the proper moment—so that not too much metal is lost, and so that the touchmarks remain distinct. You will find that pieces such as the large chargers are oil impregnated, which makes cleaning quite difficult. It is best to steer away from pewter in this condition. Avoid pewter which has been highly polished, as most collectors want it to retain a soft patina. It has been argued that the metal was originally shiny and that restoring it in this manner should not hurt it. Maybe this is true, but you must recognize that others may not share this opinion, and that the majority of buyers want pewter to have an aged look, if possible. You may have difficulty in selling the shiny product, and therefore it is not a good investment.

Brass, Iron, and Tin

Historical Overview

Brass, bronze, copper, iron, and tin are metals which have always been used for functional and decorative objects. They are less exotic than gold or silver and do not command anywhere near the same prices. Prices for most items made of these metals have not increased in the same ratio as for many of the other decorative arts because it

Metal birdcage, Tunisia, 1986. Cages of this type have been made there since the last century. Bought in Tunisia for $6.

the eighteenth century are still being made. One that is only forty years old will have acquired quite a good patina. Also, there are some shops that will antique them for you with acid, which takes only a few moments. To call some pieces old and some reproductions is not quite correct. How aged must a piece be before it is considered old? And age is not the only factor in determining value.

BRASS

Brass is an alloy of copper and zinc. The proportions of each in the mixture determine the hardness of the metal. Brass has been known since ancient times, so there is a history of brass work with which to compare contemporary pieces. As mentioned, the values of brass items pale in comparison to the prices being paid for furniture, glass, pewter, silver, ceramics, and the like. A simple redware decorated dish can command up to a thousand dollars, but there are very few pieces of brass that can equal that, no matter how exotic they are.

is impossible to document them. Craftspeople have never stopped handmaking pieces with these metals and most did not mark them. Therefore, there is no way to determine provenance. For example, brass pushup candleholders which appeared in

Most of the eighteenth-century brass you find will have originated in England. There was very little American manufacture which can be documented, and we know that very little was made because of the shortage of materials. Some good Con-

Brass stirrup, Spanish, sixteenth century. Found in South America.

Brass whale oil lamps are rare. This with the Dolphin handle is especially nice. Made in Newburyport, Massachusetts, c. 1830s.

Enterprise coffee grinder, Philadelphia. These were used in grocery stores in the late nineteenth, early twentieth centuries.

tinental brass has arrived, and more is being imported today than ever before. The Mediterranean countries are a good source of brass, as a lot is being discarded by housewives there who are turning to teflon and stainless steel for cooking. They are tired of polishing brass, and they are quite happy to relinquish this role to the American housewife, who will in time realize that it can be a chore. Dealers tell me that more brass is sold to men than to women—men will take it home as a gift, but will rarely participate in cleaning it. The abundance of the product along with the shortage of help to take care of it is a contributing factor to the lack of interest in brass as a collectible. You must survey your needs and your desire to clean it before buying.

IRON

Iron was the metal most readily available to the American colonists, as huge bogs were discovered right in New England. Bog iron was found in the area around Plymouth and throughout what is

now called the greater Boston area. Saugus was the home of the first iron works (dating back to 1636) and the location has been fully restored to its original condition for all to visit. The original pounding hammer was found beneath many layers of earth and has been re-installed to pound iron today. Bog iron is found in marshes or even at the bottom of lakes and ponds. The Saugus marshes and locations in Braintree and Needham yielded much iron. The ponds in Gilmanton, New Hampshire, were rich in a pure ore. Salisbury, New York, was the site of early ironmaking, as were many locations in Pennsylvania. Ore was mined in those states, and right after the Revolution, coal was used to melt it. The Pennsylvania Historical and Museum Commission has restored some ironmaking locations including those at Hopewell Village, near Reading, and the Cornwall Furnace, near Hershey.

In the 1800s, machines came into their own and coal became readily available to all who wanted it. This resulted in a tremendous expansion of America's iron and steelmaking facilities. The center of the business shifted toward the Pittsburgh area as both iron and coal were available there in great quantity. Birmingham, Alabama became a center for steelmaking and supplied the South during the Civil War. I would need several volumes to discuss everything that was made in iron and steel since then—much of it right through the Art Deco period which is being collected today.

TIN

Until recently, tin languished in the role of an inexpensive commodity as far as collecting was concerned. Even the Historical Society of Early American Decoration, Inc., founded in the memory of Esther Stevens Brazer, gave little impetus to collecting tin for a long time. Decorating tin is now a great and rewarding pastime

Tin hand lanterns in designs that extend back to the eighteenth century. They are designed for candles.

and more attention is being given to this poor man's metal than ever before. Decorators are looking for interesting shapes and forms on which to paint their designs, causing an upsurge in prices. You can see the patterns and research material accumulated by Esther Brazer at the Bump Tavern in Cooperstown, New York, which is part of the Farmer's Museum complex.

Early American decoration may be divided into the following classifications: stencilling on tin and wood, country painting, gold leaf painting, lace edge painting, freehand bronze, glass panels, and Chippendale painting. The Esther Stevens Brazer Guild has established specific categories of craftsmanship for the execution of techniques found in each. Chapters of the aforementioned Society are set up in all the New England states (with the exception of Rhode Island), and in New York, New Jersey, Maryland, Illinois, and Pennsylvania.

Collecting Guidelines

BRASS

Brass bells are popular, though most do not command much money. A special bell-metal was formed with the introduction of tin to the mixture and most bells are made of this. Paul Revere is noted for his bells, and if you find one bearing his stamp of manufacture, you are indeed fortunate. However, ordinary school, dinner, and farm bells are relatively inexpensive. Sleigh bells of brass or bell metal are most in demand. Some are chrome plated, so you should use a magnet to check the metal if you are not sure.

Much ecclesiastical brass was turned out in the shape of candlesticks, candelabra, votive light stands, sanctuary lights, crosses, and even entire altars. Some is sold surrepititiously on the open market, but much is sold legitimately. A transfer to a new church structure will often attract donations of new church artifacts, and the old may be sold to benefit the treasury. How-

Bronze

Since bronze is a close cousin to brass, I might note that there is tremendous interest in the decorative arts which use this metal. Notable are the bronze figures, most of which were done in France and even Russia. The signed bronzes are most popular and valuable. Subject interest is paramount and those with animals in action are quite desirable. Those with a solitary figure standing are least desired.

The bronzes which depict motion of man or beast are among the best. You must be sure of the metal before investing, as many famous renditions have been reproduced in various other alloys such as spelter, which is a cheap metal with a high zinc content, or even white metal, which is about the cheapest iron-based substitute you can find. White metal contains iron, tin, albata, electrum, argentine, and other metals of lesser nature. A class of bronzes done during the Renaissance in Italy

Bronze, The Wrestlers, *unsigned.*

Pair of nineteenth-century French Empire bronze doré candelabra, 30" high.

ever, some pastors in Europe have recently been liquidating church brass to dealers in order to raise funds for operation. Over the years, many churches have received numerous donations of objects which have fallen into disuse or disrepair and rather than continue storing them, will clandestinely dispose of them. Since a great disturbance was raised over this procedure several years ago, most of it has come to a halt.

Brass candlesticks are quite common, including those dating back to the eighteenth century. There are some from as far back as the sixteenth century that have come to America in recent years. Most were made in England, though you will is quite desirable, but it is unlikely that you will find any here. Also, these bronzes have been reproduced over the years, making attribution very difficult. Little or no serious bronze work was done in this country. The bronzes to which the Tiffany name is attached were most often done in France or Russia.

Some of the bronze work being done today is commanding huge prices if done by recognized artists. Some of those done a hundred years ago in France may languish in value because of a lack of desirability. Some collectors are happier buying the work of known contemporary makers than investing in the older pieces which have no history.

Art Deco bronze, 1920s, unsigned. This is as classic a period as any for sculpture.

Venus in bronze by Lazlo Ispanky, 1975. This is number one in a limited edition of 100.

find Flemish design in some early pieces. The early ones may have a spike or pricket on which the candle could be imbedded for support. However, these went out of favor with the appearance of the socket modified by the pushup stem beneath, which allowed one to advance the candle upward to make full use of all of it and made for easier cleaning. The dripless candle was unknown in the early days, so all holders had a drip pan to catch the residue, which could then be recast into a new candle. The bases of candlesticks are no clue to their age—they will be found in square, round, oval, octagonal, and hexagonal shapes, and perhaps in many others as well. Some col-

Engraved bone-handle knife: "Garry Olsen's Boys; We are of the brave fighting Seventh," 1862.

lectors have stated that a good candlestick would have been made in two sections with a screw assembly to tighten them together. This work was often done in the seventeenth century, and the holders would certainly show their age to confirm this. You must be careful not to confuse these with holders from the Orient which were made in great abundance in this manner in the last century and into the present one. You should accept this screw base as a sign of recent rather than old manufacture 99% of the time. When whale oil became popular

about 1820, candleholders were pressed into service to hold oil lamps which featured a candle sized peg at their base so that they might be inserted into a candleholder. These are called "peg lamps" and may sometimes be found in brass, though glass was used most often.

Furniture knobs and other pulls were fashionable as early as the seventeenth century and were designed in keeping with the styles of the day. Brass was most popular for these, though some may be found made of other metals. It was not until the Chippendale period that large backplates became popular and these were made in what is called the wing style. The Federal period featured oval and often rectangular (with cut out corner) plates. Toward the end of the Federal period, pull knobs in brass or wood were fashionable and these continued into the Victorian period. You cannot fault a chest or other piece of furniture for having new brasses, so long as they are sand cast and have the look of the old, but you must be sure they are in the same period with the piece.

Brass was used for inlaying furniture, with spectacular results. This art reached its pinnacle in France and Italy. Andre

Copper

Copper also has a close kinship to brass. Being a soft metal, it is easily formed, has good color, and can withstand the heat of cooking and other abuse. About all that can be said for brass can be said for this metal. However, there are some exceptions. Horse ornaments, bells, door knockers, fireplace equipment, warming pans and candleholders are scarce in copper. It was used a great deal in the making of cooking utensils, which were then tinned on the interior so food would not come in contact with the copper. Brass must have seemed more like gold, hence its greater popularity. Actually, copper could have been used to make just about anything in metal. There were specific uses for it, especially in weathervanes, copper and shot pouches, canteens, daggers, knives and ale warmers. Less spectacularly, it was used as a sheathing for wooden vessels as early as the mid-eighteenth century. Along with brass and bronze, it was used as a base for cloisonné, champleve, and enameling.

Copper was not favored as it turns green with age and attrition, and therefore requires more care than brass or other metals. Food could not be cooked or stored in it, nor did it have the strength of other metals for use in heavy tools. It was used in coinage, and perhaps here one will find its greatest value.

Boulle (1642–1732) worked under the patronage of Louis XIV, and succeeded in turning out work which is the epitome of this form. There was a revival of this work in the early nineteenth century, but none is known to have been done in America. Ormolu mounts of brass were popular at this time, and were used as decoration at corners, feet, and handles. This style was most popular in France and Italy, but some work was also done in England.

Brass locks and keys are popular, no matter what country they come from. The door locks are used in restorations, and the padlocks are used as decorative items. Locks for furniture did not become popular until the middle of the eighteenth century. Some of these locks are stamped with the names of makers, which will heighten interest, if not the value.

You will find skillets, shoehorns, tobacco boxes, sundials, snuffers, spirit measures, spoons, trivets, and weights and measures in brass. You must judge these on their interesting qualities and condition. Repairs to brass are quite visible and must be done in good taste and not offensive. Warming pans sell reasonably, but are of interest. They are judged by their pleasing proportions, condition and above all by the beautiful or unique pierced design in the cover. Almost all warming pans found in America came from England, though some must be from other countries. There was little or no manufacture of these pans in America. Handles have often been replaced, so you must judge the condition of it at the time of buying.

Reproductions—The problem of reproduction is present, as there are workers today still turning out products which have an eighteenth and early nineteenth century look. Banging a piece up a bit, charring it over a fire, and allowing the iron handles and fittings to rust a little can create an aura of age that can fool the neophyte. You have only to visit a country like Holland to see the tremendous amount of this work going on. The once popular coal

hods with Delft handles are now a drag on the market: the sale of the new has hurt the old.

There are several good makers of weathervanes and lighting devices whose works age rapidly in the out-of-doors. Some are antiqued with chemicals to give them a good aged look, and once they have been used for several years it is difficult to separate them from the truly old, especially if the pieces were cast in sand molds. The roughness can fool you, so you must know from whom you are buying before investing much money.

There is a lot of trinket collecting in brass. Snuff boxes, military buttons, telescopes and binoculars, sextants and octants, ship's clocks, cuspidors, horse related items (hames, stirrups, brass handled buggy whips), early belt buckles, cigar cutters, stencils, and drinking mugs are popular. Powder and shot holders from the Revolutionary War have value. Whale oil lamps are rarest of all, as most were made of glass, tin, or pewter. Those with interesting shape and proportion are most desired. Look for signed fireplace equipment, as some makers were diligent in this.

Perhaps the most reproduced forms in brass are the chamber candleholders and candle chandeliers. The former are still being turned out all over the world, with many coming from the Orient. You must understand that 90% of the world's population is still lighted by candle or oil and that these chamber holders are very much a part of present-day culture. Chandeliers are being made for historical societies and others who are restoring old homes to their original elegance. The early ones were mostly from England, so the reproductions have the same look and are quite well done. You would have to examine them closely to tell the difference. Candelabra were popular, though few early ones are found today. You will do just as well by locating contemporary reproductions as they are faithfully done and in good taste. I might note that at the Peterhof Palace of Elizabeth, Empress of Russia, near St. Petersburg, a hundred people were employed each evening just to light the candles, replace them, and put them out at dawn.

Door knockers in brass are quite popular. They are reproduced in great quantities today and as they age it becomes difficult to tell when they were made. Present-day sand casting leaves rough marks and impressions similar to those found on the old. Knockers gained popularity in England in the eighteenth century and were brought to America to become part of the popular culture. The eagle, lion, horse, and dog were popular motifs. Rams, flowers, dolphins and even clenched fists were also included.

IRON

Since iron was readily available, it was used for just about everything where a strong metal was needed. Kitchen pots, pans, and utensils; carpentry and husbandry tools, weapons, horse equipment, lighting devices, door locks, hardware of all kinds, and nails and spikes were all products of pre-1800 manufacture. These items are collectible from the eighteenth century on.

Iron lighting devices have soared in value recently. Both floor and table models of old rush holders and candleholders are of importance. There is one glaring problem, however, and that is in determining the age of iron artifacts. I have seen excellent reproductions aged in a hurry via salt and manure piles—a year or two of this unorthodox treatment can fill iron with pits, rust, and lines which can fool experienced eyes. When someone tells me a piece of iron is old and that he knows this merely by examination, I am quite suspect about his qualifications as an appraiser. I feel that too much money is being paid for "eighteenth century" iron, as I knew a blacksmith (now deceased) who could duplicate it in a year. Hang on to your money before investing great sums in old iron. You may be joining the ever growing club of losers. Buy only that iron which has documentation if you are spending a great sum.

Lynn Poirier, former director of the Mercer Museum in Doylestown, Pennsylvania has researched old lighting devices in the huge collection there. It is her opinion, after examining old records, inventories, accounts of blacksmith shops, etc., that no rush lighting devices were made in America. She has found no evidence that they were a native product, rather that they must have come from overseas. One must be careful in the use of the term "Early American lighting devices."

Likewise, iron kettles, tin trays, bun baskets, coffeepots, tea caddies, etc., are still coming from foundries, cast in the same forms which have been used for centuries and decorated in the manner of the old. Antique weathervanes, some andirons and other fireplace equipment, bedwarmers, apple butter kettles, whale oil lamps, buckets, and similar items will often rise in value if they provenance is documented.

One must be careful when buying old

Iron rush holder, eighteenth century. These are being reproduced today.

iron objects, such as rush candle holders, betty lamps, cruzies, Hessian andirons, L&H hinges, kettle cranes, etc. as they are still being made today.

TIN

Tin is an important base for decoration as many country items were made from it. There were many noted early decorators such as the Butlers in upstate New York and Zachariah Stevens at what is now Westbrook, Maine. Their work, along with that of many unrecorded others, has enabled students to classify the decorations as originating in specific regions. Tin items with existing old decoration have climbed quite high in value. Those pieces which are not decorated but are just old items used about the kitchen and home are climbing in value as artists compete with each other for unusual pieces to decorate. This is a very rewarding area of collecting. You can take classes in decorating techniques, ei-

Decorated tin document boxes, nineteenth century. Found in Maine.

ther painting or stencilling, and make yourself a good income by buying, decorating, and selling old tin items.

The late Peter Ompir from Sheffield, Massachusetts and Mona Rowell of Pepperell, Massachusetts have already created a legion of fans who have bought and are buying everything decorated by these two artisans. Tin is very prominent in their work.

Areas of Collecting Interest

Bottle Tickets

Bottle tickets were beverage labels used in eighteenth and nineteenth century England and America before modern packaging techniques. They ranged in design from early rectangles, shields and crescents to elaborate nineteenth-century labels bearing foxes, grapes, leaves and cupids. They were made primarily of silver but one can find them in ivory, mother of pearl, and Battersea and Staffordshire enamels. They can appear as boar tusks mounted to represent hunting bugles and some are even set on tiger claws.

The names on the labels provide an intriguing look at the drinking habits of our affluent ancestors. Whiskey, port, brandy and sherry were the most popular but occasionally one will find such exotic names as Vidonia, Sillery, Pommery and Vin de Grave which are drinks unknown to us today.

The earliest tickets seem to be those which came into use in the middle of the seventeenth century with the introduction of glass bottles. By 1784, an act of parliament in London officially named the labels, "Bottle Tickets" and decreed that they

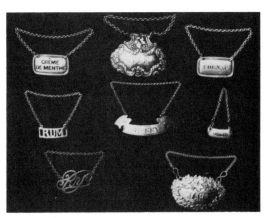

Bottle tickets made of sterling (most were made in England).

must bear the name of the maker. After the invention of die casting in 1794, the feathered borders and simple designs of the handmade examples developed into more elaborate decoration. By 1810, silversmiths were adding cupids, leaves, grapes, lions, shells, monograms and crests to their work. In the 1830s, cut out initials and names became common in design and tickets were often attached to the bottle with a silver ring instead of a chain. By 1860, the introduction of clear bottles and the sale of individual bottles rather than casks or barrels for home consumption prompted the use of paper labels. The names of American silversmiths have not been found on bottle tickets collected in this country which date before 1850. Tiffany and Gorham made them late in the last century and into this one.

Brass Beds

Most collectors are not aware that brass beds are really not made entirely of brass. The metal is an alloy of copper and zinc and is quite soft. Bedposts and rails made of it would not support the weight to which they are exposed, so one will find that the framing members are either brass-plated steel or steel posts sheathed in a brass casing. Solid brass will be found where there is ornamental decoration and filigree and often in the ball finials found atop the bedposts. Structurally, however, the base metal is steel for strength and support.

If you wish to check your bed, locate a magnet and apply it to the metal. The magnet will be attracted to steel, but not to the solid brass. One should not feel he is cheated—all brass beds are made this way.

Know the rules in brass beds—the fancier the better; the more filigree and decoration, the more desirable. Condition is important, so if the posts are worn and tarnished, most often they need replating, which is expensive. Those kept in best condition through the years were lacquered when it was fashionable to do so. This saved on frequency of polishing and pro-tected the metal from pollution and deterioration.

It was not long ago that brass beds were not in favor. In the 1950s most were thrown in the dump. A building in New Hampshire has the headboards, footboards and springs of sixty brass beds in the cement floor to reinforce it. One must note that they are being reproduced and are plentiful in furniture stores. This is bound to eventually depreciate the value of the old ones as the current beds acquire some age.

Fireplace Ovens

The fireplace oven is a product of the early eighteenth century. The English perfected the mass production of sheet tin which was the most inexpensive metal at the time and all kinds of kitchen and household items were made from it. Tinmakers who came to this country carried on the trade and the fireplace oven became almost a necessity. Until that time, baking was done in a brick oven built to one side of the fireplace. A separate fire was built in it and then the coals and ashes were raked out. Baking was done in the heated interior.

The tin fireplace oven did away with this as it could be set quickly before the fire and the reflecting interior would make the heat surround the item in it. These were

Tin fireplace oven with rear door used to check on the food cooking.

Brass four-poster bed with tester. Late nineteenth century, France.

later refined to hold a revolving spit so various meats could be barbecued with all sides of the meat receiving the heat because of the reflection of the tin.

One will find original ovens made right up to the middle of the nineteenth century. The first iron stove with an oven, as we know them today, was made by the James Stove Company in Troy, New York, patented on April 26, 1815. It was called the Baltimore Cook Stove and was the most popular in use for about twenty-five years. Expensive at the time, it found its way only into the homes of the affluent. It was not until after the Civil War that mass production brought the price down. Hence, the continued use of the tin reflector oven until then.

If you buy such an oven, be sure it is not rusted out. Those with holes have little value. They are being reproduced today, so perhaps you might be content with a new one rather than an old one in poor condition. They will age rapidly in front of a hot fire after a few years of use.

Iron Banks

The nineteenth century brought with it a changing technology, and after the Civil War the inventive genius of America was turned loose. This was a period when factories turned from war production to making goods for consumers, so all sorts of gadgets and tools made their appearance. Many are quite interesting and form the basis for numerous collections today. Notable in this respect are the iron banks, both mechanical and still, which have risen very high in value. Some have reached the five figure price range, which far exceeds anything made of metals other than silver, pewter, or gold. You must learn what is most desirable for you. Those banks which are mechanical and scarce are hot items. All have been cataloged and collectors are always on the lookout for some with which to round out their collections. You should stay abreast of the activity at auctions and shows to inform yourself of values, since they change continually. Early in the

Uncle Sam mechanical bank, c. 1895. Shepard Hardware, Buffalo, New York.

1930s, the *Book of Knowledge* brought out a series of reproductions of mechanical banks and so labeled them on the bottoms. Though not original, they have assumed a good collecting value today. Reproductions are made in Japan at this time, some being quite good and some easily told from the old, the paint jobs being the first clue as to age. It is difficult to duplicate old worn paint. You should never repaint an old bank of any kind, as this will detract from the value. Rust may be cleaned off old banks, but they should not be repainted.

Still banks (those which perform no function other than to accept money in a slot) have assumed importance, since they were made in interesting shapes and some have approached the rare status. Many people are collecting new banks in iron and as these are often made as special items in limited editions for banking institutions and others—they will have their own importance and increased value in time.

Many iron banks are being made by the John Wright Company of Pennsylvania, and are being done in exact reproduction of earlier banks. As long as a present-day bank is of iron, it can have some value in the future, but you should steer away from plastics, pottery, or other materials. Some of the old tin banks are quite important, and in recent years there have been several new versions which have been made and which have already acquired a good value. Condition is important in judging all banks.

Lithographed Tin

Until the 1870s, all printing had to be done in black and white. If coloring was needed, it would be added later by hand. New machinery was invented at that time to print in color in what is termed chromolithography (some use the shortened term "chromo" to designate a printed colored picture). It was not long before it was discovered that this printing could be done on all sorts of materials, so the creation of the colorful commercial containers, called "advertiques" today, became a reality.

In 1909, 15,822 establishments were engaged in the manufacture of tobacco products in the United States and if only a fraction of them used tin containers, this would be enough for a specialized collector today. Some companies used many types of tins for different products (biscuits, tea, coffee, lozenges, powder) which adds to the total. There are good books on collecting lithographed tin and one will learn that it is best to concentrate on a category

Lithographed tin powder can dated July 1924.

or two and build a better group of items relating to a particular product.

Original condition is important. Age, color and condition of color must be judged. Do not attempt to repaint or retouch the pieces. Old pieces will be found dull and dingy; clean them with a mild detergent in water, then use a furniture spray wax to polish and preserve them as well as bring out the old colors. Rust on a piece harms value, so lightly steel wool the rust, then protect with the spray wax. Interesting shapes should be sought. One tobacco can was made to resemble a milk can, others looked like purses, and many looked like people, such as the roly-poly tobacco tins. A relatively small investment can yield a large return.

Glossary

Bell Metal—A mixture of tin, copper and zinc used to make bells.
Brass—A mixture of copper and zinc.
Britannia (Metal)—Soft metal made of tin, copper, antimony and other alloys.

Bronze—A mixture of brass, tin and other alloys.

Champlevé—Enameling in hollowed-out surfaces.

Church Plate—An English term for church silver.

Coin—875 parts silver, 125 parts alloy.

Copper—Malleable reddish/brown metal with a specific gravity of 8.96.

Cruizie—A hanging lamp which most often burns fat.

Enamel—A protective or decorative coating baked on metal, glass or ceramics.

Gold—A malleable metal found in yellow, white and various tints with a specific gravity of 19.32.

Iron—A strong ductile metal with a specific gravity of 7.874.

Pewter—A mixture of 90% tin and 10% antimony. Some formulas include lead or other alloys.

Porringer—A shallow bowl with a handle.

Quadruple Plate—A metal which is dipped and plated with silver four times.

Rush Holder—An iron stand which holds waxed pieces of rush, burned for light.

Sheffield—The name of a city in Yorkshire County, England, famous for cutlery since the eighteenth century, where Sheffield plate (the bonding of two thin sheets of silver to a body less expensive metal) originated.

Silver—A malleable white metal with a specific gravity of 10.50.

Spangle—Sparking metal or plastic discs, often sewn on garments.

Spelter—A metal made mostly of zinc. Used in inexpensive statuary, etc.

Steel—An alloy of iron and carbon. Additional alloys are added according to specific use and formulas.

Sterling—925 parts of silver and 75 parts of alloy. This mixture may vary slightly in different countries.

Tin—A metal obtained from cassiterite. Used for plating and as an alloy.

Zinc—A mixture of brass and copper, plus alloys. Used for rustproofing other metals.

CHAPTER FIVE

Decorative Art

Folk Art

Introduction

It has only been in the last years that there has been any great appreciation of what we term "folk art." Folk art encompasses what can be considered the work of relatively untrained hands—items created by people who saw a need for a product and simply made it, or perhaps even invented a tool or kitchen aid to do a particular job in the days when one could not go to the local discount store and buy one. Some items are functional and some are decorative, but collectors today look at them in light of the latter, as most have aged and acquired a patina that endears them to the aesthete. Folk art items were made in all materials, but mostly materials that were easily available around a farm or average home. Though some bear the style of pieces made by city craftsmen for the carriage trade, most do not incorporate the quality which is turned out in the hands of those trained and skilled in their endeavor.

Some people refer to folk art items as "primitives," which is not necessarily an accurate description. Eric de Jonge, the former director of curators at the William Penn Museum in Harrisburg, Pennsylvania, has described this type of work variously as naive art and uninhibited art. There is a marked distinction between the work done by untrained hands and the work done by an uncivilized people. The term "primitive" could be more accurately applied to the workmanship done at the earliest stages of civilization when man first gathered crude tools and materials with which to work. This term should represent the beginnings of any art movement and the work done during this period. "Folk art" is a better definition of work done by a civilized people who were simply untrained in the particular field of creation or decoration in which they engaged. There are many natural artists who have a flair for quality—in form, proportion, workmanship, and beauty—and are able to express it with little or no training. These self-taught artists need not necessarily be lumped together with those whose early civilizations gave them little preparation or incentive to do this work. The term "primitive" is used loosely to indicate some early work done in this country and though it is not totally objectionable, neither is it totally accurate.

Calligraphy

FRAKTUR

The Pennsylvania German Fraktur is an excellent exercise in calligraphy and early examples are quite important and valuable today. Fraktur is a piece of very decorative calligraphy done in a traditional

Folk painting on a breadboard, done by Dorothy Davis of Cape Cod, Massachusetts. Though done in the 1970s, such examples of contemporary art have great interest and can only increase in value.

Pennsylvania German style. Practically every family had a member who was responsible for making up the certificates that documented important events, such as birth and death. Most were done in colorful fashion with floral or other decoration adding a touch of beauty. In other sections of America artists worked in this fashion as well, but the Frakturs are more plentiful than other genres and might be easier to find.

After the mechanical printing presses took over (about 1830–1840) hand work waned, and the printed certificate took its place—gone was this native bit of talent which is so highly prized now. Good collections can be seen in Pennsylvania at the Ephrata Cloister, the Farm Museum at Landis Valley near Lancaster, and the William Penn Memorial Museum in Harrisburg.

Carving

AMERICAN

There is no area in America in which such work was not done, so you have the entire country in which to collect. The greatest concentration of items has been found in the New England and Pennsylvania area, as both were quite prolific in industry, and both had substantial populations. The traditions of the British Isles are quite evident in the New England work, and those of the Germans, Dutch, and Swiss in Pennsylvania. The influence of the Dutch and later the French is felt in work from New York State.

Wood—This is a material which has always been plentiful, is easily worked, and can be carved or decorated in many ways. Many kitchen items such as dishes, bowls, butter molds, tableware, rolling pins, funnels, boxes and baskets, dough boxes, pails and buckets, sugar tubs, dippers, spatulas, washboards, and dish strainers were turned out in abundance.

For the farm chores, the man of the house turned his talents to the production of milk pails, churns, stools, watering troughs, fruit baskets, apple driers, herb driers, winnowing sieves, eel traps, bean flailers, kegs for rum and cider, water kegs, feed pails for horses, etc. The well-equipped home also needed a large (spinning) and small (flax) wheel on which to turn out the needed fibers for clothing. The more fortunate lady had a full-sized loom to make cloth, but others were content with lap looms. Some carvers turned out swizzle sticks, which were used to stir a mixture of ale and beer. Along the coast, you will find decoys carved to assist in the hunt. Wooden weathervane figures are common wherever metal was at a premium. Small boxes of all kinds are quite popular; those with carving or painted decoration are most desirable, as they reflect the industry of the man with his knife or other carving tools, and of the lady, who carefully added the flowers, leaves, and pictorial decoration to the effort with her brush and quill.

Some of the greatest work in carving was done for sailing vessels. Huge figureheads fastened to the prow were a must on every ship. Many of these were rather ex-

Carved wooden butter molds. Beauty of design and depth in cutting are important.

otic ladies or important historical figures of the times. Since it is our national symbol, eagle carving was practiced just about everywhere, and those who did this work are well recorded. Charles Bellamy, a native of Kittery, Maine, maintained studios both there and in nearby Portsmouth, New Hampshire. His doorway eagles are much desired today, although his work ranged all the way to the huge twelve-foot bird he carved for a vessel made at the Portsmouth Navy Yard. The ship is long gone, but the eagle survives at the marine museum in Newport News, Virginia. Bellmay's work is well recorded and the greatest collection of it is probably at the Shelburne Museum in Shelburne, Vermont.

Another noted carver was Wilhelm Schimmel, whose rather primitive eagles are in great demand in his native Pennsylvania as well as elsewhere. Schimmel was what is described as an "itinerant" artist, who often did his work in return for meals and lodging. His eagles feature a rare kind of bold cutting; you will know one almost instantly once you have seen some others with which to compare your example.

In recent years, a large amount of wood carving that falls into the folk art category has been imported, especially from Europe and Africa. These items are finding favor here, as their American counterparts have risen greatly in price, and in some cases can rarely be located for sale.

Collecting Tip

Carved wooden work must be in good condition. Age takes its toll, and those pieces which have not survived well may have little or no value. Old wood that has been repainted has been hurt as far as collectors are concerned. It is better to leave the faded decoration than to try to renew it. Evidence of new saw or chisel marks should make a buyer suspicious. Above all, the piece must be interesting and reflect an attempt for quality on the part of the maker. Signed pieces, which are infrequent, can have greater value if you can document the maker and the time and place where he worked. Assembling information about one maker can enhance the value of all his work, so long as it is of good quality.

Unique carving by A. Elmer Crowell of East Harwich, Massachusetts, who is best known for his decoys and shore birds. This is a carving of a woodcock.

Gatepost eagle, carved wood, nineteenth century. These were common along the eastern seaboard states in the eighteenth and nineteenth centuries.

Whirligigs were made in Europe long before the Pilgrims made them. The degree of imagination expressed in their function helps value, along with condition and good paint color.

Carved eagle by John Bellamy, 1836–1914, master ship's carver, born in Kittery, Maine. He worked at Portsmouth Navy Yard as well as for the public. Shelburne Museum, Inc., Shelburne, Vermont; staff photographer, Einars J. Mengis.

Carved wooden eagle by Wilhelm Schimmel, Pennsylvania, nineteenth century. His work is very distinctive in form and depth of cutting.

Bone/Ivory/Stone—Another form of carving is done on bone or ivory. If the work is done on materials that come from sea creatures, it is called *scrimshaw*—if the materials are from land animals, it is usually referred to as engraving or *sgraffito* work.

Powder horns, knife handles, and sword scabbards and handles were extensively decorated in this manner. Using a pointed tool, the workman incised the lines in the decoration he wanted, then rubbed ink, powder, or other colorings into the crevices, making them stand out in relief against the white substance of the bone or ivory. Actually, bone and ivory work seems to predate the work done on marine materials, as horn carving was popular during the eighteenth century. Items of Revolutionary War vintage are especially good and work on war-related items continued well through the Civil War. Many soldiers filled their idle time by making gifts for

Carved wooden figure made to stand in front of a chandler's shop during the nineteenth century. These are rare as they were carved mainly for businesses in the coastal towns.

were not necessarily made aboard ship. Most of the work we collect is from the first three-quarters of the nineteenth century (after the American merchant marine enlarged to take care of our world trade) and is made from teeth from sperm whales, whalebone only or lower jaw of the sperm whale, baleen (the tough straining fiber masses in the mouth of the sperm whale), woods available on ships from all over the world, as well as mother-of-pearl, abalone shell, and coconut shell. Whales' teeth might be found as long as $10\frac{1}{2}''$, hollow, and about two inches wide at the base, tapering to a point.

Scrimshawed whale's tooth, nineteenth century. Sailing vessels were a popular design, along with the U.S. flag.

family and friends, as well as by decorating their own possessions.

The term "scrimshaw" is believed to have originated from the Dutch word *Scrimshander*, which is a reference to a lazy fellow. In reality, the men who did this work were quite talented. It is believed that they actually competed with each other to turn out the best works of art. Such objects

Carousel Figures

One of our prime examples of American folk art is fast disappearing as we witness the sale of circus carousels. Some carved figures have sold for six-digit prices. As each carousel is dismantled and sold piece by piece, the prices just seem to go up, the demand far exceeding the supply. The names of Stein and Goldstein, Gustav and William Dentzel, Herschell-Spillman, Philadelphia Toboggan Company, and others are well known to collectors.

Animals and birds, some real and some mythical, have been the inspiration for many figures. The different forms are most interesting—for example, flying, standing, and jumping horses, kangaroos, deer, goats, griffins, sheep, lions, roosters, and many more.

Some variations of the animals are quite desirable. The most elaborately carved animals were featured on the outer ring, where they were seen more easily, and the lesser animals positioned on the inner rings. Some warlike figures feature armor. Generally, every carousel features an animal with a shield or other device with the maker's name carved on it.

The figures were carved of wood, most often in sections which were glued together for strength. Early carousels were operated by steam; some that ended up in Tahiti were fueled by coconut shells in the absence of wood or coal. The steam calliope, most often played by an employee, came into being to provide music. This gave way to the electric models, with an automatic calliope.

Signature carousel figures are not common—only one to a carousel, if that. Stein and Goldstein became partners in 1907. Stein died in 1937 and Goldstein in 1945.

Baleen

Baleen is a very hard substance found at the rear of the mouth of a whale. It forms a strainer that filters out unwanted items as the huge mammal moves through the ocean. Some refer to baleen as "bone hairs," though it does not resemble human hair. Rather, much of it is flat and can be up to several inches in width. Naturally, baleen is rare, and one must screen much of it to get enough strands of uniform size to make baskets, ship models, etc. Baskets with fine weave are most valuable, and items of this type are being made today and are valued at almost the price of the old, as the material is scarce. Once the killing of whales is stopped all over the world, no baleen will be available at all. Baleen was used by sailors around the world as a material to work on while at sea. One item which is a rarity is the sailor's valentine made of shells, coral, baleen, bone, and other items from the sea. These are a form of statuary most often kept under glass as they are great dust catchers.

The artisans began by scraping the teeth or bone with a knife or sandpaper, then scratch carving it with a steel needle. A whaling ship held up to thirty men, and quite often remained at sea for two years. One can only guess at the amount of scrimshaw that returned with them.

When ships are portrayed, you should notice how the flag is flying, as it should be in the direction of the wind, and the men on board should also be portrayed in some activity. If a picture is done, it should have a frame around it. (English scrimshaw can be judged by the length of the teeth—they are often up to ten and one-half inches long—and by the English flag. Also, the English carved more strongly than the Americans.) Scenes from *Godey's Ladies' Book* were often reproduced.

If possible, you should collect teeth in pairs, and they should point in opposite directions, being matched from opposite sides of the jaw. Some teeth feature pictures in frames in daguerreotype fashion, others may be inlaid or painted. Patriotic teeth and those that commemorate the death of famous people such as Presidents, with angels, tombstones, and the like, are

A type of engraving called sgraffito appears on this stoneware jug with brown glaze, signed by W. B. Quick, Warners, New York. It reads "Syrup & Jug 49¢." He sold a gallon of syrup, along with the jug, at that price. Warners is now part of Syracuse.

important. One tooth pictures a barber giving a haircut to William Henry Harrison—the other side reveals that it was cut too short and that the President caught cold and died. Other collectible teeth are those with harbor scenes of ships or even the sailor's home in the background. Memorial or mourning teeth might feature a lady leaning on a tombstone with space left for the name of the sailor and when he died. Others feature women and children weeping. Teeth carved in relief such as one found showing a man kissing a girl's foot are important. You may also find architectural scenes of buildings done from prints. Very rare and valuable is the "Susan's Tooth," which features a picture of the ship *Susan* and was done by a man who lived on Nantucket Island around 1820–1830. Only about a dozen have been found. You might look for the signed work of William Parry of New Bedford, who was active in the 1930s and whose work is perhaps the best among his contemporaries.

Many items were made from bone or ivory and then decorated, such as small carved boxes, sewing baskets and implements, jagging wheels, crimpers, bodkins, sewing needles, candleholders, swifts, dolls and beds, rolling pins, chess figures, chessboards, napkin rings, canes, shoehorns, doorknobs, magazine racks, dippers, water kegs, billy clubs, bird cages, and even rope bed tighteners.

Since there is an embargo on killing whales, it is only natural that even the reproductions of this work being done today will eventually rise in value. Research I did in 1975 revealed more than a thousand people still doing scrimshaw in Maine, New Hampshire, Massachusetts, and Rhode Island. Old whale teeth turn up by the basketful at marine auctions, and these are still being used. Most new work, however, lacks the dexterity in penmanship as well as the determination, follow-through, and bold strokes that characterize the old.

The Endangered Species Act of 1973 placed limitations on carrying teeth, tusk, and bone matter from marine animals

Ivory vs. Ivorine

One must be alert when collecting carved ivory. It is organic and therefore perishable if exposed to abnormal conditions. Check the size of any ivory object. The largest piece can be no wider than an elephant or rhinoceros tusk—six or eight inches at the widest point. I have seen plant stands with tops over a foot in diameter which people have bought as ivory. This is rather wide for a tusk.

Decoration is done by scratch carving teeth or bones from any sea animal or teeth, tusks, and bones of land animals. Unfortunately, companies are selling kits of vinyl teeth for carving at home, and, once decorated, can fool unsuspecting people.

Another problem lies in the use of ivorine. After ivory is carved, the shavings and other bits and pieces can be melted down with a chemical—this mass can then be molded into familiar forms. When sold, the pieces are identified as real ivory and rightly so, but the item has not been hand-carved. How does one tell ivory from ivorine? Anything that is cut or carved has sharp edges. It is impossible to mold a sharp line in ivory, glass, or any other substance. The melted

ivory should be called "ivorine," its proper name.

Also, bone carvings are limited by the size of the animal. Each bone has a marrow center that must be discarded, leaving a thinner shell, which is used. Bone and ivory will color a little with age, the former more than the latter.

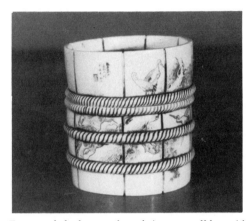

Engraved elephant tusk made into a small box with cover. It is designed to hold small carved ivory erotic figures. Signed by the carver, the decorator, and by the poet whose work is inscribed, as well.

across state borders. You might check with people from whom you buy about these restrictions.

The work of the Alaskan Eskimos, even contemporary work, is assuming new importance. Eskimo carvers are skilled with ivory, bone, and stone, creating vibrant human and animal forms which radiate a strong sense of life. It is believed that the Eskimos originally carved for religious reasons or for tribal chiefs, who gave gifts to other leaders. The carvers attempted to portray their immediate lifestyle and that of people about them, often working with a soft stone, which is abundant in the Arctic. They created works around the shapes of the chunks as they

were broken from the ground. The forms of nature inspired much of their work.

The changes in Eskimo lifestyle are noticeable in the work they do today. Although there are many regions of the Canadian and Alaskan Arctic where life is similar to what it has been for centuries, in other areas civilization has brought with it a different approach to artistic endeavors. There are the purists who say the twentieth-century Eskimo carver has gone commercial, changing from ethnological inspiration to the inspiration of the dollar. The Eskimos have even created cooperatives to market their work through a central agency, which does smack of commercialism, but you must remember that life near

Two Inuit reed baskets made in the Sitka region.

Eskimo work is also referred to as "Inuit," which means "the people." If you wish to collect Inuit artifacts, go to Lapland, Iceland, Greenland, Alaska, or Canada. Other than that, make the acquaintance of someone in the military who is to be stationed at the Dew Line or some other remote hardship post. Give him your shopping list and the amounts you wish to pay. Contemporary work is very collectible at its present prices. There are galleries in America that carry carvings and other work, but those with the widest variety, according to our travels, are in Canada. The Canadians have assembled the best collections of Eskimo art, from both their country and Alaska, and have sent exhibitions of it throughout the United States and Europe.

the North Pole is difficult and dollars hard to come by. If we are to condemn them for commercialism, we might as well condemn Toulouse-Lautrec, Wilhelm Schimmel, or John James Audubon, whose work often went for groceries and spirits to replenish their souls.

Plaque, wood, painted, by Taisia Voronetskaya, St. Petersburg. Ministry of Culture.

If you like carvings and know people going to Russia, ask them to obtain some of the artistic soft stone and bone carvings from the Ural Mountain area. The first record of stone work is from the eighteenth century, when deposits were discovered on the mountain banks of the Irgina and Sylva rivers. The stone is found in many colors and is excellent for artistic carving. Peasants of the Perm region began to make Easter eggs, picture frames, flower-petal-shaped ashtrays, and even platters of white gypsum and selenite. They imitated the forms of porcelain articles and wood carvings. When the decorative arts declined in Russia in the late nineteenth and early twentieth centuries, this work all but halted. There was a revival in this art form in the 1930s, however, and today the Russian government encourages this carving as it brings in hard currency from other nations and is a highly desired Russian export. The animals carved in the soft stone are beautifully done and on a par with the best you can find anywhere.

Bone carving in Russia has a more ancient history, as it dates back to the tenth century. Bone carvers of the Moscow Palata were quite famous in the seventeenth century. In the eighteenth and nineteenth centuries, the Kholmogory craftsmen in Archangel province began turning out intricate pieces, such as bone caskets and little cases and boxes, and doing much fretwork and adornment with carvings of men, flowers, and animals. The pieces were often colored to heighten their beauty. In the second half of the nineteenth century, craftsmen from Tobolsk turned out miniature sculptures done on mammoth bone, drawing on animals and birds for their inspiration. Some of these were brought to this country by immigrants, and some are being shipped here today by dealers who are picking them up all over Europe and Asia. These little-known collectibles are sleepers in American collecting today.

Weathervanes

Early weathervanes are often classified in the folk art category. The weathervane was the farmer's trusted friend in predicting the weather. A south wind in the summer meant fair; if the wind shifted to the east, it brought rain. West winds meant fair all year around. If the wind blew cold from the north when a storm cleared, it meant the storm had backed up and would come again. A northeast wind brought a storm that usually lasted three days, and a southeast wind brought one of lesser duration.

Not many wooden weathervanes have survived, but those in tin, copper, and brass show the ingenuity of their makers. You may find the figure of a horse, man, fish, driver and sulky, locomotive, feather, building, bird, deer, other animal, or just about anything that could have excited the maker's imagination.

Perhaps the most popular and common figure is that of a running horse. Legend has it that a pacer named Smuggler raced in the 1870s. In 1874, he was entered in a trotting race and had to wear toe weights to correct his stride. He won the then-big $10,000 purse. He was immortalized as a weathervane figure by Harris and

Copper weathervane, nineteenth century.

Important American weathervane figure, molded and gilded copper and zinc horse and rider. J. Howard and Co., West Bridgewater, Massachusetts, c. 1860. From the Barenholtz collection. Sold at auction by Sotheby's in New York for $770,000, January 27, 1990. Photo © 1990, Sotheby's, Inc.

Company in Boston between 1874 and 1881. Another model was made by W. A. Snow Company in Boston between 1883 and 1940.

If I were to calculate the rarest of the vanes, I would list these—sulky and driver, fire engine, locomotive, centaur, and oddities such as the minister in a long coat riding a high wheel bicycle. Geese are rare, roosters are common. Plows were popular, along with horses, dogs, sheep, and cows. Some vanes were even gilded for fancy homes.

It would be difficult to grade the designs as to quality, since the figure alone is not sufficient for judgment. The size, condition, and material from which the weathervane is made are important, as well as its age. Those which were used for target practice by hunters and contain bullet holes are not as desirable as those in pristine condition. Some are dimensional, with filled-out bodies rather than just

Copper weathervane of the "Smuggler" type, which was made by several concerns late in the nineteenth and early into the twentieth century.

sheets of material, and these are more desirable. One of the most impressive of these is a huge ram, which once graced the Amoskeag Mills in Manchester, New Hampshire, and is now displayed at the Currier Gallery of Art in that city.

When old weathervanes are taken down, they are often injured since the iron rod on which most are mounted is cut. The rod usually comes down through the ceiling of the cupola and is imbedded in the floor to give the weathervane strength and stability. Rather than disturb the roof, removers will often cut the rod just above it, and this does not help in its resale.

Fine reproductions are being made today and these are quite acceptable for use on an old building. The price of the old weathervanes has risen so much that perhaps a new one is a much wiser investment at this time. After all, most people cannot tell old from new when they have the item in their hands—if it is perched on your roof, forty or fifty feet away, perhaps they will never know.

Paintings

Introduction

Let us trace briefly the history of oil paintings and their care today. Western painting was influenced by the Greeks and Romans, who used tempera, a simple recipe containing either a whole egg or just the yolk mixed with gelatin made from parchment skin. The first mention of oil colors appears in thirteenth-century German manuscripts, but these were not very good, as a proper solvent had not been developed. Alchemy soon brought forth turpentine, and varnish was created from resin boiled in linseed, poppy, or walnut oil. Painting was done on wood or parchment, and gold leaf often applied by a jeweler. Early painting was featured on horse ornaments and carriages. Portrait painting soon became quite popular, followed by landscapes.

Conservators and scholars can tell much about a painting by thorough examination. Photographs, x-ray, infrared and ultraviolet lights are employed to check layers of painting, signatures, ground color, and canvas to determine age and authenticity. Experts can discover repairs, addition of new paint, loss of old paint, and even sketches beneath the paint from which the artist worked. Total examination involves measurements, as no picture is supposed to be reproduced in the exact measurements of the original and most of these are well catalogued. The expert can judge the age of the canvas, frame, ground layer, and picture layer of paint, along with the surface coating used for protection. He can tell old oil since it becomes translucent with age. You must be familiar with an artist in order to compare a picture with his known works. You should be versed in the language and literature of the country of origin, as a great deal is related by the time span and subject matter of a painting.

Paintings deteriorate slowly; they are usually brittle and fragile. It is best not to touch a damaged area with your fingers, apply a self-adhesive tape to a tear, or try to protect the surface with a blanket or wrinkled papers, which can exert pressure on the painting surface. Dust is detrimental to canvas, and the reverse of a painting should be protected with a stiff board or paper which is *not* in contact with the surface itself. Paintings suffer from extremes of dryness and humidity; a uniform 45% relative humidity is best. Paintings should not be hung in sunlight or over radiators or fireplaces.

Above all, do not attempt to clean paintings at home. Old remedies such as rubbing bread or a sliced onion over the surface to clean them are taboo. Do not use a detergent or any soap in attempting to clean a canvas. Special solutions are employed by conservators, and these range in varying strengths and solubilities. Each solution must be tested on the painting before use to make sure it will not lift the original paint with the dirt. The canvas is cleaned bit by bit with a small cotton swab in order to make sure there is no change in pigment strength or vulnerability to the solution being used. This is an art practiced by professionals, so leave the cleaning to them. At home, an occasional light dusting or gentle wiping with clear water on a damp rag is permissible once a painting has been restored properly and a protective varnish coating applied.

You must also realize that the professional has the proper materials if any repairs to tears in the canvas are required. The paint formulas used by the original artist have been catalogued so that the expert can match them exactly for touch-ups and restorations. This is important if the work is to be done properly. If the painting is worth saving, have a professional save it for you.

American Oils

In the eighteenth and nineteenth centuries many itinerant artists worked decorating walls and furniture as well as painting portraits of members of a family. It has been said that some artists prepared bodies on canvas during the winter months and during the good weather traveled to homes, painting heads for the bodies. Eric de Jonge, chief curator at the William Penn Museum, questions this notion, saying that no unfinished body pictures have ever turned up to confirm this tale. He feels that no woman, especially, would want to be painted in any finery other than her own.

In family portraits, it was not uncommon for a new baby to be added to an old picture as the artist made his rounds from year to year. Many old portraits such as these are unsigned, but there is new interest in them. Their value is measured by the ability of the artist, the interest he conveys, and the condition of the work. Years ago

Trade sign painted by Gibeon E. Bradbury, Salmon Falls, Maine, 1833–1904. Bradbury was typical of many who painted wagons, landscapes, and portraits to trade for produce and other commodities. He painted on mattress ticking, linoleum, and even tar paper, as he was a man of little wealth.

many such pictures were thrown away and the frames adapted for other use. This practice has driven the price up on the remaining pictures. Of special interest are groups of people engaged in some activity, such as a battle, party, band concert, or some other facet of life, whether peaceful or brutal. Some pictures are painted on materials as common as a mattress cover, but do not worry about this as it may enhance the value.

WHITE MOUNTAIN AND HUDSON RIVER SCHOOLS

The eighteenth century produced little or no American landscape work. The settlers were surrounded by the beauty of the outdoors, and did not need to capture it to bring into their homes. Without photography, portrait painting flourished as a means of preserving the images of family

Primitive or flat painting, which has no dimension. Typical of the work done by the traveling limner, who worked for bed and board.

Oil on canvas, The Travelers's Return *by Alvin Fisher, American. Fisher was one of the earliest of the landscape painters in America. He went to the White Mountains in New Hampshire as early as 1830 with Thomas Cole to paint, and later went to the Hudson River region. This era was the beginning of the Barbizon style of painting in this country.*

and friends. Early in the nineteenth century, as America's cities grew and the great outdoors became more remote, landscape work flourished. The industrial age brought with it teeming cities, tenements, and pollution from smokestacks. Even the factory worker attempted to bring some of the outdoors into his home via a painting or even a print. Thomas Cole, Alvin Fisher, and other artists went to the top of Mount Washington to paint as early as 1825—beginning what is now referred to as the White Mountain School of painters. Their New Hampshire landscapes created a great impression, and soon artists were seeking out other places of beauty to capture on canvas. The Hudson River area gave birth to a school of painters who did fine landscape work, and it was not long before many painters headed west to capture the mountains and scenery there. These were schools of realism in that the artist attempted to portray a scene faithfully with no attempt to alter it. This is a photo-technique that has gradually been challenged by succeeding generations. Such artists worked well into this century, and are well documented in the books listed in the bibliography. A good rule is that if an artist does not appear in the books, he has not arrived as far as collecting is concerned. These two schools of painters are highly

Hudson River landscape, c. 1830s, painted in Barbizon style. The men and animals on the bank, fishing boats and sailboats, and smoke coming from the town at right all contribute to interest and value.

desired today, and prices are rising on their work every year. You would do well to invest in works by known American artists of this period who are recorded, as they represent perhaps the finest investment in antiques today.

MODERN ART

Unfortunately, there has been, in my opinion, little painting of great renown done since the Depression, which spawned a group of artists who lived mostly in major cities, some existing on funds from the WPA. This program granted them survival and freedom to work, but much of what they turned out was revolutionary with a Bolshevik tint. Communism was being preached everywhere as the solution to America's economic problems, and art naturally reflected this. Some Depression art is being collected today and touted as great art, but in my opinion, you should be very careful before you invest in it.

The period that followed World War II brought with it perhaps the greatest era of mediocrity in the history of art. We have been subjected to rather amateur work in most of the arts: painting, sculpting, ceramics, and even music. There are those who have found a formula for becoming rich by thrusting upon the public the most devious and garish work in an attempt to be so different that they stand apart from everything else. These practitioners have succeeded in luring supporters to their work, whether it is good, bad, or indifferent. The most tragic consequence has been that museums and galleries are lending their space to exhibit this work regardless of quality. Some analyze this as the "Art Institute syndrome," in that the museums do not want to be left behind again as they were in the exhibition of Impressionism, and therefore will exhibit just about anything today. It is a situation which will reverse itself in time, since new young artists are coming along who will have nothing to do with such mediocrity. A new school of realism is already at work throughout the

Marine Paintings

Marine paintings are what the name implies—scenes of ships at sail, in a harbor, or docked. America had many fine marine artists from the eighteenth century all the way into the twentieth. Works by accomplished artists will have value, as is the case with most art. Condition is important and the scene portrayed has a bearing on the value. The better artists are listed in the books cited in the bibliography and those of the earlier period usually command better prices. Scenes of ships should include men in action on board, and the introduction of whales, sea gulls, or other marine life is important. Flags, preferably American, should fly. Size is quite important, since most collectors like large marine paintings because of their panoramic quality.

Many English and French marine paintings turn up in this country which are quite well done. Again, those by famous artists are of importance in America. The next most important school of marine painters flourished in Chinese ports during the last century. Artists often painted the sailing vessels that dropped anchor and sold the finished products to the captains. Some of these were probably exported to America as part of the active America-China trade. The background of an Oriental city with an American ship in the foreground makes for quite an interesting painting and you are well rewarded in collecting them.

country and the small exhibitions at crafts festivals and fairs reflect this.

On examination, you must concede that to achieve the workmanship necessary to the Realist, Barbizon, and Impressionist schools, one must be an accomplished painter, since these are the most challenging and difficult styles to do well. Those who indulge in the action school (which is nothing more than what appears to be paint thrown at a canvas) and those who paint in geometric forms are just exhibiting to us their inability to really do anything with a brush and canvas. Those who attempt to interpret a mess of gobbledygook as projecting a message are being rather demagogic in relation to good art. Creating good art makes demands on the ability, time, and patience of the artist. Those works that can be splashed out in five or ten minutes in kindergarten fashion certainly do not meet this test. All the explaining in the world cannot compensate for this, any more than all the talking in the world can improve the quality of a piece of furniture ground out by machine in Grand Rapids, Michigan, in the 1920s. When you invest in modern art, you must judge the work on its quality—good taste, good design, and

good workmanship. The minute you stray away from this, you are gambling. Those who gambled on Picasso years ago have made out quite well, but he is an exception—how well can you pick the exceptions today?

At a talk with college students, the noted cartoonist Al Capp was asked, "I look at a Picasso painting and I think it is garbage. How can I learn to appreciate art?" Capp replied, "You understand it well, it is garbage." Which prompted a further question, "Who determines that a Picasso painting is worth five hundred thousand dollars?" Capp's answer was, "The dealer who just paid one hundred thousand for it." The price of art is relative to those who appreciate it and also depends on who owns it. In the hands of a well-known person, some oils are valuable, but if you own them, you may have long trying days to dispose of them at any price.

European Styles and Influences

Investment in European paintings by unknown artists is hazardous, as years ago (as well as today) paintings were turned out almost on a mass-production basis. If the artists are not regarded highly enough to receive acclaim in their native countries, they do not represent a good investment. Many travelers buy such oils on trips, hoping they have uncovered an artist who someday may be famous. You should buy these unknown Europeans for enjoyment alone, and invest in the American paintings for enjoyment as well as future reward.

BARBIZON SCHOOL

When landscapes came into fashion early in the nineteenth century, a group of artists began painting scenes in places such as the Black Forest near Dusseldorf in Germany. The French picked this up in their forests at Fontainebleau, and both efforts resulted in what is termed the Barbizon School of painting. It is characterized by dark foregrounds which frame the lighted middle ground, which is the central theme of the picture, then a luminescent or silhouetted background, which creates a three-dimensional effect. This school

served as an inspiration to many American painters who came to Europe to study. Corot, Daubigny, Millet, and Rousseau are among those who painted during this period.

IMPRESSIONISM

Impressionism followed the Barbizon School and was pioneered by Monet, Renoir, Cezanne, and others. These artists created their atmospheric impressions of nature by breaking up the lines of light and substance to give a rather dreamy quality to their work. Impressionism was not readily accepted either in Europe or in America, and it was not until the Art Institute of Chicago hung some Impressionist works in the 1890s that any measure of appreciation was shown. At the time, the Institute was the target of many critics who felt the work was quite inferior, and today it still tries to protect its reputation for being first in the exhibition of new works in order to live up to its late nineteenth-century success. Im-

Indian Encampment on the Platte River, Colorado, *1868, by Worthington Whittredge, American, 1820–1910. Sold for $280,000, September 23, 1981, by William Doyle Galleries, Inc., New York City.*

pressionism is quite popular today, with the work of some artists selling in the millions.

CUBISM

Picasso revolted against Impressionism with a form generally referred to as cubism. This is a technique of breaking down and taking apart forms of nature. It has a geometric quality which reshapes known forms to the ideas of the artists and is not bound by any rules of conformity to accepted forms. There have been few successful practitioners of cubism, with Picasso remaining as the leader and the best known. Though other styles have succeeded it, some work in cubism is still being done.

SURREALISM AND THE ASHCAN SCHOOL

The twenties brought the Ashcan School, which was nothing more than a realistic portrayal of life in the city. The street or alley scene usually contained the inevitable waste receptacle, which gave this school its name. Much of this is good art and the supply is quite limited. Though it was not appreciated very much at the time, values on this school have risen a great deal today.

A new idea was also brewing, at the same time: surrealism, or super reality. Its goal is to liberate man's unconscious personality from the chains of reason and inhibition; its best known exponent is Salvador Dali. Surrealism could well be called a partner to abstractionism, and uses shapes, forms, and colors that have no counterparts in nature. Though this school has its investors and afficionados, it has not yet taken the country by storm, and only time will tell if it can repeat the successes of early styles which had to wait years before being appreciated.

EXPRESSIONISM

There has been one constant in all the painting styles which were instituted thousands of years ago, and that is the work of the expressionists. Expressionism is a revelation of the artist's personal emotions which may be traced throughout his or her lifetime. This style, more than any other, conveys feelings on a canvas through the use of brush and paint. In 1975, the Tate Gallery in London staged a retrospective of the works of John Constable. Moving from picture to picture, one could see the changing emotions of the artist. He painted three canvases of his father's farm in Dedham, each with a different perspective. The gallery indicated that the best version is at the Currier Gallery of Art in Manchester, New Hampshire.

El Greco, who made his fame and fortune in Spain, was very religious. All of his figures, whether human, animal, or imaginary are elongated toward heaven in search of the Divinity. El Greco's work is easily identified because of this personal expression.

Van Gogh's work clearly reflects his tormented passion as he painted before, during, and after his period of madness. When you see a complete showing of his work, such as the one staged in the 1960s at the Guggenheim Museum in New York, you can trace his emotions quite easily as you view successive canvases.

Prints

Engraving

The first plates from which prints were made were wood engravings, which produce what are now called wood-block prints. This work had been done in Europe for many years, but the first recorded American artist in this medium was John Foster of Boston, who did a likeness of the Reverend Richard Mather.

Where the artist wants a white space, he carves out the wood, leaving the remaining surface to receive the ink. Printing is done by rolling the paper over the inked

View of Hellgate from Great Barn Island, *Hudson River. Steel engraved as a book print.*

block. This crude work, an early form of the art of reproducing likenesses, has great appeal. Many newspapers and periodicals relied on woodcuts for printing pictures right into the nineteenth century.

Line engravings were made in eighteenth-century America by cutting or incising a design or picture on a soft copper plate with a sharp tool. Paul Revere made many of these, including his famous "Boston Massacre." This type of cutting is known as "intaglio" work. In "relief" work, the engraving is left raised above the plate. Intaglio and relief work are done by putting ink into the cut lines, wiping the plate clean, and then rolling damp paper against the surface on a press and forcing it into the lines, where it picks up the ink. The work was later done on steel plates, as copper was quite soft and could not make as many impressions as the harder metal. This technique was developed about 1820, so steel engravings may all be dated after that time.

Stipple engraving is done by impressing a design in dots rather than lines. An artist coats a plate with wax, and then stipples through it to the metal beneath. An acid which does not penetrate the wax is then spread over the plate, eating out holes in the metal at the points where the stippling was done. After the wax has been removed, the design is printed from the acid etched plate.

Mezzotints were first made in the early part of the seventeenth century. A copper plate is roughened by crisscrossing it with

lines, using a sharp tool. This roughness is smoothed out and shaded in areas to create the picture in reverse. After being inked, these plates are used for printing and several colors can be employed at one time. Shading to give better dimension to the work is possible with this technique. The English and French did excellent eighteenth-century mezzotint work, which is very collectible today.

Etching is done in much the same manner as line engravings in relief, in that acid is used to score unprotected areas on the plate's surface. It was refined so that an artist might repeat the acid baths in certain areas to effect shading. In dry-point etching, no acid is used, and a pointed tool is employed to do the entire job, requiring the hand of a master.

Aquatint was developed at the end of the eighteenth century. It is a refined form of etching in which masses are printed more easily. A finely powdered resin is spread over the plate and solidified by heat. After the design is traced through it, acid is applied and reapplied to create the design and shading.

Lithography

Lithography is a process in which a greasy crayon is used to trace a design on a

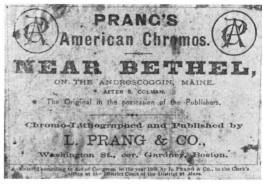

Louis Prang of Boston was known as the father of the American greeting card. He worked late in the nineteenth century. This label appears at the back of chromolithographed prints he made of paintings that were purchased by known artists. Samuel Colman worked between Portland and Boston.

The Horse Shoe Falls, Niagara—With the Tower *is a fine early print, engraved by R. Brandard from the mid-nineteenth-century painting by W. H. Bartlett. Since it shows a tower that is no longer there, this print illustrates the interest in prints and paintings that preserve scenes long since gone.*

very porous stone. The stone is then soaked in water, and it absorbs the moisture in its clear areas. Ink is rolled on the surface and it clings to the crayon areas and is repelled by the wet stone. A sheet of paper is rolled on the stone, picking up the design from the remaining ink. Most colored lithographs were painted by artists after printing. There is a revival in this form of work today and some fine artists are quickly being recognized for their work.

This work by contemporary artists is not to be confused with the reprints of old work being turned out on sophisticated presses today. The offset method of print-

ing has made faithful reproduction of old work possible, and you must be careful to examine prints to determine their age and authenticity. Also, beware of the practice of turning out prints by contemporary artists, numbering them in a short series, and then selling the complete series in different areas of the country. Buyers have been deluded into thinking they are getting limited edition originals. Most are dressed up in expensive frames which enhance their appearance. Although the prints cost only a few cents to make, their frame dressings and a gullible public have resulted in quite a profitable business for the fakers.

Areas of Collecting Interest

Frederic Remington

Painters of the old West are very much in demand these days. One name that

stands above most is Frederic Remington. Born in Canton, New York, in 1861, he migrated to the West, where he proceeded to capture the American scene in paintings,

Watercolor on paper, The Couriers, *American, Frederic Remington, 1885. Sold for $88,000 by Butterfield & Butterfield, Los Angeles and San Francisco. Photo courtesy of Butterfield & Butterfield.*

sketches, and bronzes. In 1990, one of his paintings sold for almost $4.5 million.

Most people cannot afford the luxury of such a painting, but there is one area of Remington collecting that is still open to most. Early in his career, he worked for

Harper's Weekly, creating woodblocks of western scenes. This is the only place such work appears, as the originals and woodblocks have literally disappeared. Several museums as diverse as the Remington Art Memorial in Ogdensburg, New York, and the Bowdoin College Museum of Art in Brunswick, Maine, display collections from time to time. You can find an example in the book *Frederic Remington: Artist of the Old West,* by Harold McCracken (Lippincott). Though this book is no longer in print, perhaps your local library has a copy. These prints in *Harper's Weekly* date as early as 1886. Some are signed, some not. In 1890, 119 of his works appeared in the publication.

During this period in the latter 1880s, several Remington watercolors appeared in exhibitions in New York City, guaranteeing him a future as an artist. Some of the early *Harper's* prints sell in the three figures, so they are worth collecting. Often

The Battle of Bunker Hill, *John Trumbull, 1756–1843. Trumbull is famous for his huge canvases of Revolutionary War action. Courtesy Wadsworth Antheneum, Hartford, Connecticut. Purchased by Daniel Wadsworth and members of the Atheneum Committee. Photo by E. Irving Blomstrann.*

boxfuls of the papers are sold at auction. Any from 1886 on are worth inspecting and possibly buying.

Historical Paintings

Paintings that depict the history of our country are much in demand. Many artists traveled from coast to coast to record the scene as they saw it in the nineteenth century. Along with photographers, they have made it possible for us to see our country as it was. Some of these paintings were repro-duced as prints so that they might be made available to even those with meager means.

It is only recently that illustrative artists have come into their own. General opinion was that they painted quickly, only for money. Of course, they were commissioned to do their work under publishing deadlines. Many turned out fine work.

At the time of our centennial in the 1870s, many paintings with patriotic themes appeared and were quite popular. They still are today. They represent perhaps some of the best investment in art, as the big galleries have all but ignored the

The New Century Begins, *Joseph Boggs Beale, 1841–1926, American. Wash drawing. From the collection of the American National Insurance Company, Galveston, Texas.*

Washington Greeting Lafayette at Valley Forge, *oil on canvas, R. Atkinson Fox, Philadelphia, c. 1870s. Fox was an illustrator/artist noted for the many prints of his work which are available today.*

illustrative artists, so prices have not yet risen too high.

Original paintings or sketches by book illustrators appear at auction from time to time. If you can locate a copy of the book for which the work was done, you have a very interesting combination.

Collect historical paintings, etchings, and prints. They are much better than those with nebulous themes.

Japanese Woodblock Prints

A wide range of Japanese woodblock prints appear on the market and in auctions. They depict scenery of that country as well as portraits of the people in it. The most fascinating I have seen are those that portray Japan's modern wars, late in the last century and early into this one.

All in color, many in triptych, they portray battles on land and sea and present a view of the development of Japan as an industrial and militant nation. This art documents events in a manner that photography could never capture. Many of the artists are better known for their prints of life in the Meiji Period, 1868–1912. They excelled in their use of color. The stark

Rare triptych showing a view of Kanazawa at night, by Hiroshige, nineteenth century, Japan. During the 1920s, many folios of Japanese prints were sold in this country and abroad. One must examine them to determine vintage.

Japanese woodblock tryptych, Great Naval Battle and Great Victory Near Haiyang Island at Sunset, *from the collection of Jean S. and Frederic A. Sharf. Photo courtesy of Worcester Art Museum.*

coldness of winter battle and experiences are expressed with dramatic detail.

The golden age of Japanese woodblock printing generally is judged to be the eighteenth and early nineteenth centuries. The artist-designer, publisher, wood engraver, and printer together created masterful prints using the sophisticated techniques of embossing, color gradation, and overprinting. Probably few Japanese artists actually went to the battlefronts. Rather, their information came from photos or published accounts. They must have appealed to the pride of the Japanese as more than 100,000 impressions were made of some prints. Throughout history, the Japanese have enjoyed anything that conveys the bravery and loyalty of the military class (samurai).

Nantucket Baskets

The island of Nantucket is full of history and folklore. It is also the source of a very popular collectible—the Nantucket basket. The design for it was basically copied from that of the Native Americans who lived there for centuries. The baskets are also called Nantucket Lightship baskets, as many were made on the South Shoal Nantucket Lightship between 1854 and 1890. They are unique in that they show the influence of the coopers, with bottoms, staves (vertical splints), and hoops (tops) in the manner of the whale oil barrels. Most were made by men aboard ship during lax hours, or around an iron stove ashore during the bad winter weather.

Nantucket baskets vary in size from quite small to about a peck capacity. In early baskets, two boards might make up the bottom; later ones had a single board with grooved channels to receive the splint. Staves were mostly of ash, oak, or hickory. Often, they were split of cordwood brought from the mainland. The weaving strands are cane or rattan. Most handles are eared so they can swing; very few are rigid. Some may be brass-eared. Nails are mostly copper, but later baskets have brass or iron nails. The baskets are characterized by their extremely tight weave, strength, and durability. Tops of Nantucket handbags most often feature a carved ivory or bone, or exotic wood panel, attached or embedded for decoration. A

Collection of Nantucket Lightship baskets. The old examples command a lot of money, but the new are expensive as well.

An Eskimo (Inuit) carving from Povungnituk on the eastern shore of Hudson Bay, Canada. Executed in gray stone, bone, and skin by Joe Talirunili in 1964. Canadian Eskimo Arts Council.

nest of eight baskets in different sizes today sells in the four figures.

There are contemporary makers whose output is spoken for many months in advance; in fact, some of the new sells for more than the old. Be aware, however, that they are being imitated, and quite well, by artisans in China who are sending them to us via Hong Kong. Look for labels or get other certification that yours is a real Nantucket basket. Unless you know how to tell them apart, you may be purchasing an import.

Native American and Eskimo Artifacts

Native American artifacts have soared in value, although most are not really very old. In fact, newer pieces are commanding more attention, especially those made in this century, because they are in better condition.

New England is not a good place in which to collect, as few items have survived. Most Native Americans had left the area by the time of the Revolutionary War, so New Englanders must content themselves with

broken sherds of pottery, glass, arrowheads, and some metal items found in burial grounds years ago. None of the cloth, baskets, or decorated bone and ivory have survived in this area. Pennsylvanians have been able to come up with some later objects, but it is in the Far West that most collecting can be done. When Native Americans migrated from the East to es-

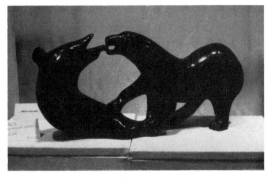

Carving of a bear attacking a whale, by B. Osowetok, Cape Dorset Masterworks Exhibitor, 1980. Carved from black serpentine. Inuit Gallery, Vancouver, British Columbia.

cape the oncoming settlers, they took everything with them, often even the bones of their ancestors, which were dug up, bagged, and reburied at their new homesite.

The Hershey Museum in Hershey, Pennsylvania, features a large collection of Native American artifacts. The Mount Kearsage Indian Museum in Warner, New Hampshire, also has exceptional artifacts, which its owners have collected over a period of many years.

Poster Art

Posters are known to have been made during the time of the early Egyptians and Romans. About 1840, posters gained popularity in France when they were used to advertise books. The female figure was added about 1880, and a whole new area of advertising was born. The advent of color lithography made it possible to reproduce huge paintings in billboard size, often in sections. Circuses, theaters, and businesses

Poster of Santa promoting Schumacher's grains of gold.

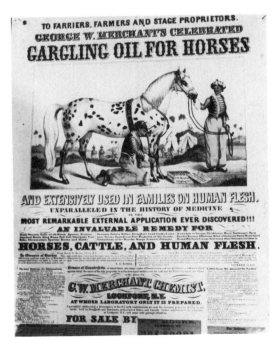

Poster advertising gargling oil for horses. Hangs in the shed at the Calvin Coolidge Homestead in Plymouth, Vermont.

of all kinds seized on this method of attracting a crowd to their offerings and products. Noted artists whose work is sought today, such as R. Atkinson Fox, Maxfield Parrish, and Henry Herrick, were among those who centered their work for commercial purposes and illustrated everything from newspapers and books to large posters and billboards. By 1895, poster art was well accepted; its popularity continues undiminished to this day.

Collectors are centering their activity on the older work which pictures the nostalgic years behind us. Some collect in categories, such as circuses, movie stars, theaters, etc. Others acquire what they can just for decoration. The most desired posters seem to be those from France, particularly those by noted artists such as Manet and Toulouse-Lautrec.

The rules for collecting are quite simple. Subject matter is important—it must be of interest. Condition must be good. Many posters are water-stained from being framed with glass against them or foxed (discolored) from being backed with wooden boards (the pitch from the old boards will stain them). Rips and tears are a no-no. Color must be bold. Known artists are most collectible.

Theorem Painting

Most old homes out in the country contain at least one painting on velvet, a product of the first half of the nineteenth century. Most are still lifes of fruit or flowers. Historians tell us the artists traced a stencil on the cloth, then painting the design with watercolors directly on the cloth. Some feel this was a type of seminary art, learned by young girls along with household duties such as spinning and weaving. Yet there is evidence that many such paintings were done by housewives as an extra-curricular activity. None that I have seen has ever been attributed to a male artist, nor has any been attributed to a known painter.

Velvet is quite fragile, so many theorems have not aged well. Putting them into frames with glass against them and wooden pine boards behind has contributed to the

Theorem painting, done on velvet, was popular early in the last century. Condition is most important to value.

attrition of many. Changing temperature in a home creates condensation on the underside of the glass, staining the cloth and removing the color.

The value of theorems is based on their condition as well as the ability of the artist. Most of good quality are selling into the four figures, so are worth seeking at country auctions. Most are not signed, so this is really not a factor in desirability. Louise Karr wrote an excellent article on theorem paintings in the September 1931 issue of the magazine *Antiques*. Many museums and libraries keep back issues for reference.

CHAPTER SIX

Textiles

Wall Hangings

Samplers

A sampler is a wall decoration created by embroidering handwoven cloth. Most samplers were done on linen until the middle of the nineteenth century, when the less expensive cotton took over. Samplers tested a young girl's ability to sew an alphabet and figures and to create an interesting and pleasing design. Those of the eighteenth century are the most desired, because of their age and primitive quality. They were not originally made to be framed, but in the early part of the nineteenth century it became fashionable to hang them as interesting works of art. They were more appreciated by the descendants of those who made them. In the second quarter of the nineteenth century, less attention was paid to the letters and figures and more to scenic decoration, such as farm buildings, trees, flowers, and animals. These pictorial samplers are judged not only on quality of work, but also on design. These were the work of the younger girls, with the older girls turning their attention to embroidered pictures.

The nineteenth century saw the arrival of "Berlin Work," named after a light wool used to make clothing and gloves. Designs were woven to a base cloth in artistic fashion, and a three-dimensional effect could be achieved because the thread could be raised at the whim of the artist. Most designs were made on canvas, but some were done on the combed or worsted wools of the day. Patterns were copied from publications such as *Godey's Ladies Book* and some were copied from the paisleys done in Scotland at the time.

Stevengraphs

Another product of the Victorian era is the Stevengraph, a silk picture framed as a wall hanging. The Jacquard loom was invented in France in 1810 and made weaving pictures into any fabric possible. Soon manufacturers everywhere were using it. The loom was computer-operated in that pierced cards were used to direct the pattern being woven. French silk was permitted free entry to England at the time of the Cobden Treaty in 1860 and this harmed the economy of the English mills. Coventry was a center of this work and the enterprising Thomas Stevens of Coventry created bookmarks that caught the public fancy. He later turned to the production of pictures in silk. Even those made by the other firms that followed are given the generic name Stevengraph. The first of these was made about 1879 and was introduced at an exhibition in York. Even postcards were made with woven silk panels and these are collectors' items. Condition is most important in determining value today; many are water-stained and/or faded. Some were unmounted, but those with aged frames are best.

Tapestries

Let me touch briefly on tapestries. It is not likely that you will be able to locate and purchase a tapestry wall hanging made before the seventeenth century. Tapestry weaving was a going art in the Netherlands then. Many artists were at work designing tapestries, while many others were engaged in making them. Even artists like Peter Paul Rubens were employed since most work was being done for the wealthy and for royalty. Tapestry work in wool and silk was later taken over by the Jacquard loom. At the end of the seventeenth century, a new type of tapestry called *Tenieres* was created featuring rustic scenes full of people and animals. These are highly colored and quite lifelike. Commemorative scenes were in vogue later on, and even war events were immortalized in this manner. There is limited demand in America for even the large, important hangings, since most end up in museums or in a few wealthy homes. The lesser tapestries which were ground out on looms by the thousands in the last century have little or no value and should not be acquired as an investment. The handmade items are of more interest and value if you can find them. Since there is no easy rule to follow in determining the manner of work, you must seek competent advice before investing much money, or else study the field yourself in order to make your own appraisal.

Rugs

Early American

Early rugs are one of the most expressive forms of American folk art. When you consider that practically every young lady was taught to spin, weave, and sew, you would think there should be an abundance of floor coverings as millions must have been made since the Pilgrims landed. However, collectors do not find it easy to locate outstanding examples since, as with most art, few fit this description. While thousands of artisans plied every trade, only a few set themselves apart as true artists whose work is of great quality. Though many girls were proficient with tools such as looms, wheels, and winders, not all could be classified as true artists in their work— they made necessities for the home, perhaps with little or no talent for good design and decoration.

Hooked rugs made of wool on a foundation of homespun linen between 1775 and 1840 are direct and original in design. Folk rugs were given an added brilliance with the introduction of turkey red dye in 1829. Chenille, the rarest product of hand manufacture, is made by threading a half-inch strip of cloth lengthwise, gathering and rolling it to appear like a furry caterpillar, and then stitching it on to a closely woven fabric.

Naturalistic floral medallions with scroll borders and corner spandrels appear frequently in rugs made in the latter part of the nineteenth century. These were first popularized by Edward Sands Frost of Biddeford, Maine, a tin peddler, whose stenciled burlap designs tolled the knell of the bold original patterns of the earlier period. While peddling tinware, Frost had noted many housewives at work at their rug frames, and vowed he could create better designs than the housewives had available. He traced and cut out tin stencils using his shears, reproduced them on burlap,

Well-designed Navajo rug, c. 1920.

linoleums. Braided rugs are in keeping with early homes, as are oriental rugs.

Oriental

Oriental rugs represent a complete study in themselves, as they are judged by pattern and workmanship. They were popular in wealthy homes, and many were carried here in the China-American trade. Rugs from the Near East gradually assumed greater importance to buyers in America, and the rugs from old Persia, now Iran, are among the best to collect. Rug weaving by hand is tiresome work and a large rug will often consume up to five years in the making, with several people working at it. It is said that the art of making them may die out since young people are not eager to take on such a chore. I wonder at the abundance of these rugs coming into America at this time, which are often sold in major cities at auction in order to dispose of them. Can it be possible that some machinery has been smuggled into the hills to help out in production? If this is a dying art, how can so many be offered at auction brand new?

The People's Republic of China is responsible for some exceedingly fine rugs that are finding their way out to the open market via Hong Kong. The workmanship is superb, and prices for these rugs are on a par with the best from Iran and in some cases exceed them. There has been a continual output of "oriental" rugs from Belgium; during the 1950s thousands must have been sold here at low prices. Dealers purchased the 9 × 12 size at three for $100 and pitched them out at auctions for $50 apiece. Although beautiful in design and color, they are quite thin and wrinkle easily on the floor. Those from the Orient and Middle East are much heavier and of better quality.

and began peddling these along with his other products. His designs soon caught on and he created a full line, many of which are reproduced for visitors at Greenfield Village at the Henry Ford Museum in Dearborn, Michigan. Frost's pattern Number Two features the initials of a bride and groom worked into the border, about four feet apart. On the facing border is a place for the minister to stand, and all step into position for the wedding vows.

Large rugs were used as bed coverings at first, since they were considered too fine to suffer abuse on the floor. Their quality of warmth and the greater availability of materials soon resulted in their common use as floor coverings. Until that time, it had been popular to paint floors in colorful designs. Later on, canvas might be painted to spread as a covering, and this may have been the forerunner of the gaily printed

Quilts

Quilts are common, as most old homes have a trunk or two full of them. The quality of each piece must be judged on the

originality of the design, quality of work, color, and condition. If it is documented with the year and possibly the name of the

The Jacquard loom was invented about 1810 in France. Coverlets made in this country with such a loom exhibit great expression in the designs and colors used. Some designs, such as the Hemfield Railroad shown here, are well identified.

maker or owner woven into it, a quilt will assume much more importance. Pennsylvania, Ohio, and New York take top marks for the production of quilts in the nineteenth century, as the designs are colorful, reflecting the German-Dutch heritage of many of their settlers. New England can be credited with much fine work, but there was less attention given to dating and naming these.

Construction Techniques

A quilt is made up of three parts—the top, which carries a main design, the filler, and the back. In the old days, cotton and wool were favorite fillers, but many synthetics are used today. Quilts were not always fancy looking; many of the earliest were called *white-on-white*, the design being impressed as the upper cover was stitched to the backing. When the stitches are spaced apart to form ridges that outline a design, it is called *trapunto* work. A *pieced quilt* is made by stitching different pieces, often of different colors and patterns, together to form a design. *Appliqué quilts* are made by sewing different pieces to the top cover, forming the design in this manner. *Crazy quilts* were made in the Victorian era and were so called because they consisted of such random pieces as parade ribbons, flags of all countries, advertising flags, and even neckties. These are judged in the

Appliquéd and embroidered "Hudson River Quilt", made c. 1969–1972. Sold for $23,100, January 27, 1990 at Sotheby's. © 1990 Sotheby's, Inc.

Coverlet, c. 1920s, made of felt sections which came as premiums with tobacco purchases early in this century. Sewn together, they are colorful and very different.

same manner as the earlier ones, and should be preserved as interesting bits of Americana.

It is thought that the *patchwork quilt* was a creation of the New World, where cloth was at a premium. The economy of the times is reflected in the quilts; clothing and other cloth items eventually appeared as patches in quilts. In the eighteenth and nineteenth centuries, young girls were expected to have at least thirteen quilt tops—twelve for everyday and one special top to show their most elegant work before becoming engaged. When betrothed, a young woman would invite friends to a quilting bee, and after setting up the bridal top on a frame, all would join in quilting it.

Quilt designs have names, and patterns for quilts were circulated for all to use. Most were made from scrap material and old discarded clothing. Cooperative quilts were made by members of churches or organizations. Each member contributed a square of work, often signed, and these were later sewn together to make the finished product. Some quilts relate the history of a group or an event. For example, the English regimental quilt at the Shelburne Museum in Shelburne, Vermont, depicts scenes from the many countries in which this regiment served, along with views of its permanent station in the British Isles. Others were made with materials from France, which might be separate squares with pictures of U.S. Presidents or other famous people printed in the fabric. Some were made from cloth with designs already worked in it on Jacquard looms. Exotic fabrics such as silk and embroidered cottons found their way here from India and were used to good advantage.

Designs were printed in many of the women's magazines of the day, but most quilts were the result of the material available and the individual taste of the maker. Some designs are geometric, others floral, and some even approach pure abstract art.

Collectible Coverlets

A coverlet is a woven bed cover made on a loom. Our earliest collectible coverlet is called a linsey-woolsey. Those eighteenth-century examples that have survived are treasured today. There is still a question as to whether they are all wool, or part linen, as the name implies. Late research suggests they are named for the town of Linsey in England where they were reportedly first made. Identified by their wool-like quality, linsey-woolsies are really two layers of homespun stitched together, often in design. Each layer is a different color, with a lighter side for summer and a darker for winter. The cloth was dyed with readily available materials, such as onion skins, beets, bark, and ochres. They are subject to damage by moths, so most reveal a hole or two, but some were protected in cedar chests over the years and have found their way to some historic home or restoration. In later years, coverlets were decorated with embroidery, and some are works of art. The Shelburne Museum features a sample quilt on which the maker worked the alphabet and numerals in several different fashions, along with floral motifs and other decorations. A person ordering a coverlet from this maker would be able to choose a design and a type of lettering and numbering. Such sample quilts are rare.

Making a quilt is rather like painting with cloth, and it is in this light that each is judged today.

One of the most desired pieces is a Baltimore quilt, so named because of the city in which they were made. These were made by girls facing marriage, and most are really great works of art. Some have sold well into the four figures because of their superb quality and beauty. It would seem that the young ladies vied to outdo their friends and that such competition resulted in greatness.

It is felt by some historians that, during the middle of the last century, the quilters in Baltimore raised this work to the level of an art form. Tradition tells us that most young ladies were expected to make at least thirteen quilts before becoming really proficient in creating one of this category. These final efforts are among the best ever made in this country and are sought by collectors. Perhaps one of the best examples one might see is at Claverton Manor in Bath, England, the site of the American Museum in Britain.

Today quilt makers are still at work, working in traditional as well as contemporary designs. Whether their work will be revered as much as those of the last century must be left to the judgment of time. The outstanding place to see and buy contemporary quilts is the annual Mennonite auction held in Harrisburg, Pennsylvania. The women of this religious group spend the year making up to 300 quilts, which are sold to raise money for relief purposes throughout the world. The quality is very good, and because of this, the auction attracts about ten thousand people, which must make it the largest in the world.

Areas of Collecting Interest

Clothing

In the past two centuries, there have been three basic skirt forms: the hoop, the bustle, and the sheath. The latter is the only style to survive. In the last century a poet immortalized the plight of a suitor, saying, "He must stand and bellow in thundertones, across half an acre of skirts and bones, as if hailing a ship on the ocean."

Simple turn-of-the-century cotton dress. There is interest in clothing of any period, from the lowest to the highest of styles.

With the demise of the hoop and bustle, the fashion world lost some colorful and graceful styling in feminine apparel.

At the time of the Revolution the bustle was in, but shortly thereafter there was a return to the simple sheath, examples of which were found during excavations in the Mediterranean area. About 1820, the hoop was introduced and grew wider and wider until it reached its maximum width before the War Between the States. After the war, in a time of conservatism and restraint, it lost its popularity. Women fought for suffrage and for liberation from the old ways, including dress.

However, the wealthy preferred a fancier look and the bustle returned in the late 1860s. It was once termed the "upholstered" look because every inch of fabric was secured by hundreds of tuckings. Never has a period known more opulent materials, color combinations or lavish use of trimmings. Homemakers and working girls, however, had to content themselves with what they could turn out on their sewing machines or, toward the end of the century, what was available from a Sears Roebuck or Montgomery Ward catalog.

With the advent of mail order, styles were kept simple for ease of packaging. Huge textile mills were supplying the world with inexpensive fabrics from which clothing could be made quickly for all members of the family, but most of this lacked high style. It was left to the major stores in the large cities to import the newest fashions from overseas for the wealthy, who would have nothing to do with production fabrics and so helped keep a modicum of style here.

Around 1879, skirts narrowed, with long, slim trains supported by a bustle-like pad with a tied-back look. The largest bustle size was reached by 1885, then the style gradually faded away early in the twentieth century.

Some of the most desirable clothing was made during the Deco period between 1920 and 1940, when designers were dressing the movie stars in regal attire. Boas and sequins over form-fitting silks made quite an impression, still enjoyed today. At home, the wealthy sought out the services of such independent designers to make their high-style clothing as well. This gave rise to the boutique, run by many who are legends today.

Until our bicentennial, few people saw value in keeping old garments. Actually, not many survived as they were cut up for quilting or rug making, or handed down until worn out and eventually used as rags. Those locked in old trucks were most often sold with the trunk at auction. Few museums paid attention to garments, as they are fragile, take much room to exhibit, and models for them are costly.

At the Smithsonian, however, an exhibit of the inaugural dresses worn by our first ladies stimulated interest. More recently, some museums have added old "costumes" to their collections. Collectors entered the competition to be ready for the bicentennial celebrations, which many felt would create a demand for period clothing.

In the late sixties and early seventies young people began dressing in offbeat clothing as a rebellion against conformity. They haunted auctions and thrift shops, searching out the bizarre as well as practical. Some have told me they did not have money and this was the only clothing they could afford. Whatever the reason, the interest in old clothing has grown and one must compete for the old clothing now.

"Flame" Stitching

If your have an old handbag or chair seat covering with a V-shaped, rather jagged design, it could be very old. This design is known as Irish stitching; in this country, some refer to it as "flame" stitching. In the seventeenth and eighteenth centuries, the most popular work done on canvas used the Irish, tent, cross or queen's stitches. The latter is the most difficult of all and very few examples have survived from that period.

The Irish stitch is vertical on the front and diagonal on the reverse side. It was relatively easy to do as thread went over

The flame stitch, or Irish stitch, was popular in the eighteenth century. Here it appears on a pocketbook of that period.

three or four weft yarns, while in other stitches the thread might pass over only one yarn. With the Irish stitch it was possible to create large areas of cloth suitable for such big jobs as upholstering a chair. Anyone who has a chair with this original flame stitch upholstery has a treasure indeed. The Irish stitch takes several forms: a diamond within a diamond, flowers, or even geometric shapes. Today, some use it in bargello work.

Flame stitching is one of the earliest forms of needlework in which the artisan might sign the work by stitching in a name, year of manufacture, and possibly location—something that was done extensively in the jacquard coverlets of the early nineteenth century in this country. The Irish stitch can be found on panels used in early fire screens, chair seats, and footstools, and also on tablecloths.

Most of the early Irish stitchwork found in this country was probably done here. Immigrants from the British Isles brought the tradition with them. One should seek advice on the care of such fabric, as it is highly sought by museums and collectors.

Oriental Rugs

More and more people are turning to oriental rugs not only as a floor covering, but also as an investment. Homer mentions them in his *Odyssey* as early as 800 B.C. and even the great philosopher Plato is known to have had an outstanding collection. The turbulence in Iran has created pressures on the rug market as it is not known how dependable the supply will be—hence the growing interest in those already in this country.

There is perhaps no field of collecting in which the majority of buyers know so little about the product, so much education is needed before one ventures out into the world of oriental rugs. One must identify origin, material, weave, and dyes, and should ask the following questions as well: Does it lie flat or is it crooked? Has it been washed and repainted to brighten the colors? Are the edges bound? Has it been clipped and possibly made up from several rugs? Do the colors bleed? Does it have jufti knots (knots tied in four rows of warp threads instead of two, which takes less time to weave)? Was it made of dead wool (that taken from a dead animal), which will wear more rapidly? And on and on. The rules in oriental rug collecting are numerous, and one must be well advised before investing.

Many antique items bought for investment are relatively low in cost, but the investment in a good rug may run into the

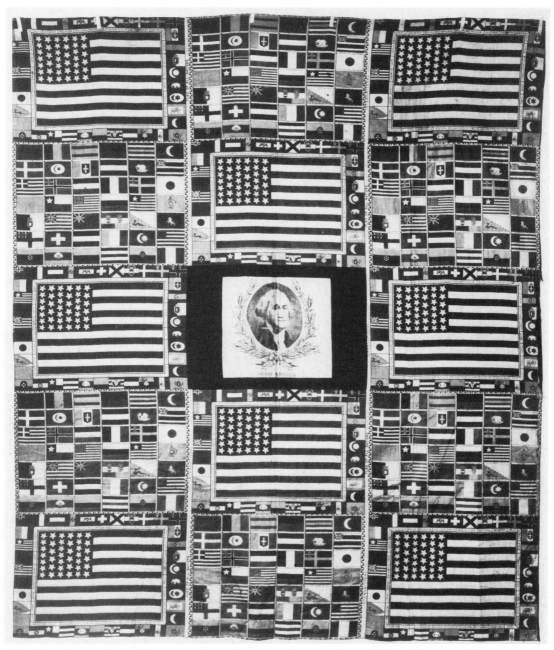

Printed textiles have been with us since the early nineteenth century. Presidents and flags were favorite subjects. Sections were sewn together to make this coverlet top.

thousands. This is why reading good literature and doing business with reputable people in the field is most important.

Condition of a rug is also important. Keep animals from soiling your rug. Keep it out of the sun so an end won't fade, and, above all, change the position of your furniture from time to time to even the wear.

Printed Textiles

Printed scenic wallpapers, printed ceramics, and printed cloth all seem to have had their beginnings in the eighteenth century. Textiles were printed from wood blocks, which had been cut to the desired pattern. The durability of the inks is attested by examples in museums today. In the beginning, such printing was used for decoration alone. The cut surfaces of the blocks were inked with the colors desired, then pressed one by one alongside each other to create the picture. An artist was at hand to ink in the borders where the lines might not join as accurately as desired.

Late in the century, the English used this technique to create such mundane objects as handkerchiefs. Some featured noted events of the day, such as the opening of a bridge or the creation of a new building. Early in the nineteenth century, events such as the first railroad to go into operation were memorialized on cloth. Soon, printed squares were sewn together to create coverlets, pillows, and the like.

In our country, printed cloth was soon used to promote patriotism as well as politics. With the machine age came the engraved rollers, which could print the cloth as rapidly as it could be fed through them. In France, copper plate printing was developed early in the century and combined in the roller plates. One will find panels with likenesses of Washington, Lincoln, and other patriots. They can be framed and preserved as excellent wall hangings.

CHAPTER SEVEN

Collectibles and Collecting

Introduction

Collecting for collecting's sake began after World War II. In the 1950s, an occasional auction gallery helped people dispose of items they had kept during the conflict and now were ready to sell. Industry had retooled quickly, and new furniture, kitchen items, appliances, tools, clothing, cars, and other items filled a pent-up demand. Consumers who had made good money in war industries and many returning servicemen had pocketfuls of money. Delayed weddings prompted the need for homes and everything to fill them. Many with less money bought used merchandise that appeared in the marketplace. Good antique items were in demand, but those pieces made from about 1830 on languished as the undesirables. Most of the Empire, Victorian, Eastlake, Art Nouveau, and Art Deco pieces were something we *had* to sell just to keep an auction gallery full for business. During this period, Tiffany vases sold for between $2 and $5; leaded shade lamps were plentiful for 50¢; much oak furniture was chopped up to burn in the wood heaters in auction barns. Vases with Native Americans painted on them (Rookwood) went begging. Ice boxes and rolltop desks were not carried out of a house as they fetched so little, or nothing at all. Even the junk dealers didn't want brass beds.

Kitchen items such as Fiesta ware, Depression and carnival glass, graniteware pots and pans, stoneware crocks and jugs, and spongeware were liquidated for but a few dollars.

In 1963, my National Educational Television series on antiques began, seen coast to coast. I had discovered the prices of prime antiques were rising and a new breed of collector was appearing. These collectors were settling for common, inexpensive items which fulfilled their desire to collect something at prices they could afford. Shows on collectible bottles that could be dug up in dumps prompted thousands of letters for bibliographies of the then few books on the subject. Folk art, dolls, buttons, quilts, stoneware, pewter, silver, postcards and other ephemera, stereopticon viewers, decoys—the list is endless—captured the fancy of young and old alike.

At that time, there were but a few antiques shows—no flea markets, no barn and yard sales, no group shops, no outdoor auctions in the winter. One could attend auctions only in good weather. Antiques shops in the North Country closed for the winter. The auction barn became the center of year-round activity for buying and selling.

It took about twenty years before the

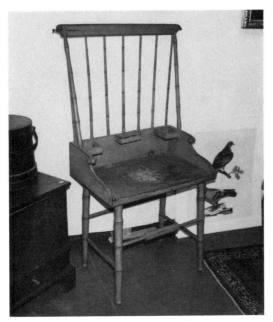

Strange pieces keep turning up. Witness this chair made up of the back of a Windsor, the top of a washstand, and the leg frame of a Sheraton fancy chair.

In the early 1950s, an Empire chest like this would have sold for $10.

items that had been sold by the boxful were considered important enough to be sold by the piece. Suddenly it seemed people were collecting everything. Books appeared on old water pumps, manhole covers, beer cans, iron wagon steps, barbed

wire, mourning pictures (rather gloomy wall hangings), and the numerous items created in every medium by relatively untrained, naive, or uninhibited artisans, lumped together in the category of "folk art." Once the objects began appearing in museums, the frenzy rose. Everyone wanted to buy a winner before the price went up.

In the mid-1960s, more than 300 dealers staged an "Art Deco" show at the Coliseum in New York City. In all their glory, out came the artifacts of the 1920–1950 period. Old toasters, mantel lamps with horses or with President Roosevelt at the wheel of the ship of state, spelter (zinc) statues of the Eiffel Tower and Statue of Liberty, mesh and other handbags, strange hats, buttons, Fiesta ware, carnival and Depression glass, costume jewelry, along with just about everything imaginable appeared before a capacity crowd. The real age of collecting had begun.

A dealer who appeared on one of my TV shows stated that a collectible is collectable—i.e., one is able to collect it. Before

Bronze leaded shade lamps like this would have sold for $1 or less in the early 1950s.

fire comes out of your nostrils at this observation, rest assured, I am comfortable with either usage.

Once the genie had been let out of the bottle, she was never to be put back. Collecting knows only the limits of imagination, taste, and desire. However, I caution the many students I teach to keep in mind that it may be necessary someday to sell what you buy. Many people tell me they buy objects because they like them. This is fine if you have plenty of money. However, there are circumstances such as death, separation, divorce, illness, bankruptcy and even moving that may necessitate the disposal of your collection. All of a sudden, the aesthetics fall by the wayside, and the money realized by selling becomes most important. It is just as easy to learn to like good, desirable items as it is to get caught up collecting what is junk to begin with and always will be junk. Do not expect a dealer or auctioneer to bail you out if you have bought unwisely.

So many items were made by machine and can still be made by machine. Some buyers have learned this to their sorrow, as repros keep appearing on the market. The early handmade items can be considered works of art and should be called antiques. Their true reproduction is impossible, so most rise in value. Collectibles must have something special about them. Desirability sets the price; contributing factors are rarity, condition, and, often, function. Many collectors of tools like their warmth and beauty, yet some use them as well. Many use their Fiesta ware daily, as it is colorful and different from the table wares of today. Many items should not be used, such as tin windup toys, mechanical banks, ivory fans, and even the electrical toys of the fifties and sixties. Original boxes can add up to 25 percent of value. Collectors of new

At auctions in the 1950s no one would have bid on these colorful advertising lithographs.

items of today have the advantage of knowing what the future holds. When you buy, keep the boxes, labels, instructions, and even bill of sale, as documentation of the piece. Twenty years from now, most everything of interest made today will have increased in value.

In this chapter, you will find observations on new as well as old items. While I cannot cover the entire spectrum of collecting in a book chapter, I have tried to illustrate the range of collectibles and to offer tips on identification and how to grade them.

The field of collecting is limitless. Let your eye be your guide as to quality, and your experiences at auctions, shows, and flea markets your guide to values. One must be immersed in this business to buy and sell wisely—a part-time, on-again, off-again collector will not keep himself advised sufficiently to do well at it. Talk with dealers and collectors in the field in which you are interested. Go to museums to see the objects on display and study their characteristics. Above all, read good books on the subject—you will find there is a wealth of material that will help you, if you will but seek it out.

Advertising Memorabilia

Fans

Paper and cardboard advertising fans were used during the late nineteenth cen-

tury. Some of these were made to open a full 360 degrees. A color picture of a product, establishment, or pretty girl might appear on one side, with the reverse carrying the advertising message. These were issued at many public functions in an era when air conditioning was unknown. Most are on inexpensive wooden sticks. Although these fans are of interest, most do not command much money. Buy what appeals to you in fans of this type, with little thought of what you might get at resale someday. Because the number of collectors of these is quite limited, you may have difficulty in getting your money back when you are ready to sell.

Trade Figures

In the eighteenth century, when many people could not read, merchants relied on trade figures in front of their establishments to let the public know the work in which they were engaged. A large gilded watch appeared in front of a watch repair shop; a pig or other animal in front of a butcher shop or on a sign cutout; a large pair of gilded spectacles at an optometrist's office.

We are all familiar with the cigar store Indian, most carved of wood, standing outside the tobacconist's shop. As a boy, I can remember them being left outside all night with no thought of anyone stealing them. Today, with some selling in the five figures, one has to go to museums to see them, where they are guarded day and night.

Figures of this type appeared in England in front of chandlery shops on the docks, most often in the form of a sea captain decked out in full regalia. Figureheads on ships have been around since the time of Cleopatra, but the British elevated

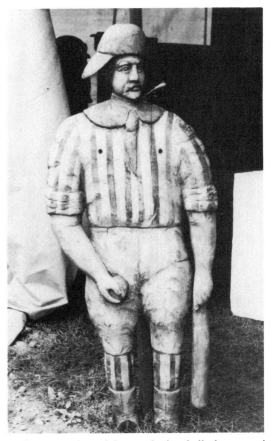

Unique carved wood figure of a baseball player, used to advertise a sporting goods shop early in this century.

this art form and immortalized naval and national heroes.

The carved wood figure is most desired, but other materials such as papier mâché, plaster, and even ceramics were used. I recall one blacksmith shop in Vermont that had a team with two horses standing out front, lifesize. Trade figures are not common today, and the old ones are not easy to find—good luck.

Animation Art

On June 18, 1991, Sotheby's in New York conducted an auction of animation art. Dana Hawkes, director of Sotheby's Collectibles Department, stated in a press release that the "sale of Animation Art was very exciting with a full salesroom and keen competition for celluloids from a variety of different areas and studios. The market for animation art continues to be steady and strong with the finest materials bringing extremely bouyant prices. The most exciting section of today's sales were the 'Peanuts' cels from the Bill Melendez studios which in many cases brought several times their high estimates. Also, a wonderful cel from Alice in Wonderland brought $47,300 against a pre-sale estimate of $15–20,000."

We have watched the growing interest in the sale of cels—those individually created paintings, thousands of which are needed to create animation in cartoon features. They are being framed as decorator's pieces. This type of art has its own afficianados. Since they have arrived at the five-figure mark, collectors have become more serious about collecting them. Years ago, they were just thrown away, once the cartoon or full-length feature was completed. Today, large studios such as Disney are planning their own auctions to capitalize on the demand. Disney retains a corporate auctioneer who sells outdated and outmoded and unneeded equipment. All studios sell artifacts and clothing from famous stars and movies—witness the interest in anything connected with Elvis. There are reproductions of the cels—one must obtain a warranty of authenticity before parting with big bucks. At least the auction houses certify what they sell.

Baseball Memorabilia

Most people are aware of the interest in collecting baseball cards. Books on the subject indicate their rarity and desirability. This is a world of changing values, so one must keep abreast of prices to play this game. Recently, the prices received for some of the early rarities have encouraged more collectors to get involved, which has helped drive up prices. I will not dwell on this subject, as there is much good written material out there to help you.

There is, however, one rarity that may interest you. It is the baseball "silk." These are small-sized portraits, about two by four inches, of famous players on silk, issued early in this century. They were given with packages of various cigarettes, such as Helmar, Turkey Red, and Old Mill. Over a hundred players were immortalized, some in black and white and some in color. Baseball card collectors are prime customers for these. They are so rare that not enough have been sold to establish prices for various players. Maybe you will help set the prices when you buy and sell.

Box-Top Collectibles

Back in the 1930s, during the heyday of radio, such notable stars of serial programs as Jack Armstrong, Tom Mix, Orphan Annie, and Buck Rogers were the idols of most youngsters. Advertisers, particularly the large cereal companies, realized the potential of such listenership and responded with premium offers that are the rage of collecting today. After the hero finished an exciting bout with some black-hatted villain, the announcers offered the magic watch or compass that was used to bring him down. Just 10¢ and a cereal box-top would bring you the identical gadgets used by your hero.

Let's look at some of them today. When Jack Armstrong took to the air in 1933, he soon offered his dandy shooting plane gun, which fired discs from a spring-wound mechanism. This device cleared the shelves of Wheaties in short order. It sells in the three figures now. Researchers guessed that over a million youngsters watched the daring feats of the all-American boy, so they represented quite a market for cereal sales.

Aviation was still in its infancy in the 1930s, and anything to do with flying was an instant hit. Jack Armstrong was an intrepid pilot who frequently jumped into the cockpit to chase and foil dastardly villains. One could join his Tru-Flite Club and get a set of cardboard fighters. The club continued into World War II, when it was called the WAFC Club (Write A Fighter Corps) to encourage writing to our servicemen. A real Piper cub was once offered as a giant premium in a contest—where is this, today?

The writers of Jack Armstrong were so imaginative that just before the war, our hero formed his own SBI, Scientific Bureau of Investigation. J. Edgar Hoover was consulted on the similarity of title to the FBI, and he voiced no objection. However, the writers anticipated so many scientific military inventions that our government censored the program for security reasons.

In 1935, the darling of the screen, Shirley Temple, became a big star, and soon the makers of Wheaties were offering cereal bowls, dishes, tumblers, and mugs with her picture decorating them. More than 5 million of these blue and white pieces were sent out as premiums. Needless to say, they are very desirable.

In a unique twist, Shirley herself sent in a boxtop and dimes to Jack Armstrong for a hike-ometer. The company responded by sending it via air mail special delivery. One of these is a goodie today.

Another desirable is the Frank Buck explorer's watch, which appeared in 1948. It was a reworked version of Orphan Annie's Miracle Sun Watch, which was offered by Ovaltine, a popular hot drink. One with the sun god motif on the back is worth more than one without.

If you join those in the box-top collectible field today, you will find the rewards are more than money; the stories that come with them are lots of fun.

Candle Molds

More candles are used in this country today than at any other time in our history, though perhaps 99 percent of our homes have electricity. Candlemaking abounds, especially in tourist areas, with New England in the forefront of manufacture. Colonial homes lend themselves to such lighting, and most people enjoy the traditional feeling that candles give. Many restorations feature candlelight tours, showing preserved or restored homes in an eighteenth-century atmosphere. A restaurant in Colonial Williamsburg, Virginia, uses nothing but candlelight at its entry and throughout its dining areas.

Generally, candles are made of tallow, which is rendered fat. Over the years, just about any substance that could be liquefied and burned was used in their making. Our settlers did not have cattle to slaughter, so they depended on the fat from deer and bear. When this was scarce, they burned pine knots, which gave off a rather smoky but effective light. Strands of rush taken from the marshes were soaked with anything that would burn and used as well. As soon as cattle became plentiful, all the fat was melted down and skimmed several times to purify it.

Wicks were made of coarse fibers of flax and spun on a wheel into balls, like twine. The fat was boiled with water in a kettle and into this were dipped the wicks, which were fastened to a slender rod, then suspended, perhaps between the backs of two chairs, while another group of wicks was dipped. This process might take about twenty minutes or more, as layer after layer of tallow was built up until the candles were of proper size.

For men of muscle, large racks were designed in the shape of a cross; as many as fifty candles might be dipped from this frame. Once they hardened, the candles were stored in a box and enough for each day placed near the fireplace. Some were

Tin candle molds and dipping racks, which still can be used. The many varieties can add up to an interesting collection.

stored in a cold place, as it was believed a cold candle would burn longer.

Candle molds came into use at the end of the eighteenth century, but it was not until the tin knocking trade expanded that they were in general use. "Tin knocking" is an old English term used to identify those who made their living by fashioning functional items from metal. Tin was the earliest metal used, but later, many turned to brass and copper. Shem Drowne was an English tin knocker who came to Boston. His greatest work is the grasshopper weathervane which is atop Faneuil Hall in Boston. It has been there since 1754.

Wooden molds, the size of candle desired, were used to fashion a tin covering, which was soldered to the exact size of the candle to be made. A hole was left at either end so the wick could be fastened in both places. Tin pouring scoops were made so one could pour several candles at a time.

The largest tin mold I have ever seen has space for sixty candles. In Pennsylvania, one is likely to find them made of clay in many kinds of ceramics such as redware, stoneware, semiporcelain, and Rockinghamware. I have seen them in brass, wood, glass, and iron as well.

There was a time when itinerant candlemakers would stop at homes to make candles just for bed and board. They were much needed: one candle might last three to five hours, and the average single-room household might burn three or four a night. As houses were enlarged, more candles were needed. A table in the downstairs hall would hold many chamber candleholders, which were taken aloft as everyone retired.

Clothing Accessories

Buttons

Button collecting first took hold in this country during the Depression. The National Button Society of America was organized to promote collection and display of buttons.

There are many classifications of this collectible, with a wide range of types to choose from. Eighteenth-century buttons are rare since not many have survived. The most familiar are the military buttons, which were saved because of an attachment to the history of the American Revolution which prompted many people to save the uniforms of their ancestors. While the uniforms disappeared due to the ravages of moths or time, the buttons were most often saved as a final remembrance. Much of the clothing of the eighteenth century was held together by sashes, belts, and hooks.

In the early nineteenth century, fashionable women were dressed in the Greek Revival style, and buttons were used sparingly on their draped clothing. Buttons were used mostly by men. It was not until the change of styles after the Civil War that buttons came into general use on clothing for all members of the family. Early buttons were made of copper, porcelain, precious metals such as gold and silver, glass, steel, bone, ivory, and even wood. Decoration was done by enameling, carving, molding, and gilding. Some buttons were silver plated after this technique was developed in the 1840s. Many housewives made buttons from the bones of farm animals by cutting, shaping, and polishing, and these were used frequently on undergarments. You can tell bone from ivory by examining the material with a magnifying glass—bone will have small black specks throughout, whereas ivory is clear. Many "gold" buttons are actually made of pinchbeck, which is a manmade product, so you must judge most of these in this light. The technique of decorating buttons by enameling them originated overseas many years ago and was not practiced much in America, so most enameled buttons we find are probably European. Metal buttons were chased and engraved with decorations, and some are now called "steel cut," referring to the bright facets left by such work. Hunt clubs often had sporting buttons with hunting scenes on them made up for their members. Some buttons were enameled on metal, and others were done on porcelain. Some buttons were made in concave or convex fashion and joined together at the rims to form a hollow button. Exotic materials such as shell, mother-of-pearl, and tortoise are found, but although these are not common, they do not command much interest. Housewives often made fabric buttons by sewing material over a shaped disc and then drilling holes to accommodate the thread. Some of the early steel buttons will rust and must be oiled or otherwise protected. Gems were used on royal buttons, but it is unlikely that you will find any of these in America.

Horn was sometimes used for button making; some was simply carved, and another technique involved molding the material by using heat. Most American "pearl-looking" buttons came from Birmingham, England, where they were made in abundance during the middle of the last century. This pearl look was later duplicated in plastic, which eventually dominated other materials in button manufacture. Compositions of plastic and other synthetic materials became the rule in button making and fine quality gradually disappeared except in buttons made for the carriage trade.

Other materials of exotic nature used in buttons were vegetables, ivory, nuts, and even seeds. Jet is best known for its use in jewelry, but it was also used for buttons. It is actually a natural material called lignite, which has a coal black quality that was eventually reproduced in a black glass which can fool the uninitiated. Pressed glass buttons were turned out by major factories, but the quality of most is not great, and they are collected for their curiosity

value alone. Paperweight buttons were made to look like the larger weights and are interesting to collect. Then there are the charm string buttons—every string contains at least a thousand small buttons, each different from the others. A girl would collect these buttons until, supposedly, the final one was put on by the man she married. Some doubt that they ever existed, while others feel that the strings were long ago broken up as a practical matter when clothing needed mending.

The decorating motifs and shapes of buttons were influenced by the art forms prevalent in other decorative items, so a true collector can soon learn to classify his collection into different periods. You must keep abreast of the action in button buying and selling, but this can be difficult as there are few specialists in the field because of the low rewards. There are many buttons selling for just a few cents and this brings a much lower return than antiques, which sell for many dollars. You can learn a lot on your own by buying boxes of buttons at auctions and then sorting them out. Those of interesting and/or valuable materials, those with good design and decoration, and those that show some handwork in their making are ones you can consider saving. You will assimilate much knowledge if you deal in buttons and keep buying and selling until you learn what the collectors want, and this will guide you in what you should be collecting if profit is important to you. If buttons are represented as having come from the garments of famous people, be sure you have documentation before buying. The woods are full of good story tellers.

Fans

Not many realize that men as well as women carried fans as far back as the seventeenth century. Their origin is lost in history, but it is known that fans were used in the Orient many centuries ago. The Egyptians pictured huge fans which were used to cool the reigning Pharaohs, and smaller ones must have been in use even in their day. Those that are collectible today could have been made in the Orient, Europe, or America, but the fanciest came from overseas. French fans were most popular in the eighteenth century, since this was an age of elegance there, and fans were a social necessity almost as important as good clothing if one wished to be properly dressed.

It is felt that the first hand fans did not fold, but were made in square, rectangular, round, or oval shapes. Materials were silk, parchment, leather, paper, bamboo, grass, linen, and even cane. The folding fans use framing (called the "sticks") which is held together by the mount (the axis at which they open). In the sixteenth century a fan opened about 120 degrees. They continued to progress in size until they could be spread beyond 180 degrees. The folding fan probably originated in the Orient and spread to Europe through the growing trade. Some fans were made totally of carved ivory, tortoiseshell, horn, or bone,

and some featured these materials along with lacquered wood used as framing in the sticks and mount. Gold, silver, and jewels were imbedded in fans for the wealthy, and some fans even contained a small mirror which milady could use to look over her shoulder as she pretended to cool herself.

Painted decoration was popular, and was done on almost all the materials, particularly wood and cloth. Some fans had mounts covered with vellum (lamb skin); others were decorated by cut or open work. Some of the painting was done by artists who signed their creations. Other fans feature spangle and sequin decorations.

The addition of a small scent pad or box near the mount was a helpful innovation for an area where the air was bad. A bride's fan could have been made of lace and that of a portly matron may have had feathers attached as a decorative touch. You can look for the cords from which fans dangled from the wrist, since these can be quite fancy and made with good metals and

Fans can be framed and hung as wall decorations. Note the elegant gilt frame surrounding this painted silk and ivory stick example.

decorations. Fan boxes were popular, and you will find them in a variety of materials. Papier-mâché must have been the most popular, perhaps because these boxes were inexpensive to make.

As with anything else, a fan must be judged according to the requirements of being an antique. Fans showing fine handwork and good taste, design, and workmanship are the most desired. Carving, painting, and other decorations are important. Precious metals and gems and exotic materials such as ivory, bone, horn, and tortoiseshell contribute to desirability. Condition is important, so you must be careful not to invest in those which cannot be restored properly. Those with fine carvings and paintings are often framed as wall hangings and are quite effective. It is the workmanship, beautification, and art on the fans which generally give them the most value.

Parasols

Back in the Victorian era, when walking was the method used by most people to get from place to place, the parasol was considered a definite part of a lady's costume. A woman had to be quite strong to carry one, as many parasols weighed eight or ten pounds.

The oldest and heaviest parasols seem to be in demand today. The handles are the key to desirability. One will find handles in carved bone, walrus tusk, horn, tortoise, precious metals, gem encrusted, bamboo, and many other kinds of wood.

Early in the last century, parasols were quite small, designed more as protection from the sun. By the 1880s, they were made of a variety of materials and were much larger. Some were made of colorful silk and even striped with red tassels and cords. In the 1880s, an inventor created one whose cloth might be changed to complement whatever costume its owner wore.

Once parasols had to be crammed into trains and automobiles, they were transferred into functional protection against wet weather, streamlined, and reduced in size. Those most favored today collapse and can be place in a large handbag. Buy the old for decoration, not use, as the old materials have become fragile with age.

Dolls

As with many other types of antiques and collectibles, dolls just seem to be going up in price. Seemingly, the fashion dolls are highest on the list, along with rarities, of course. Dolls of clay have been found in excavations in Egypt dating back to about 5,000 B.C.

Perhaps the most interesting and valuable dolls I have ever seen are the Tanagra at the archeological museum in Athens. Tanagra was a city between Attica and Boeotia where there was a great terra-cotta industry. According to museum literature, when a woman of means died, a clay figure was created in her image, usually standing less than a foot. These show the dress and hairdos and facial characteristics of the times; hence their importance to historians. They were painted, and much paint remains on those we have seen. The figures were buried with the deceased; hence their good condition today.

Collectible dolls come from almost every country. Excellent examples have been found in pre-Columbian ruins in Mexico and South America as well as from early civilizations in Europe and Asia. Dolls have been made in a variety of materials including clay, wood, wax, rubber, parian porcelain, glazed porcelain, metals, bisque porcelain, papier-mâché, and celluoid.

Wooden dolls were evident during the eighteenth century and into the early part of the nineteenth century, when the industrial revolution allowed mass production of dolls in other materials. The good early

Group of dolls seen at a show. Most have bisque heads and are German or French.

wooden dolls are rarities and are therefore high in price. The primitive ones were carved rigidly, while the better ones had pegged joints which allowed motion. These were gessoed or painted in a lifelike manner. Wooden dolls were made until the late nineteenth century, but these are inferior in quality to the earlier ones. Some were made with hinge joints which could rust over the years, so check this. During this time, the heads, hands, and feet might have been made of wood, and a stuffed body, arms, and legs attached. Some early dolls had plaster heads on wooden bodies, and these are quite rare. Springfield, Vermont, was a doll-making center in the late nineteenth century, and dolls made by Joel Ellis and Mason and Taylor are very desirable. Wooden dolls were also made as late as the 1920s by A. Schoenhut & Company of Philadelphia.

Porcelain dolls varied in their glazes, which included the shiny, bisque, and parian. In the dolls with a shiny glaze, you should look for those with brown hair, as this is rarer than black. Brown eyes are also rarer. Facial coloring is important, and it should be as natural as possible. Dolls with set-in glass eyes are not common. Shoes with flat soles were used until about the time of the Civil War, when heels began to be added. As with most dolls, the style of

Unusual bisque-head doll carrying sewing gear, plus suggested items that could be made, such as socks, hats, and handbags. She is called an English Notion Nanny.

clothing used can help determine when they were made.

Parian is an unglazed porcelain, generally pure white. The hair of parian dolls is generally molded; they have glass or painted eyes and some fancy ones even had pierced ears. Bisque doll heads are unglazed, and the coloring is generally more pronounced than on dolls in parian since the doll makers were not held rigidly to the white texture. The French and German makers are best known for bisque dolls—they made the busts (and often feet and arms to match) and the purchaser could add the body and clothing she wished. You can check the provenance of a doll by lowering its dress at the back of the neck, as this is where many manufacturers stamped their names and marks.

Papier-mâché is made of paper which has been torn to shreds and mixed with paste. This can be molded, will harden, and can then be gessoed or painted with ease. Papier-mâché dolls may have either painted or glass eyes. These were popular in the nineteenth century until dolls of this type and class gave way to other compositions which might have been made of similar materials. Ludwig Greiner of Philadelphia patented a method for making papier-mâché dolls in 1858 and some may be found with his mark on the upper back.

Rubber, both hard and soft, has been used to make dolls. Charles Goodyear patented a process for making rubber, and this material was first used for dolls in the middle of the nineteenth century. This has

A group of papier mâché dolls of the nineteenth century. Most are not found in good condition. These are very good examples, well dressed for the period.

been modified by the use of foam and related materials in today's dolls. Not many of these dolls survived as they could go out of shape if they were stored with weight against them.

Wax was one of the earliest materials used in doll making. Some dolls were molded directly into shape and others were made of wax poured over some other type of body material such as papier-mâché or cardboard. These are quite perishable as they are subject to heat, and therefore most are high in price due to the small supply. These dolls were popular until the end of the last century.

Metal dolls are interesting, but do not command the high prices of most of those made with more exotic materials. They seem to have originated in Germany and at one time were popular because of their durability. Most were made in this century and metal heads, legs, and arms were often used as replacements for broken parts of other dolls.

Cloth, perhaps the most basic doll material, was readily available in every home and a mother could easily fashion her own gift to a child. Rag dolls fall into this category, as do those which were designed with a great deal more finesse. Companies were set up to print complete doll bodies in color and these could then be stuffed and stitched up at home. These were offered as premiums for cereal box tops as recently as the Depression—not only in doll forms, but in animal forms as well. The Arnold Print Company of North Adams, Massachusetts, is well known for this work.

Celluloid was first perfected just after the middle of the nineteenth century and was immediately put to use in making doll heads and bodies. Almost everyone has seen one of the celluloid Kewpie dolls that have been given away as prizes at fairs for years.

Dolls were made to walk and "talk" in the second quarter of the nineteenth century. They were used on pull toys, some were designed with mechanical features which permitted them to perform, others

Annalee

The first Annalee doll was made in 1934. Since that time, many have been made to depict everything from Santa Claus to bunny rabbits. Their fame has spread throughout the world as they embody the creativeness and handwork that has great appeal to collectors. From this has come a collectors' club as well as a museum where they are made in Meredith, New Hampshire.

Annalee Thorndike, the creator of the dolls, started making them as an in-home business during the Depression. As early as 1955, she did a series of ski dolls for the New Hampshire Office of Vacation Travel. If you own one with signed skis, you have a classic. Several years ago, she created the New Hampshire State Trooper in limited edition. Originally, they sold for $144, but the last one to be sold at auction brought $1,000. High on the collecting list today are some of the early Santas with hand-painted features and a bean for a nose, a kangaroo made in plush velour instead of felt, and the Yankee Doodle jockey boy. Many tourists have taken these home, and throughout the country not enough is known about how very collectible

1965 14" photographer, one of fourteen designed by Annalee Thorndike of Meredith, New Hampshire. It sold at a recent auction for $925.

they are. This is a sleeper item—all today are worth much more than when they were sold originally.

American Girls Collection

The latest in dolls is the American Girls Collection, brought out by the Pleasant Company in Middleton, Wisconsin. There are four, in what can be considered a historical series; Felicity Merriman, 1774; Kirsten Larson, 1854; Samantha Parkington, 1904; and Molly McIntire, 1944. They are targeted to the seven- to twelve-year-old group. Each is dressed in clothing of the times, which provides a lesson in history. Along with the dolls are books that tell their life stories. Each doll, with accessories, can cost well over a thousand dollars. Accessories include cookbooks and craft sets, which are geared to the activities of a young lady in each of the periods. These dolls fall into an educational toy category and may lead the way to more. Perhaps they will become the hot collectibles of the future. The cost may narrow down the number sold, so supply may not be able to meet the demand when the secondary collector enters the market some years hence.

fell into the puppet category, and some were incorporated into music boxes where they danced to a tune. More recently, dolls have been made to cry, wet, and talk via a built-in tape recorder. The Barbie doll of today with all her attendant paraphernalia, which includes not only her clothing, but also sporting equipment, cars, boats, and campers will certainly be of interest to the collectors of the future. Many women who were girls during the Depression are seeing the type of dolls they played with on the flea market counters today. The Shirley Temple and Raggedy Anne dolls have their buyers, which indicates that you should preserve anything related to dolls of any period. Someday, someone will want them—and that day may not be far off in our quickly changing world.

Novelty Dolls and Accessories

There is great interest today in collecting doll-related items. Many dolls themselves have risen to astronomical prices, so attention is being diverted to items used in the making and enjoyment of them.

Rare are the Roly Poly Dolls sold extensively by Sears. These have rounded, weighted bases so they will not tip when baby plays with them. Miniature Hoosier cupboards were made for doll use. Collapsible cardboard doll houses were made for use where space was limited. Wooden washing machines, $16\frac{1}{2}''$ in height, could actually be used to wash doll clothing. Japanese nodding-head dolls were popular after World War II. These were made of papier mâché, about five inches in height, and moved their heads on coiled wire springs. A crying Schoenhut novelty doll is quite rare, although originally they ranged in price from 25¢ for a baby to only $1.95 for the adult. These have papier mâché bodies with fine bisque china heads and were sold in 1912 by Sears.

With the craze for wicker now, wicker rocking doll cradles would be of great interest, but in my years, I have never seen one. They sold originally for 45¢ to 95¢, quite expensive in their time for a doll-re-

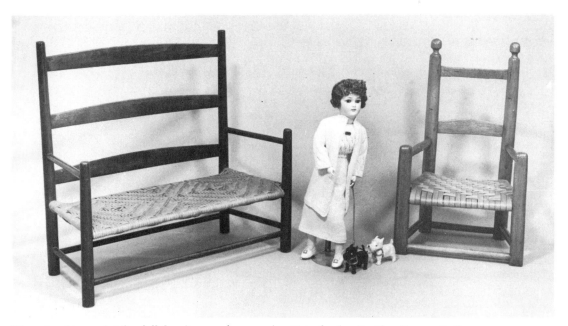

There is a big market for doll furniture and accessories. Note the tiny Scotties. Bourne Gallery.

lated item. There are many rarities out there—check old copies of Sears or Ward's catalogs. They are a good guide to this collecting.

Enamel

The art of enameling reached its peak many centuries ago in Byzantium and Georgia. There are three ways it was done. The first, called champlevé, is probably a lost art today. Cavities are punched, ground, or chiseled into the surface of a material, often gold, and then filled with colored smalt. Smalt is made of powdered glass that is colored and then mixed with an adhesive that binds it to the surface. Colors are put into the cavities to form a picture or design, and then the entire work is fired, then polished to remove the excess material, leaving behind a true work of art. When you consider that much of this work was done on gold, often on items as tiny as beads and hanging pendants, it is little wonder that artisans today marvel at it.

The second technique, called cloisonné, involves raising a wall of material on a surface. The early work was done by soldering fine gold wire to a gold surface in the desired design. This was done by the cold solder method, using mercury as a flux, since mercury is a solvent of gold. The outlined areas were filled with smalt and then polished. Cloisonné was used extensively not only in the Georgian area, but also in the Orient and in France. It is mostly cloisonné from China and France that we collect today, since their output during the last century must have been tremendous. Cloisonné was done in a less expensive manner, using brass or bronze as the metals and is quite desirable as it is demanding on the artist. The production coming out of the People's Republic of China today is very good. A simple new eight- to-ten-inch vase will command over a hundred dollars.

The third technique is simply called enameling. Materials such as those used to beautify porcelain and glass are merely painted on the surface, with lines of gilding detailing the design between the colors. This line can be mistaken for the raised brass wall in cloisonné, so you must examine it carefully to determine what you are buying. The value of enameled metal pieces is not as high as that of those made with the raised walls and smalt. Much imitation cloisonné has been made and is still being made today, so be careful when you buy.

Fire Buckets

A necessity in the early American household was the fire bucket. You might recall seeing them passed along a line of people between the well and the burning structure in old movies. The earliest, of leather, were made in Europe. We are most conscious of the English product as the mother country provided them in our trade. After the Revolutionary War, however, local artisans began making them as well. An average household had eight to twelve.

Look for those made completely in leather; other materials were used, but leather is most desirable. Condition is important, with no cracks or damages. Decoration heightens value, and it should be clearly defined and recognizable. Those which are dated have the most interest. Most of these will be from the early nineteenth century; earlier ones have a low survival rate because of time and attrition. Fighting fires was a community effort, and all would show up with their buckets to

Leather fire buckets decorate many early American homes. Those with names of owners and dates, such as these (1815) are the most desired.

assist. Most fire buckets had family names painted on them, which made it easier to return them to owners after a fire.

One should not repaint a leather fire bucket. It's best to retain the old faded look; however, the brighter they are in color, the better.

You may take care of the leather with saddle soap or another good preservative. Do not apply this to the painted areas. A good harness maker can help in repairs if straps are broken or bottoms are loose. (You can find harness makers at racetracks during the busy season doing repairs on harnesses.)

Fishing Gear

Over the last seveal years a great interest has developed in fishing gear. Fine bamboo trout rods and old custom reels have always sold well, but the fascination for handmade lures has pushed many of them into very high prices. Some people collect old flies to use them for fishing, but others are mounting them in deep frames for display.

Hand-carved wooden lures seem to be the big thing now. Many are beautifully painted, and some are considered folk art. My concern is that too many have been appearing on the market. Shortly after an auction in New England, where many sold in the three figures, I noted dozens of them on the tables at a show in upstate New York, priced at less than $50. I do not know the reason for the disparity in price, but be sure the item is an old American piece, rather than a reproduction from the Orient.

Gibson Girls

Gibson Girls blossomed from the hand of Charles Dana Gibson, a noted artist at the turn of the century. As ubiquitous as Mickey Mouse is today, the Gibson Girl was immortalized on shirts, hats, china, shoes, buttons, and even corsets. Rare was the home not adorned with a Gibson Girl pillow top.

Even the English got into the act. Royal Doulton Pottery made china plates in sets of twenty-four and vases on which the lovely faces and figures were imprinted. It is unlikely that the dishes will grace your table for dinner, though, as a dishwasher would be very unkind to them.

Some china in this country was imprinted with transfer prints, which look almost photographic. These must be considered decorative items as one would not want to take the chance of breaking them by using them for dining.

Guns

Most guns with any age are of interest, but you must acquaint yourself with the go-ing market price before investing. The popular Model 62, 22-calibre Winchester

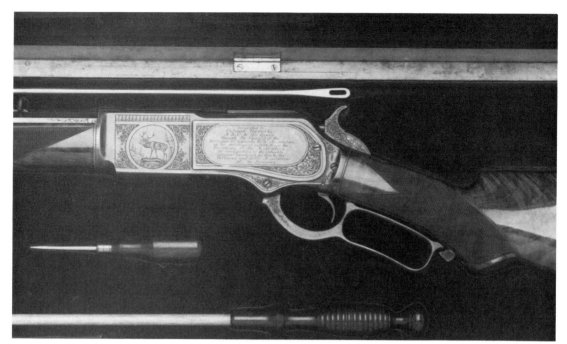

Winchester presentation rifle, Model 1876, Signed C.F. Ulrich; presented to Col. Gzowski, Queen Victoria's aide de camp in 1884. Butterfield & Butterfield, San Francisco.

Pepperbox pistol, perscussion, made by Allen and Thurber in Grafton, Massachusetts, c. 1860s. A weapon of this type was used in the assassination of President Lincoln.

pump gun sold in the late 1930s for $18, but is up in the hundreds now because the model has been discontinued. This is the type of gun still used in shooting galleries. It is next to impossible to wear them out, and they are very accurate and reliable. This proves that age is not the only factor in determining value.

Most gun parts are marked with the same serial number, which makes it possible to check the originality of the pieces and to look for replacements. It is important that all parts be original to the gun. If you are collecting weapons from the first half of the nineteenth century, check to make sure they are not conversions. The early ones used a flintlock firing mechanism, and many were later converted to the more reliable percussion cap. This alteration must be taken into consideration. Some gunsmiths are clever in returning these pieces to their original flintlock condition with another lock not original to the piece.

There are many foreign guns in America. Perhaps the most collectible are those which are rarities in their country of origin. About 2,590 percussion-operated and reliable Tower rifles were sent to the Confederate forces during the Civil War. These turn up from time to time, but their quantity is limited. The famed Luger, Mannlicker, Haenel, and Mauser sporting and military arms are very fine collectibles of the twentieth century.

War-Related

Weapons related to American wars are very desirable; especially those from the Revolution, the War of 1812, and the Civil War. Insist on documentation if someone tells you that a gun was carried in certain battles, as family history is often not too reliable. A museum curator in Pennsylvania was approached by the descendants of a man who served in the Civil War. They claimed he had served with distinction as a captain, and they wanted more information about a sword that had been handed down in the family as having been carried by him in some very famous battles. The curator recognized the "sword" as one of the long bayonets which were in use at that time, but rather than debate it with them, took down the man's name, regiment, and other pertinent information. His research revealed the man in question had deserted the Army two weeks after his induction and was given a dishonorable discharge.

During the Revolution, most guns in use were of British origin. Others were made by local gunsmiths, or were French guns that had been taken as prizes in the French and Indian War of 1754–1760. Locating weapons made in America before the Revolution is rather fruitless, since most people who own them will not sell them.

Rapid-fire mechanisms popular during the Civil War have also grown in value. The North entered the war with an arsenal of about 9,000 rifles, 7,000 of which were the old flintlocks, which had long been out of favor due to the advent of the percussion cap. By the time the war ended, the men had been equipped with all sorts of rifles and handguns, and the first brass cartridges had completely outdated all of the previous firing mechanisms. Samuel Colt of Connecticut perfected the five shot pistol as early as 1834, but the government did not give him the expected orders for these, and their production was low. Colt's principal customers were the wealthy since his guns were expensive. The war changed this, and the many Colt models made at that time are very desirable today. Colt is best known for his handguns, but he made rifles as well. The multi-shot Henrys and Spencers along with the Remington handguns are very good items. Winchesters were not made until 1866, when Oliver Winchester, who until this time had been a textile manufacturer, bought the patents and rights to both the Henry and Spencer rifles—the latter, just to remove the company from competition. The model 1873 Winchester was the first rifle to use a center fire cartridge and also had a chamber for

Miscellaneous group of Colt revolvers, nineteenth century. Butterfield & Butterfield, San Francisco.

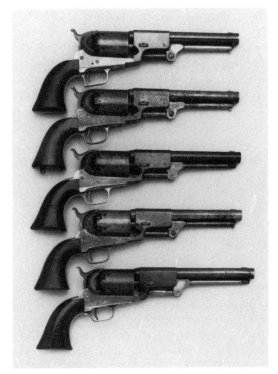

Selection of Colt Dragoon revolvers, mid–nineteenth century. Butterfield & Butterfield, San Francisco.

twelve .44-caliber bullets. This is the weapon credited with helping win the West. The first rifle designed to shoot the new smokeless powder was the model 1894 Winchester in a 30-30 caliber. This is still one of the most popular hunting weapons and is available at sporting goods stores with only minor modifications of the original patent.

Various mechanisms were tried to give greater safety and rapidity of fire before Colt brought out his famous multi-shot guns. Double-barrel rifles came into use, often with one barrel smooth for bird hunting and the other rifled for long-range slugs. Though the over-and-under barrels were known in Germany at the time, few of these were made in America. The swivel breach weapon was not commonly made, although it was popular on the frontier.

Gunsmiths in Pennsylvania and elsewhere are still making long rifles, so you must check your prospective purchases carefully to make sure you are not buying one of these. With the growing popularity of black powder shoots, some companies have begun reproducing all types of muzzle-loaders and these are available for sale everywhere. The originals will always be prized for their beauty, workmanship, and

age, so be sure this is what you buy when you invest.

Kentucky Rifles

The first truly important American native rifle was the Kentucky rifle. About 2,000 Kentuckians fought with Andrew Jackson at New Orleans during the War of 1812, giving their name to the Kentucky rifle. However, the rifles probably did not come from Kentucky, but rather from Pennsylvania, though others in this style were made in Ohio, Indiana, and even Tennessee. Very few, if any, had been made in Kentucky when they first saw service in the Revolutionary War. Legend grew around the rifles after the Battle of Saratoga. General Washington assigned southern sharpshooters equipped with these long rifles to every regiment because he had seen their effectiveness many times during the French and Indian War. At Saratoga, British General Fraser was at the head of his troops just before a decisive attack on the Americans. A sharpshooter in the Continental Army was called on to fire on him at a distance of more than 300 yards—a distance well out of range for most of the weapons then in use. He fired once, killing an aide next to the general. Another aide remarked, "It is evident you are marked out for particular aim; would it not be prudent for you to retire from this duty?" To which Fraser replied, "My duty forbids me to fly from danger." He was killed a moment later by the sharpshooter's next bullet, fired from a Kentucky rifle. This helped to disorganize the British, and they lost the day.

Rifle buffs are torn between called them Kentucky rifles or Pennsylvania rifles—although most were made in Pennsylvania, they found their fame in the hands of southerners. All of the experts agree that the weapon is uniquely American and represents the final stage in the development of the muzzle-loader. It evolved from two basic types—the graceful fowling pieces developed by the English and French, and the rifled "Jaeger," which was first developed in central Europe. Many of these rifles were made by blacksmiths in Pennsylvania, notably in the Lancaster area, between 1760 and 1860. They embellished their rifles with polished brass patchbox covers, butt plates, and decorative devices. This work spread into other regions; similar rifles were made as far north as New England and as far south as the Carolinas.

Kentucky rifles fall into three categories: those made before the Revolution, those made during the war, and those made in the nineteenth century before the

Group of "Pennsylvania" flintlock rifles, late eighteenth and early nineteenth century. Pennsylvania Farm Museum.

percussion cap became common and replaced the earlier flintlock mechanism. Some rifles made in the early nineteenth century were decorated with silver, giving rise to the speculation that these were more important as presentation pieces than as actual hunting weapons. The most popular wood for the butt and stock was tiger maple, whose striping gave beautiful contrast to the iron, brass, or silver. It is said that some wood was striped by wrapping it with a waxed string, and then setting fire to the string and burning the pattern into the wood.

Gutta-Percha

There is a growing interest in early photography; witness the rise in prices for old tintype, ambrotypes, and daguerreotypes. What some may not realize is that the

bidding might be more on the case which houses the picture than on the picture itself. Deeply molded cases in unusual designs and made of gutta-percha are the

Collecting tintypes is fun. They are a lesson in history and can be made into decorative wall hangings. Most were housed individually in a folding case. The best are those well molded of gutta-percha, made from gum rubber, in the mid—nineteenth century.

most desired. Some people remove the photos and put the cases to a variety of other uses, relining them as cigarette cases or jewelry cases, for example.

Gutta-percha is a rubber-like product that was unknown to science until 1735. That year, a Frenchman traveling the Amazon noted bottles, boots, and waterproof cloth made by the natives from this strange substance, which was the gum of what we now call the rubber tree. Later, more was found in the East Indies and South America. In 1770 this hardened gum was found to erase pencil marks. In 1823, in Scotland, a Mr. Mackintosh dissolved the gum in oil of turpentine, alcohol, and coal tar naphtha. He found it could be formed into a rubbery state or hardened with added adhesives. Soon it was being used as a waterproof varnish, a coating for fabrics and sails, the packing of valves in steam engines, and also as a marine cement to tighten masts to the decks of ships. A patent was issued to make railroad rails from the product. Soon, there were inkstands, pens, bottles, pails, buttons, jewelry, canes, cups, toys, and cases of all sorts.

It seems to have been our first effective plastic compound, and it is only natural that it was used to protect the valuable photographs of the day. Collect these gutta-percha cases, as the supply is dwindling. You can tell them from the cloth and leather that were in abundance as well. Look for interesting designs with birds and flowers.

Jade

Jadeite and nephrite are two minerals to which the name jade is given. The former ranges from almost white to a dark green and the latter from black to a red/grey. It is mined in a rather primitive manner: fires are built on the open beds of rock at night and, when they are put out, the cold air contracts the rock quickly, causing it to split into many pieces. The internal fibers of jade are so closely knit that it is difficult to carve and work, which heightens the value of the art pieces made from it.

The first jade carving dates back to about 1000 B.C., when religious objects were made. Dating it from that time takes the work of a scholar as it is not until after the sixteenth century that work can be identified more easily. One must study the designs in the carving and the patina of stone as clues. In the seventeenth century, foot-operated machinery was used to turn some of it; the marks of such work are evident to those who know how to identify this.

The best of the work seems to have been done between the middle of the fourteenth and eighteenth centuries. The artisans carved jade into dragons, flowers, other foliage, and animals, and helped set the stage for the designs popularly used in Europe in later years in ceramics and silver. In the latter part of the seventeenth century, Oriental craftsmen reached their pinnacle in carvings of animals, birds, and

the like. Mythical animals and birds were particularly popular, due in part to the varied colored stone from which they were made. One emperor had a goldfish bowl about two feet in diameter, carved from a single piece of clear jade, with the outer surface carved with many forms of marine life.

There is little evidence that any jade was made into useful vessels for food or serving. Rather, it was used for art objects and other decorative devices that might be an aid to scholars, emperors, and religious leaders. Jade chimes have been found, carved to perfection to ring with a bold tone when struck.

Jade has been used extensively in jewelry. Artisans found that it was a perfect bed into which they could set precious stones to harmonize with the colors. Perhaps beads were the first form of jade jewelry made in ancient times, with intricately carved necklaces, brooches, and pins following. Pure, old, original jade may be more valuable today than the gems set in it, as early gemstones were often poorly cut and lack the brilliance of those done today. Jewelry inlaid with gold foil for dramatic highlights is quite rare.

Unfortunately, the general public is not well informed on how to tell quality and age in a jade piece. Buyers in Mexico are besieged by street urchins to purchase the green stone which they represent as jade, but is really just a green stone without much value. At the pyramids to the sun and the moon, some years ago, I purchased small carved figures (most likely done by machine) for a dollar apiece. They were touted as hand-carved jade, but at that price, as they say, if it looks too good to be true, it is not hand-carved. California jade has turned up in Indochina for sale to the tourists. The pieces end up in remote villages, where unsuspecting buyers part with too much money for an inferior product. Real jade does not come from China; it is mined in Indochina, notably, Burma. Much of it is carved in China.

Jewelry

If you want to collect jewelry, you must first learn to identify the metals and gems. This is not as difficult as it sounds, as there are really very few with which you must become familiar. Beyond that, you must appraise a piece in light of its design and condition. Age enhances a piece, but it must be of quality to begin with. Most of the better nineteenth-century jewelry you might find today came from overseas, while quality costume jewelry was made in great quantities in America, particularly in the Attleboro and Fall River areas in Massachusetts. Good costume jewelry is in great demand and relatively inexpensive. The design of costume jewelry is more important than its material content. Earrings, brooches, lockets, and chains are always good sellers. Bar pins and bracelets are plentiful and less in demand, so prices are lower.

Jewelry designs were influenced by the prevailing styles in the decorative arts. The Georgian designs of the eighteenth century were classic and those of the Victorian period of the nineteenth century were rococo with floral inspiration. The designs of the Edwardian era that followed were bold and austere. The Art Nouveau period was reflected in light and airy creations and those of Art Deco are garish by comparison.

Metals

Jewelry is made up of minerals and metals. The more valuable these are, the higher the cost of the jewelry. Gold is rated in carats by weight (1 carat = 200 milligrams). Pure gold is rated at 24 carats (24K). A 14K gold piece or plating is made of 14 parts of gold and 10 parts of alloy. Most good gold jewelry is made with gold of at least 14K. In the better grade 18K is used, but pure 24K gold is rarely used because it is too soft. The carat weight is required to be stamped on all gold items of 10K and above. The term "gold-filled" or "gold-plated" is used to designate a base metal that is covered with a layer of gold of the grade indicated by its carat weight stamp. There is some electroplating in gold, but the thickness is minute and can even be measured in millionths of an inch. Gold wash, which is a method of dipping of

Jewelry of the Victorian period is quite fancy. This magnificant parure and earring set is delicately enameled.

Pinchbeck

Back in the eighteenth century, Christopher Pinchbeck invented a metal that bears his name. It is a gold substitute so good that royalty had pieces made from it. Some of the crown jewels we see today may be imbedded in this phony metal. Age has given it great patina. Historians tell us that royalty often sold real gems and jewelry to raise money and would have pieces made to resemble them until the originals might be reclaimed.

Here is how he made it: 100 pure parts of copper by weight are melted in a crucible; then 6 parts of magnesia, 3.6 parts of sal ammoniac, 1.8 parts of quicklime, and 9 parts of tartar are added separately and gradually in the form of a powder. The whole is then stirred about half an hour, then 17 parts of zinc or tin in small grains are thrown in and thoroughly mixed. The crucible is not covered and the mixture kept melted for half an hour longer, when it is skimmed and poured out.

Any imitiation of gold can be detected by weight. It will dissolve in nitric acid whereas real gold will not.

I do not know whether eighteenth-century pinchbeck is a good investment; we see little in this country. I would expect the jewelry or other item made from it would have value as a functional item of great age and unusual material.

---

another metal to brighten it with a gold finish, may be even thinner.

Silver plate has a greater thickness than gold plate. Silver plate made before World War II is marked accordingly with the plating designations. Other important metals used in jewelry are platinum, palladium, iridium, ruthenium, and rhodium. Although it is a member of this family, osmium is not used in jewelry. These metals are alloyed with others to make expensive pieces, and they are often used in plating to give an expensive finish to lesser metals.

Stones

The diamond is the hardest and brightest of any of the gems. Diamonds are graded, flawless (or perfect); very, very slightly imperfect—VVS; very slightly imperfect—VS; slightly imperfect—SI; and imperfect—I. Diamonds come in tints of yellow or blue. A clear stone is most desired, although some of bluish tint are quite rare and good. Diamond weights are measured in carats and points. A carat contains 100 points.

Early diamonds were cut in as few as 24 facets, which accounts for their lack of brilliance when they are compared with modern diamonds cut in 58 facets. Some people buy old diamonds, have them recut to today's standards and feel that they have improved them. The present-day, man-made diamond was created for industry alone, but are used extensively for jewelry.

Emeralds and rubies are next in line in importance as gems. Genuine emerald is one of the gemstones most easily identified by its natural occlusions. A genuine emerald totally without occlusions is practically impossible to acquire. Following behind these are the semiprecious stones such as aquamarine, jade, garnet, lapis lazuli, opal, pearl, topaz, zircon, and turquoise. Good imitations of all of these are made, so you must do business with reliable people, or else learn the game. This field is full of imitations, so be careful.

Amber has been and is popular, but you must be sure you are buying the real thing. Amber is petrified pitch which has lain for millions of years at the bottom of the sea, notably the Finnish gulf, and it often contains bits of insects, bark, and other impurities. Most buyers feel that this enhances its value, and they look for deeper-toned pieces filled with the relics of a long gone age. Amber comes in shades all the way from white to black, but the most popular color is a rich amber brown; followed by the opaque amber; then the cloudy buttercup yellow; and finally the golden transparent yellow. Amber shares the distinction of being a gem of vegetable origin with the diamond alone. It was used in the earliest known jewelry, and the ancients thought it had curative powers because you can generate electricity on its surface by rubbing it rapidly. Some of the world's best rosaries are made of amber and collectors vie to locate these, some of which date all the way back to the fifteenth century.

Fine amber jewelry is obtainable today in Eastern Europe at a fraction of its cost in the west and most tourists avail themselves of some of it. The Beriovska stores, which are maintained for the sale of such items to tourists in exchange for foreign currency,

are the best places in which to buy. Amber has been copied in glass, but you can tell the imitations quite quickly, as the true amber is warm to the touch. If you are still in doubt, do what the dealers do—heat the end of a needle or pin, and apply it to a relatively hidden surface, such as the inside of a hole where a bead is strung. If the piece is amber, smoke and the odor of pine will rise from it.

Be sure that you ask for "natural amber" and that you are not sold "real amber." Natural amber is that which is found in its natural state and cut into stones from which jewelry is made. The chips from such cutting and carving, along with other bits and pieces not big enough to be used in fine jewelry, are melted down and poured into molds to form amber stones. This material is called real amber; it is not a synthetic substitute, but the melting process deprives it of its natural luster and shine and destroys the depth and brilliance one can expect from the natural stones.

Diamond and emerald necklace with diamond "idol's eye" pendant.

Strass

A paste known as strass was invented in the eighteenth century. It can be turned into gems that rival the finest diamonds in brilliance. Much phony jewelry has been turned out in strass, and you have to be an expert to detect it today.

Collecting Guidelines

When buying what most call costume jewelry, be on the lookout for certain gemstones that have risen in value. For years, boxes of gaudy pieces have been liquidated at auctions with little thought to whether there were precious gems or metals in them.

A new market has been created in semiprecious stones by dealers in South America, notably Rio de Janeiro.

While in the United States little attention has been given to aquamarine, in South America some jewelers have convinced buyers they should part with up to $1,000 per carat for a three-carat stone or better. Most people cannot identify real amethyst and will pay very little for it. Yet I have seen pendants of this stone, surrounded by 14K gold and a few diamond chips, selling for between $2,000 and $3,000.

Citrine is another little-known gemstone, yet it goes for as much as $500 a carat. Rubellite, which is really red tourmaline, is a stone most people cannot identify, yet I saw one pendant in a gold frame that sold for $2,500.

Topaz, tourmaline, garnet, and other semiprecious stones have become very popular in Brazil, and one can only guess when the hysteria for these stones will hit here, but it must be coming if Americans are willing to spend these prices now. We have visited the shops of H. Stern, Roditi,

Maximino, Jimmy's and many others in Rio quite a few times over the past ten years and have anticipated this trend. Rio is the center of this activity, although gemstones are featured all through Brazil.

Here are some rules that may help. Aquamarine is the most popular in Brazil. It shades from a light bluish green to deep blue, which is the rarest. The deeper the blue, the better.

When buying diamonds, look for the four C's: cutting, clarity, color, and carat weight. It must be crystal clear and absent of any color in the body. It must be free of interior and exterior blemishes.

Rubellite runs from pink to dark red—the rarest stones look like rubies. Most have feathers or silky inclusions. Perfectly clear stones are extremely rare.

This is true also of the emerald. Rare is the emerald without an occlusion. I have examined $3\frac{1}{2}$-carat stones in Cartagena, Columbia, the center for them, and noted occlusions, which really are a guarantee that the piece is not glass. Some emeralds are worth more than diamonds. Grass green is the best color—and a true gem will not change color under a bright light.

Tourmaline stones come in many colors and shades, or even a mixture. Many are mistaken for emeralds, so beware.

Topaz ranges from fine golden to brown in color. Some are oxblood in color, yet some are cognac shade. There is a classification of precious topaz to separate this stone from the less expensive citrine. Precious topaz is orange/pink/brown in color and is rare, even in Brazil. Those who wore it years ago felt it would cure insanity and insomnia and that it averted sudden death.

Amethyst was known to the ancient Egyptians and in other Mediterranean countries. Buyers feel the best comes from Brazil. It can have a violet hue in several shades. The ancients wore the stone to protect themselves from intoxication. The rich royal purple is the most desired color.

In opals, look for the milk white, fiery stone. Some are tinted with colors; others are called black opals because of their dark

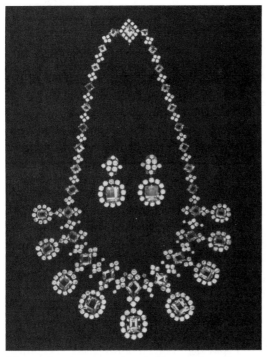

Diamond and aquamarine necklace and earring set, Van Cleef and Arpels. William Doyle Galleries, Inc., New York.

Native American Jewelry

A few years ago, there was a flush of interest in Native American jewelry, but it has worn off somewhat. Buyers have become disillusioned because of imitations and lack of knowledge as to what they are buying.

According to the Arts and Crafts Association (an organization formed in 1974 to promote the public image and ethics of the Native American arts and crafts industry) in Gallup, New Mexico, questionable business firms are producing pieces with imitation, treated, or plasticized turquoise and attempting to pass them off as genuine. They caution buyers to beware of bargain sales, where such jewelry is offered at low prices. Sometimes sellers in shops or at auctions have been found to mix genuine pieces with the bogus. Also of concern is the theft of good jewelry, which has occurred throughout the country, with such items being disposed of at auctions and in shops. Dealers and auctioneers have begun exchanging bulletins to warn of such losses. New Mexico alone generates about $250 million in the Native American crafts business each year, so you can see why the Native Americans and the state are very concerned.

Years ago at a "ghost town" in Colorado, I saw Native Americans hammering out jewelry. I then went into the gift shop next door and purchased a bracelet with turquoise.

Back east, a friend showed me the mark of an Attleboro, Massachusetts, maker under the rim. Watch out.

If you are planning to buy such jewelry, make sure you receive a valid bill of sale guaranteeing what you buy. The Indian Arts and Crafts council in Washington has published a Source Directory, which lists more than 150 legitimate makers. For a free copy, write to the Council at Room 4004, U.S. Department of the Interior, Washington, D.C., 20240.

Sterling and turquoise bear claw necklace, Arizona, 1970s. An excellent example of Native American work.

color. Brazilian opals are rich in reds and yellows, giving them a fine, fiery look.

Ruby is one of the four precious gemstones, emerald, diamond, and sapphire being the other three. The name "ruby" comes from the latin word "ruber," which means red. The stone that resembles the blood of a pigeon (an orange-yellow) is most desired. The prized star rubies reveal a star after cutting. Rubies were said to preserve the body and health of the wearer and to remove evil thoughts. The name "sapphire" is derived from the Greek word meaning blue, although sapphires are known to come in blue, violet, yellow, or green shades. A star may appear after cutting, as with the ruby. Sapphire is known as the gemstone of the soul.

Garnet is found in several colors, though most regard it a cousin to the ruby in color. Garnet in a violet shade is called rhodolite. The stones will change color under light, which makes them attractive, but they are not yet really expensive.

Blue topaz is a stone commanding some attention. It looks so much like aquamarine that few can tell the difference. It is a good substitute at much less cost.

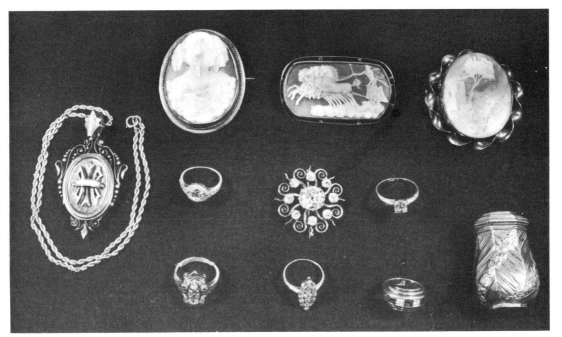

Carved cameos made from abalone shell. Also shown are gold and silver rings and trinkets which are affordable, yet made with good metals and minerals.

Kitchen Utensils

Old kitchen utensils fascinate just about everyone. Some people seek them out more to use than to look at. Favorites are those with wooden handles. Modern homemakers see charm in these utensils and also marvel at how well the wood insulates the handles.

Wooden handles appeared before the turn of the century, but not many from that era have survived, and they are not as colorful as those from after World War II. The most popular color for wooden handles seems to be green, although blue and white are not far behind.

Utensils made completely of wood, such as spoons, paddles, spatulas, hand measures, butter paddles, and even salad forks and spoons, have been used for hundreds of years. Wrought-iron implements were still in vogue at the turn of the century. I recall kitchens in the 1930s still using nothing but iron cooking utensils. They never seemed to wear out, and during the

Depression no one felt the need to throw them away. But eventually, gaily colored wooden handled spoons, pancake turners, egg beaters, whisks, and food choppers did replace much of the iron and tin.

On most old utensils the metal is nickel-plated, which gives good durability. Once this nickel wears, the utensils will rust, so check pieces carefully.

Treenware

Until the seventeenth century, most dishware and utensils used by the common people were made of wood or clay. Some people collect wooden spoons from that era. Carved of hardwoods, they had a life span of but a few years—hence the rarity today of really old examples. The English coined the word "treenware" to encompass items made from wood. Hardwoods such as hickory, oak, and ash were favored. Walnut was in general use on the continent as it

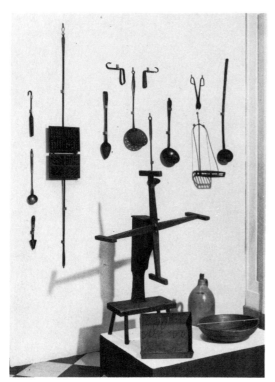

Hanging on the wall are iron kitchen utensils, many still usable today. Below the yarn winder is a tin pigeon roaster, which was placed in front of an open fire.

Treenware, collection of Mary Earle Gould. Wooden dishes, spoons, mortar and pestles, breadboards, and other useful kitchen items. Much of this was given to Hancock Shaker Village upon her death, by terms of her will. Photo by Mary Earle Gould.

was plentiful there, especially in France and Italy.

In this country, early settlers used pine because it was soft and easy to carve with primitive tools, but one will find examples in maple, birch, oak, hickory, and ash as well. Collectors seek out the burl bowls made from highly grained woods, often coming from the area where branches join the trunk or from trunks. The stress created in these sections from heavy wind and storms is what ruptures the wood and leaves it with lines of wear where the tree has healed itself.

Many cooks today like to use wood. Candy makers use wooden spoons as the mixtures are less inclined to stick to wood, and wooden spoons are easy to clean. Wooden spatulas are used on pans with nonstick surfaces because they will not scratch. The Russians are known for lacquering spoons; I have used such utensils to eat soup on visits there.

One must realize that wood is still used extensively in kitchenware, so there are many reproductions out there. If you are interested in collecting only the old, you have your work cut out for you. Wood wears and ages quickly when used to stir anything that contains fats or grease. Candy mixtures are very hot, so wooden spoons will acquire a patina quickly in such a mixture. Look for wear and good patina.

Lamps and Lighting

Fuel-Burning

A great deal of the world is still lighted by oil, which means that many of the lighting devices we consider antique are still in use in various lands. Fats and oils of all kinds were common fuel for early American lamps, and many homes were lighted with them well into the nineteenth century. Lard was a popular fuel at the end of the eighteenth century, but this gave way to whale oil early in the nineteenth century. Whale oil was made by rendering the blubber from a sperm whale. In the mid-1830s a new fuel, camphene, was introduced and widely accepted because it was cleaner burning and gave off less odor and smoke than the whale oil. Camphene was made of about one part turpentine to seven parts alcohol. Lemon, balsam, and juniper were among the other ingredients introduced to camphene fluid to give it a better scent and burning quality. Unfortunately, camphene was quite volatile and many fires were started by careless people who put it into lamps other than those designed for it. Camphene lamps look almost identical to whale oil lamps, but you can tell them apart by the length of their wick spouts. Camphene lamp spouts are longer in order to keep the flame farther away from the fuel supply.

The Argand lamp was invented in Switzerland in 1783 and was the first radical change in lighting since the beginning of time. Until then, fats and oils were burned in the open, either in cruzie or Betty lamps or hardened into candle form. The new principle allowed fats to be burned through a wick, using a draft of air introduced beneath the wick and a glass chimney to draw the air upward. All oil lamps operate on this principle to this day. However, it was not until the first oil well was drilled at Titusville, Pennsylvania, by Colonel Edwin Drake, beginning the petroleum industry, that petroleum oil lamps began to dominate lighting. Coal oil (a residue from diggings at mines) had been used before that time, but it did not have much impact as production was limited.

The birth of kerosene as a fuel during the growing industrial age brought with it a tremendous surge toward making lighting devices, notably the glass oil lamp. These lamps could be pressed out cheaply and soon practically every home had one or more. The multitude of such lamps made

These whale oil lamps can be described identically: pressed clear glass, dome top, heart design, hexagonal bulbous knop, and hexagonal base. Yet there is a difference in size. (Made at the Boston and Sandwich Glass Company.) When matching anything that comes in pairs, put them together to make sure they are identical.

in glass as well as in metal provides enough information to make another book. However, here are some tips that can be useful. Any color glass is important, as well as the type of decoration, especially that of hand-painted shades. Some people collect lamps by pattern. The popular "Gone with the Wind Lamp" which made its appearance in that movie, was actually not around at the time of the Civil War. This is the double-globed type, usually with painted decoration on the upper and lower sections. The upper globe has quite often been broken and replaced with a reproduction. If this is well done it is acceptable, but if the replacement is obvious, it harms the value. Many lamps were made with bases of metals of all kinds and even of marble and alabaster, either in simple turned style or else fancied up with figurines. These must be judged on their quality and appeal.

Miniature kerosene oil lamps, nineteenth century. Most are less than 9" high and were used as hall or night lights.

The astral lamp was designed to carry fuel from a font to the burner via a tube, which made an overhanging light possible. A special fuel, called astral oil, was created for this lamp. Many of the old astral lamps are high on the desirable list since they were made with cut glass shades and prisms for elegant homes.

The advent of gas and electricity for lighting at the end of the nineteenth century caused the slow demise of oil lamps as lighting devices in America, but it was not until after the implementation of the rural electrification program in the 1920s and 1930s that they made a rapid disappearance. Most country people keep a supply of oil lamps in case of power failures, and oil lamps keep turning up at auctions when old estates are liquidated.

The hand lantern was a necessary device, whether it burned oil or used a candle. The early pierced tin lanterns date back to before the Revolution. At the turn of the century these gave way to lanterns faced with glass as the glass industry grew to meet the demand. The Dietz Company is still very much in the lantern business, and advertises that it has a plant in Hong Kong which turns out over a million units a year—mostly for the underdeveloped na-

Various types of oil railroad lanterns, used into the twentieth century.

Pairpoint lamps made in New Bedford, Massachusetts, early twentieth century. Clockwise from left: *dragonfly, puffy floral, puffy floral with bronze base, New Bedford Harbor lamp with dolphin base.*

tions. More lanterns are being made today than at any other time in history, so you must never regard the oil lantern as a disappearing item. However, some of the old ones make good collectibles, especially those made for the railroads. Some utilize brass, and these are the best. You can see a great collection of lanterns of all generations at the Canal Museum in Syracuse, New York.

Old coach lanterns and automobile lights are rising in value. The early ones burned carbide gas which is given off when calcium carbide is moistened with water.

Aladdin Lamps

Aladdin is one of the great names in lamps of the early part of this century. Practically every farm home had one or more. Now they are being sold at auctions and by dealers as collectible antiques. A club called the Aladdin Knights of the Mystic Lamp has been organized.

Victor Samuel Johnson formed the Mantle Lamp Company of America in Chicago in 1908. He was born in Minden, Nebraska, in 1882 and died in 1943. In 1949, it became the Aladdin Industries and today is headquartered in Nashville, Tennessee.

The company gained fame at the Panama-Pacific International Exposition in San Francisco in 1915 by being awarded a gold model for its Number 6 lamp. The company advertised it made the best kerosene lamp in the world and offered $1,000 for any lamp that could equal it. The offer was never collected.

Sixteen models of Aladdin lamps were made from 1909 to 1968. They can be found in combinations of bright nickel, satin brass, Old English brass, and glass. Most are identified easily by the special $12\frac{1}{2}$-inch-tall chimney designed for this company alone. The extra height created better combustion. In an Aladdin kerosene mantle lamp, the kerosene is burned primarily not to produce light, but rather to produce heat. The heat of the nonluminous blue flame causes the nonburning mantle to incandesce and emit its pure white light.

Aladdin table electric lamps are a new area of collecting interest. Some of these have soared in price. In the bibliography you'll find a book by J. W. Courter in which you can see pictures and obtain information on what you should seek.

Aladdin oil lamps made c. 1940. Left, *alacite*; right, *clear. J.W. Courter.*

Art Deco lamp in aluminum and brass, Pierro and Pierette, made by Bally in France, c. 1920s.

Kerosene was used in some as late as World War I, and many have turned up from government warehouses still dressed in their khaki color. These must be judged on interest and condition. As is the case with many types of collectibles, pairs of lanterns are more desired than singles.

Electric

The most desirable of the electric lights are those which are popularly called "Tiffany type" lamps (see Chapter Two for more information on Tiffany). These feature shades of iridescent or colored glass set in either leaded or bronze framing. Those made by Tiffany are commanding huge prices. The workmanship in the coloring, design, and iridescence of his lamps is unmatched. Some of the lesser types are referred to as oyster shell shaded lamps and are quite Gothic in their look. The coloring and design in the glass is most important in judging their values.

Lantern Slides

Lantern slides are a form of reverse painting on glass. They were the first type of projected picture, and there is evidence that primitive versions of such devices were made as early as the seventeenth century. An oil light inside a tin housing amplified the picture through a ground lens in the manner of picture projection today. The Magic Lanterns, as they were called, were quite popular in the last century, and children used them extensively right into the 1920s. Many of the best slides were made overseas, and one can identify them by the color of tape used to bind the glass edge. Red, blue, and gilded borders were often used in Germany, while the French favored a plaid pattern tape. Yellow was also used by the Austrians and Germans.

Not all glass slides were used by children. Lecturers and teachers—for example, in the field of medicine—used them as well.

Noted American artists such as Joseph Boggs Beal are known to have painted such slides. The slides were usually made in four- to sixteen-inch lengths, but some were round, with different scenes coming into focus as they were rotated.

The best slides to collect are hand-painted. Once the chromolithography process was perfected in the 1870s, it became possible for scenes to be printed on glass. Though these are still collectible, the handwork made in the last century is preferred.

Marbles and Agates

A popular sport years ago was "pitching marbles." Every boy and many girls carried a pocketful to school for competitions which were held at recess time. A large glass agate or clay marble was placed next to the school wall and the first competitor pitched marbles to score a hit. The owner of the large agate would then claim all the marbles thrown; then it was his turn to hit the competitor's target marble. This continued until one or the other was cleaned out of marbles, or until the bell rang. These were exciting games and many stood by to cheer on their favorites.

The clay marbles were painted in different colors. The glass agates, or aggies as they were called, were colored with all shades of the rainbow and are quite pretty. Clay marbles came in a smaller size, in various shades depending on the glass. Aggies were larger and reflected the activity in colored glass making at the time. All were popular right up until World War II.

In collecting, condition and color are

most important. Throwing them at other marbles resulted in chips and cracks. Most were made by machine, but some of the glass marbles were made of handblown glass cut from a round cylinder, leaving what some call the pontil mark. Others were cut from stone, such as quartz, and some are made of semiprecious materials such as green malachite. In foreign countries, I have seen them in what appears to be agate, lapis, jadeite, and marble. Years ago, in many countries, such stones were so common that people didn't realize these marbles would be considered semiprecious some day. Perhaps some of the earliest marbles really were made of marble and agate.

Marbles can be traced back to the time of the early Egyptians as they have been found in ruins. The clay marbles are often attributed to the potteries in Bennington, Vermont, as it is known some were made there. Actually, most were made in Ohio. Glass agates were also made in the Midwest. Some marbles feature swirl patterns as well as various colors like clambroth, vaseline, and cobalt. Some, referred to as sulphides, feature small ceramic figures inside. The Lutz design, named after Nicholas Lutz, who worked at Sandwich, Massachusetts, is much in demand. He is known for his threaded glass, which was made overseas as well.

Perhaps most of the glass agates worthy of collecting were made in Europe. Many were made in Germany and Italy at the turn of the century. Rarities are the onionskin variety, which features a clear coating over a body that resembles an onion in color and texture, as well as the latticinio, which resembles the glass of this type, rather lacy in its look, made at Murano, Italy.

The late Jabe Tartar, whose passing late in 1991 was a great loss to the antiques community, was an antiques columnist for the the *Akron Beacon Journal*. He wrote about Akro Agate, saying that many people felt the first aggies were made in Akron in 1911. However, he related that Bud Appleton, in his book *Akro Agate Glass*, said that the production of aggies began in Navarre, Ohio, in 1890. The first factory failed in 1897, and many workers moved to Steubenville, Ohio. In 1901, a man named M. F. Christensen, who had been with the Navarre firm, improved the method of making marbles by dropping a blob of molten glass between two slowly revolving cast iron sheets. The gradually cooling glass formed a perfect sphere, reducing the cost of production and making it competitive with the foreign market. Marbles comprised the major output until 1911, when the company turned its attention to producing bowls, vases, lamps, and planters in simulated stained glass.

The astute collector must know how to grade them as to condition, which affects value. If one is chipped, polishing it can destroy the value. It is best to leave all in original condition and buy and sell them accordingly.

Musical Instruments

There is some interest in old musical instruments, but collectors are few and far between. Prices are not high, so you must regard these more as curiosity pieces than as antiques. Brass instruments have little value, and the woodwinds are mere curiosity items. Zithers and other stringed instruments have had a brief revival due to the current trends in music, but most are still low in value.

Pianos

Rarely is the price of a piano ever listed in an auction report. There is little mention of this instrument in books on antiques and collecting. Once I asked a metropolitan dealer about this, and he remarked that nobody collects pianos because they take up too much room. There are a couple of museums that display them, but individual collectors must be rare.

The history of the piano, or pianoforte, as it was once called, is sketchy. The harpsichord with keys that activate hammers against strings seems to have been made as far back as the seventeenth century. Out of this instrument the spinet evolved, and, early in the last century, the piano. The rectangular design of the 1840s gave way late in the century to uprights and the triangular grands. The latter are still bought and sold for use in the home.

The rectangulars are interesting. They had sixty-six keys, rather than the 88 we enjoy today. They are massive and quite heavy. Back in the 1950s, when they appeared at house auctions, most sold for between $5 and $10. They were bought by cabinetmakers who dismantled them for the boards. The tops were made of two long single boards, well aged and most often of mahogany or walnut or even rosewood. The latter is a generic name for more than thirty kinds of oriental tree. The frames were tossed away. Today, unless they are very well painted or decorated—I have seen them in gilt and semiprecious stones—they still do not command much.

Violins

Old violins keep turning up at auctions and buyers often get excited: through the cutouts on top, they see a label that reads, "A. Stradivarius, Anno 1730," with perhaps a variation on the date. They visualize a trip around the world after reselling the violin, until the truth comes home after appraisal. These violins are no more than reproductions made in the Black Forest in Germany or even in Switzerland late in the nineteenth century or early in the twentieth. Violins were quite popular then and the fine woodworkers in those countries took advantage of this, modeling their

Violins, made in the style of, left to right, *Nicolo Amati, Guiseppe Antonin Guarnerius, and Antonio Stradivarius. All worked in the late seventeenth and early eighteenth century. You will find violins of this type with paper labels inside, which indicate the maker's design. These are reproductions made late in the nineteenth or early twentieth centuries in Europe. Many were sold by Sears Roebuck.*

products after those of famous makers. You can find the names of Stradivarius, Nicolo Amati, or Guiseppe Antonio Guarnerius as they were often copied.

Antonio Stradivarius was born in 1644, and by the time of his death in 1737 is known to have made about 1100 violins. Violin purchasers hope to gain ownership of one of the 500 or so that have never turned up or been accounted for. It is unlikely that such fine instruments would have been destroyed willfully, so there is always the chance that an original will turn up. Most Strads sell well into the five-figure price range, so you can understand the excitement someone feels when he thinks he has discovered one. The ones with paper labels are reproductions, so curb your enthusiasm.

If your violin happens to be in a wooden case that resembles a coffin, it was probably made by a coffin maker near Charleston, New Hampshire, who must have gotten rich on this product. The cases are just about indestructible and saved many a violin from unfortunate death.

Guarnerius was born in Italy in 1683 and died in 1745. His violins rank with the Strads. The only other maker whose work approaches theirs is Amati, who was a teacher to Stradivarius. You should also look for cellos made by Carlo Berkonzi of Italy, who worked early in the eighteenth century. Many of his instruments are missing.

The average instrument turning up at auctions is worth little, and a hundred dollars is a lot to pay. Most sell in the $5 to $35 price range, which is enough. Actually, many people feel that these old violins are much better than the new ones, so if your child is going to learn this instrument, one of the Black Forest models might be the best investment. At least it will be cheaper than a new one.

Painted Eggs

Colored eggs are a tradition associated with Easter inspired by the decorated eggs that have been made for centuries in countries such as Ukraine, Poland, Czechoslovakia, and Lithuania. The Poles and Ukrainians decorate eggs with plain colors or simple designs; these are called "Kransanki." The "Pysanki" are the ones most sought-after, for they are exceptionally beautiful in design, made in a most distinctive manner with unusual ornamentation. Each is a masterpiece of skill and patience. First, the contents of white eggs is blown out. Next, melted beeswax is applied with a stylus to the eggs. Then the eggs are dipped in successive baths of dye. After each dipping, wax is painted over the area where the preceding color is to remain. Gradually, the whole complex of lines, colors, and geometric splendor emerges. No two Pysanki are alike. Although the same symbols may be reused, each egg is designed with originality. The sun stands for good fortune, the hen or rooster for fulfillment of wishes, the stag or deer for good health, and flowers for love and charity. Intersecting ribbons, dots, checkerboards, and rhombic designs are employed by the egg artists. In the old countries, the Pysanki as well as all eggs used at

People have been painting eggs for centuries. Though fragile, many early examples have survived. Quality, present-day work should be collected. This one is late nineteenth century, resting atop a brass stand.

Easter are blessed by a priest before they are given to recipients. Many are kept as heirlooms.

It takes about six or seven hours to decorate an egg properly. There are several egg-decorating clubs in this country whose members hold exhibitions of their work. These clubs are found in southern New York State, parts of Pennsylvania, and in the northern Midwest, where many Polish and Ukranian people settled.

Paper Ephemera

Ephemera is a word used to describe collectible items on paper. It encompasses postcards, trade cards, greeting cards, rewards of merit, menus, programs, and just about everything else published or written on paper or cardboard. There are many categories in which you may collect and the items in each seem endless.

For instance, in postcards and pictures, your tastes may run to train wrecks. This seemed to be a popular disaster to portray. Other subjects are floods, war, fires, churches, Santa Claus, castles, beach scenes, humor, and on and on. By focusing on one such subject, collectors have a direction, rather than trying to collect everything just because it is old. Many postcards are regional, in that they portray buildings, parks, monuments, street scenes, and more within a particular community. Their value lies in that community unless they are exceptional. Some feel the stamps on them may in time be worth more than the postcards.

Rules in collecting ephemera are basic: look for interesting content, good color, and good condition. At this time, stamps are secondary, unless very old and on a collecting list as well. Some collectors frame their cards in groups to make interesting wall hangings—and good conversation pieces. Postcards make nice inexpensive gifts for friends at home—look for them when you travel. I have found very good examples in foreign countries.

Bibles

The Bible is the most frequently printed book and this keeps the price down on most. It is a book that survives because no one willingly destroys a copy, and the supply is large. However, some of the very early Bibles are valuable, and the following tips may help. The Bible has been published in more editions and in more countries than any other book. Many large-sized old ones turn up in country homes, with the inner pages containing records of births, deaths, and marriages—many telling a rather poignant history of a family. As a basic rule, to be of collecting interest a Bible must go back to the eighteenth century when early presses and wooden type were still in use. Those with woodblock pictures are valuable, more for the pictures

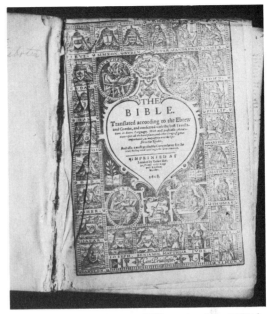

Title page of the Genevan Bible, printed in 1608 by Robert Barker, "Printer to the King's Most Excellent Majesty." Bound in calf, this is a good early Bible. Most are not valuable because the supply exceeds the demand.

than for the Bible itself. If the pictures are hand-colored, it will help raise the value.

The German Pietists at the Ephrata Cloister in Pennsylvania were the first to be able to take on the task of printing Bibles, and in the 1740s they turned out a massive copy, printed in German, for their neighbors the Mennonites. A Bible from the seventeenth century or earlier is preferable and those printed in England turn up from time to time. Metal type was in use during this century, but some might still have been printed using wooden type. In the less expensive volumes there are few or no pictures, although some decorations can be found at the title page in the front and at the chapter headings. The best volumes had hand illumination done by painting and gilding, since this was painstaking work most often undertaken by monks. This handwork was a holdover from the Bibles that were completely handwritten by monks—very few of which have survived. When a buyer finds a Bible that has been handwritten and hand-illuminated, he has the best that he can collect. Single pages from such Bibles sell for enormous sums, which is unfortunate because they must be torn apart for this purpose.

Other rare Bibles you might look for are those which have errors in print. There is the Place Makers Bible, which stated, "Blessed are the place makers, for they shall be called the children of God" ("place" should have been "peace"). This extraordinary misprint occurred in the second edition of the Geneva Bible published in England in 1561–62. Then there is the Vinegar Bible, in which "The Parable of the Vinegar" instead of the "Parable of the Vineyard" appears in the chapter heading according to Luke XX in an Oxford edition of the authorized version, said to be the most sumptuous of all the Oxford Bibles. Then there is the Basket Bible, which had a "basketful of errors" according to critics. An edition printed by Robert Barker and Martin Lucas in England in 1631 is rare. It is called the Wicked Bible because the negative was left out of the seventh commandment. The printers were fined several thousand pounds by the king and most copies were destroyed, with only four known to exist today. While searching out copies of this Bible to destroy, the censors found a German edition repeating the error.

Books, Manuscripts, and Documents

Book and manuscript collecting is an area that requires considerable study if you want to keep aware of the value and desirability of each item. As with any antique, age alone is not enough. Desirability and the law of supply and demand set the prices for old books and if you do not know these, you can get burned financially.

One category of books that seems to command a great deal of attention comprises histories of towns and counties and atlases of states made in the nineteenth century. These are invaluable to researchers of American history and are of special interest to residents of the areas that are covered in the books. Lawyers also make good customers for the atlases and histories of the communities in which they practice, since genealogies, property lines, and past ownership of items are often revealed in these old books. Writers are continually preparing stories on the history of communities and the people in them. This is a relatively safe area of collecting, and you can learn it quickly since the number of books written about any area is usually quite limited. Age helps value, because probably not many copies of a particular printing survived. However, publishers today are issuing reprints of old books in order to fill the demand for them. This can hurt the value of the old books, as most buyers want them not for their historical value, but for the information in them instead, and could care less whether the printing is old or new. Keep in touch with your local friendly book dealer to find out what books are being reprinted and what is in demand.

Next in importance in book collecting, but in many cases much higher in value, are first editions of works by noted authors. You will have to study to find out which books are most in demand. The demand changes from year to year, making it inadvisable to list any here. Usually the publisher states which printing the book is from. Some publishers use the numeral system, printing numbers from 1 through 10. As each successive printing is done, a numeral is dropped to indicate which printing it is. In the past, some editions were not marked, and many others have been found marked with the first year the book was published, although they may have been issued years later from a new press run.

Perhaps the ultimate triumph is to acquire first editions signed by the author. The signatures alone are good documentation and may have value in themselves. When you buy books today, try to have the author sign them wherever possible, since this enhances their value.

The earliest state history was probably Jeremy Belknap's History of New Hampshire, first published in 1794. Belknap was responsible for forming the New Hampshire Historical Society as well as the Massachusetts Historical Society, which, because of the early start in collecting important documents, has remarkable rarities in printed material.

The famed Ulster County Gazette, *Kingston, New York, which carried the account of the death of George Washington, dated January 4, 1800. Be cautioned that this was reprinted at least thirty-five times during the nineteenth century, so not all copies are original.*

Old books on art and antiques are in great demand. Buyers hunted for years for copies of Alice Morse Earle's *China Hunting in America*, first published in 1892. It was recently reissued by the Charles E. Tuttle Company in Vermont, making it available to all and this must have reduced the value of the early editions. Ledlie Laughlin's *Pewter in America: Its Makers And Their Marks* was originally issued in two volumes, which were sold only a few years ago for as much as $250 when they could be found. Both were recently combined into one volume and made available at $27.50, which reinforces the fact that you must be aware of possible republication before investing too much money. However, many books would be too expensive to reprint today, although they are valuable research tools for antiquarians, writers and collectors. Do not hesitate to buy books on antiques and art, as long as you do not have to pay high prices. These books are rising in value every day. Old auction catalogs, with the prices written in, are also in demand. Museum exhibitions often result in catalogs being printed. These are valuable because they are a record of the public's taste at the time, and they also serve as valuable research tools because of the accuracy of the information gathered by the museum staff.

Old school books are plentiful, and there is little demand for them. Books about our native heros are quite valuable and those relating the deeds of Paul Revere, Kit Carson, Daniel Boone, and others bring the days in which they lived home to us. Diaries are good, as they can furnish a record of events, times, and places. Among the most collectible items today are sailors' logs, as these are personal accounts of voyages and adventures. Those that include experiences with mutiny, pirates, storms, and other disasters are especially desirable. Captains' logs are always of interest, but there are few to be found. Most were turned in to the shipping companies, or were handed down in families which will not part with them.

Many books are collected because of their pretty covers. Leather bindings are most popular as decorators like them to create an authentic look in Early American restoration. Covers in colorful buckram with gilded lettering will add to the look of bookcases in any library.

Many nineteenth-century books are collected for the woodblock prints they contain. These can be cut out and framed and sold individually, realizing much more money than selling the book alone. Some of these woodblock prints or steel engravings are often the only rendition of work done by some artists. They would be commissioned to paint certain scenes and once the picture was reproduced for the book print, the painting most often disappeared, leaving the print as the only record of the work. Many woodblock renditions of work by Winslow Homer and Frederick Remington are the only record of certain scenes they did.

Comic Books

There was a time when collecting comic books was looked upon as just a passing fancy. Little did anyone realize that some would reach values in the four figures. This has priced many would-be collectors out of the present-day market, though good buys can still be found at markets and shows. Most hardcover books are never thrown away. Somehow there is reverence for a book as it represents learning, which is something few would destroy. Comic books, however, have been tossed out when children grew up and left home.

Auctions often yield up boxes of comics that have been stored in the attic for years, so this is a good place to seek them out. Condition is important; they should not be torn or faded. The earlier the better; some of the best go back no farther than the 1930s. I have been asked about

---

Superman Collectibles

One of the most popular comic book character is Superman. His first comic book is quoted in the four figures if it is in good condition. Other Superman items have value because of it. He made his appearance in 1938 and by 1940, he was a radio star. It was only natural that movies and television would follow. Benny Goodman recorded Superman which was written and arranged by Eddie Sauter. One of the first alarm clocks with the man of steel on it, dating to 1940, is quoted at over $500. There are lunchboxes, ray guns, toys, dolls, and games inspired by him as well.

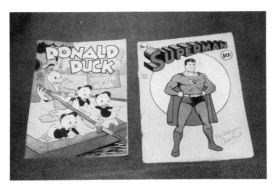

Donald Duck adventure comic and a Superman comic book autographed by Clark Kent.

collecting today's comics. The first of any series should be good in the future. Keep them in good condition, separated by acid-free paper.

Foredge Books

One has a foredge book if a painting appears when the edges of the pages of the book are spread slightly. When the book is closed, the painting cannot be seen. This technique of decorating books, called foredge painting, appeared as early as the seventeenth century and was done by a Stephen and Thomas Lewis of England. It is known to have been done not only in the British Isles, but also in France, Italy, Ger-

Foredge book. Spreading the front edge of the pages reveals the painting. When the book is closed, the painting cannot be seen.

many and China. There seems to have been no tradition for it here in America.

To create the paintings, artists would spread the edges of the pages and hold them with clamps. The paintings were done in watercolor. Then the book was closed and gilt applied to the edges so that there was no indication of the painting. One of the best collections of foredge books is at the Margaret Woodbury Strong Museum in Rochester, New York, where more than seventy volumes are studied by historians and researchers. They are not put out for the general public because of their rarity and fragility. The New York Public Library has a Bible dating from 1651 decorated in this manner. The prime years for this type of work seem to be between 1650 and 1850.

In some volumes two different scenes are evident when the pages are spread in opposite directions. A few books have turned up with the paintings done directly on the edges, with no attempt to conceal them. American book painting came after 1856, and there are some with scenes of Philadelphia and New York City in the eighteenth century.

Greeting and Trade Cards

Advertising and trade cards are fun collectibles, but few sell for much money. Some people collect cardboard fans which bear advertising messages on one side and colorful pictures on the other. These were given away at theaters on hot nights as promotional gimmicks.

Postcards are fun, as they are numerous and varied. Louis Prang of Boston is considered to be the father of American greeting cards. Born in Prussia in 1824, he later moved to New York, where he was unable to find work in the lithography field for which he was trained. After moving to Boston, Prang set up his own business and in time produced cards of all types. In 1874 his production of Christmas cards was very well accepted and his name became a household word. From this fine start, he went on to make cards for other holidays such as Easter and New Year's. Prang solicited the work of known artists and paid them well. He also developed a technique of printing as many as twenty colors to produce the finished product he wanted. Some of these cards were fringed with tassels, and others were made partly of silk and other cloth. Prang's floral designs were among the best and he created exquisite Easter cards with the theme of spring. Some sold for 75¢ a dozen, and others cost as much as a dollar apiece, which was a lot of money at the time.

Santa Claus was a popular subject. Many makers, including foreign ones, portrayed the jolly gent in different situations and likenesses. Cards with a standing Santa are worth more than those with a sitting Santa.

Some collect cards by artists, and others by makers. Some want them merely for the old stamps, while others are looking for those with Christmas seals which have been canceled by the postmark, as these bring good money. There are many collectors of specific scenes such as lighthouses, trains, seaside resorts, churches, etc., and all will pay according to their eagerness. Most cards are sold by the boxful to dealers who are much more canny about reselling them. The dealers allow buyers to examine the cards, hoping that they will show an interest which will help set a higher price. Get a price quoted on cards before you buy—this is one area where games can be played.

Maps, Deeds, and Wills

Old maps, deeds, wills, and other documents are academic in their value. Those relating to people who are historically important are, of course, the best, and the average ones found in boxes of papers during estate auctions are of little value. These can probably serve their best purpose as a gift to the local historical society, which will preserve them for research. Old newspapers have research value only, and books like *Godey's Ladies Book* and magazines like *Petersons* and *Frank Harper's Weekly* serve as interesting references to the life and times in which they were printed, but have little material value. The *Godey's Ladies Books* are often stripped of their colored prints, which are then individually framed for resale.

Rewards of Merit

In the early part of the last century, teachers began rewarding conscientious students with rewards of merit, slips of paper indicating some scholastic achievement. Rewards of merit were hand printed and colored by the teachers, who signed and dated them. They are considered a pure form of folk art. Those done completely by hand are the most treasured. Some took the form of little stickers applied to a successful paper. Sheets of such stickers bring good money, but those on individual school papers have little value.

After the 1830s, when printing presses were mechanized, printed rewards appeared. Though they are still collectible, most do not have the value of those handdone. The awards continued into this century before being replaced by red and gold stars and other printed tokens.

Valentines

Fortunately, February 14th has not been changed by our politicians as the traditional Valentine's Day. Its traditions go back to St. Valentine, the patron saint of lovers. The day is celebrated around most of the world with cards and tokens of love and friendship, yet the Church does nothing to honor the saint. He was put to death by Claudius II in Rome for not renouncing his faith, about the year 270. Some historians challenge his designation as the patron saint of lovers, but his memory has triumphed nevertheless, and he is celebrated to this day.

The first written reference to Valentine's Day appeared in a work by Chaucer

Reward of merit, c. 1840s. In this period, they would be hand-colored.

Cut valentine by Esther Howland of Worcester, Massachusetts, c. 1840s.

about 1370–1380; "For this was on St. Valentine's Day, when every fowl cometh to choose his make [mate]." It was not until the eighteenth century, however, that there was any record of a written card or message being given or sent in honor of the day. In France in the seventeenth century, Valentine cards appeared but were limited.

Best to collect are embossed and cut cards made by hand sometime during the middle of the last century. These are considered works of art by collectors and are highly prized. If you are settling an estate, check the boxes in the attic as these items were treasured by the young ladies who received them. Many fine examples were created in Fraktur style in Pennsylvania. One made in Denmark about 1800 pictures a young man holding his heart at the feet of his beloved, but she can be seen only when the card is held to the light. The variations are endless. A fine reference is *The Valentine and Its Origins*, by Frank Staff (Praeger, 1969).

One important name in early American valentines is Esther Howland of Worcester, Massachusetts, who in the 1840s began making valentines for sale to the public. These are quite fancy with lace cutouts, flowers made of paper, and small talismans. Her parents owned a stationery store, and soon their efforts in marketing them paid off. Today they represent some of the earliest and finest one can collect.

Care and Preservation

It is sobering to speculate that about 90 percent of book paper made in the first half of this century has a life expectancy of only about 50 years. It is possible that only about 1 percent of the books published early in this century will be with us to welcome in the twenty-first. This revelation appeared in an article in *The Laboratory*, published in Pittsburgh in 1964. Robert E. Kingery, then preparations chief at the New York Public Library, stated that his institution should be spending about $12 million a year just to keep its paper collections in good condition.

How does this information affect the small collector who is interested in books, prints, lithographs, and photographs? It should be of great concern, as silent killers are at work in almost every home, destroying much of our precious heritage, yet few people are aware it is happening. The value of a picture or document suffers greatly when condition is impaired. Eventually, it becomes worthless.

Early papers were permanent and durable, as they were often made from linen rags which had been bleached by alternate rinses in sour milk and wood ashes, followed by exposure to sunlight and nascent oxygen from the grass of bleaching meadows. After washing in hard water, calcium and magnesium carbonates were left in the finished paper. This helped in their preservation.

In the last century, the fibers in wood pulp were discovered to be usable in paper manufacture and the trend toward the inexpensive, nondurable product resulted in the near disappearance of the fine-quality bonds which had been in use. Unfortunately, this was a period of mass production of prints which are highly collectible today. Some made by the famous Currier and Ives firm in New York City are selling for many thousands of dollars, when a little over a hundred years ago, they were selling for cents. Today the condition of the print is important to its value.

In some of these cloth-fiber papers, acidity has set in and many compounds used in making paper have, over a period of time, discolored and ruined items made from it. It is believed there is a migration of chemicals when various papers or paperboards are stored next to each other. Chlorine and alum are two great offenders.

When one purchased a print for as little as 10¢ years ago, it was not inconceivable to take it home, get out the scissors, and trim the generous margin so it would fit in a frame at hand. This was the first step in its destruction. Most were mounted with the print directly against the glass,

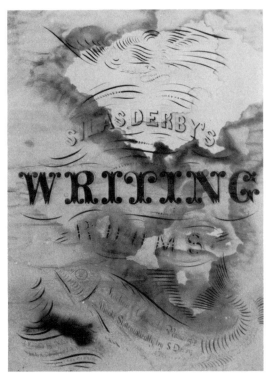

Calligraphy done by Silas Derby at his writing rooms in East Randolph, Vermont, 1845. Because it was framed improperly, this document suffers from foxing, caused by moisture.

with no mat to hold it away. This was the second point of destruction. With changing temperatures in a home, condensation will form on the underside of the glass and this will fade colors and stain and rot the paper.

Lastly, most of the old pictures have rough sawed pine boards as backing. Novice collectors do all they can to preserve these as evidence of age and authenticity. This is the third point of destruction. In a hot and humid home, pitch and dampness will ooze from the wood, causing a reddish brown stain called "foxing" because of its color. So long as these boards remain against the print, there can only be further destruction. The old boards can be retained, but a layer of nonacid paper or museum board must be placed in between to stop the foxing action.

Placing a heavy, acid-free mat around a watercolor painting when framing it is the only way to preserve its colors when condensation forms. It is important for the same reason to mat anything which is framed. If you treasure grandmother's sampler and you have it framed with glass against it, you are contributing to its destruction. Colors are fading, and the cloth and threads are rotting. If you frame photographs, prints, or lithos of any kind, they must be matted to be saved. In short, keep the glass away from them and separate any backing with museum board.

Document conservation centers have been set to restore and preserve old paper items, but their services are costly. If you cannot avail yourself of their services, at least you can institute a program of preservation in your home. Francis W. Dolloff and Roy L. Perkinson, former conservators at the Boston Museum of Fine Arts, collaborated on an excellent pamphlet, "How to Care for Works on Paper." They warn against stacking together unmatted pictures or papers; they should be separated by acid-free paper. Pictures hung in a cellar playroom may be susceptible to moisture, which comes into such areas through the walls. This can cause growth of mold, which will harm any paper. Intense light can fade a print. They also caution against insects, giving as an example a print that had been partially eaten by silverfish, which devoured the gelatin sizing in the paper. The booklet is available at the bookstore at the museum.

Acid-free matting is available at framing shops. Now is the time to start a campaign of properly framing and caring for all your treasured items. The longer you wait, the greater the deterioration.

Perry Pictures

I have an advertising circular in its original envelope touting Perry Pictures of Malden, Massachusetts. This concern brought art to the general public for as little as 1¢ per picture early in this century. Some pictures, printed in black and white, about 4″ × 6″, sold for as little as one-half cent. However, a minimum order of 50 was required for this bargain.

More than 2,250 pictures are listed in their catalog, which was available to those who sent three 2¢ stamps. With the catalog came various order blanks as well as money-order certificates for post office use. The "shipping and handling charge" was 3¢ for an order up to $2.50 and 30¢ for a $100 order. My catalog is dated 1906.

Listed in the catalog are many birds, flowers, and butterflies. These pictures were in color and sold for 2¢ each. There are series on foreign countries, history and geography, modern and ancient sculpture, as well as the art from all nations.

The fine art work includes such notables as Ruysdale, Da Vinci, Sir Joshua Reynolds, Millet, and Rosa Bonheur. For a 10″ × 12″ size, the cost was 7¢ each, or fifteen for a dollar. One wonders at the success of this venture. In my experience liquidating homes, I do not recall seeing such pictures—at least not those marked by Perry, whose name was on all those sold.

The cost was not prohibitive, so many must have been sold.

Peter Ompir

Collecting decorated tin, wood, papier mâché, and other materials is extremely popular. Early painted tin items have soared into the four figures. Those in the know, however, have just as much interest in collecting the work of contemporary makers, notably Peter Ompir, who has been called the "dean of decor painters." Ompir died recently, which has only fueled the desire of many to get some of his work before it totally disappears.

Peter Ompir lived near Great Barrington, Massachusetts. Early in the Depression, he left his native Pennsylvania to go to New York to seek work. He turned to painting as a means of survival. Eventually, he traveled to New England to find interesting items to paint and finally settled in the Berkshires, where he set up his studio. He was a student of the Art Institute in Chicago and the National and American Art Academies.

The beauty of his work in the eyes of antiquarians is that it looked a hundred years old the day it was painted. He mixed all his own colors, then worked in designs of fruit, flowers, birds, and even mannequins. He said it took almost two weeks to

Decorated tin coffeepot by Peter Ompir, Sheffield, Massachusetts, c. 1970s. His work, though newly done, looks very aged.

complete some of his choice pieces. He decorated furniture as well as small tin table items and boxes. Back in 1970, one of his tea caddies fetched $150 or more.

One would be well advised to search out the pieces done by Mr. Ompir, as they are excellent investments as well as beautiful work.

Radios

Old radios fall into the collectible category since most date from after World War I. Early sets were completely battery-operated, but also very popular were the crystal receivers that were put together by children as well as amateurs. High-power stations were set up in the 1920s, among them WGY in Schenectady, XERA in Del Rio, Texas, and WLW in Cincinnati, all with 500,000 watts of output. If you compare this with the maximum of 50,000 watts allowed clear-channel stations today, you can

understand why it was easy to build almost anything to receive such a strong signal. The TRF (tuned radio frequency) receivers were the rule until the mid-1920s when the superheterodyne came along to replace them. Tinny magnetic speakers gave way to the more resonant dynamic speakers, and electricity became the universal power for them.

If you are looking for exotic early radios, concentrate on early Atwater Kent, Majestic, RCA, and Polle Royal. There are

Many old radios still play well today. Many have excellent tonal quality and short wave, which is not available on most of today's sets. These are well documented, as they are recent.

many others that are good to collect whose names disappeared years ago. Perhaps most desired are the Scott all-wave receivers of the 1930s. They were built on two chrome chassis: the upper tuning section, and the lower amplifying section. As many as thirty tubes were in these sets, guaranteeing worldwide reception of the highest order. A sleeper is the Philco 690 XX made in 1937. With six speakers, it heralded the oncoming hi-fi boom and could tune the world. The less expensive 490 XX had four speakers, woofers and tweeters, making it quite a set as well.

There is growing interest today in short-wave reception. The old sets were designed to pull in the farthest stations. I would look for the early Scotts. Those built today probably cannot exceed their quality and reception.

Rogers Groups

John Rogers was born in Salem, Massachusetts, in 1829. At one time he worked in a railroad repair shop in Hannibal, Missouri, and in Spain as a designer of cloth. His travels led him to Manchester, New Hampshire, in the employ of the huge Amoskeag Manufacturing Company. Artistically inclined, he began modeling figures from clay taken from the Merrimack River, which adjoined the factory complex. They were well received by ready buyers, which encouraged him to open a shop in New York City in 1859. His first offering was a group of figures titled "The Slave Auction." During the Civil War, he turned out many groups comprising soldiers, blacks, and politicians, all of whom played some part in the great conflict.

Rogers groups were turned out until 1892, when he retired to a farm in Connecticut. Made of plaster, they were prone to absorb dirt and polluting materials in the air. One of the greatest problems is that in an oil-heated house, the fumes from the fire blackened these pieces, thereby

Rogers Group made by John Rogers, New York City, mid-nineteenth century. The Traveling Magician *is by one of more than 300 designs available to collect.*

lessening their value today. Years ago, many pieces were painted, which also decreased their value. Condition of a Rogers Group is most important: there should be no chips or cracks in the plaster, they should be as clean as possible, and they must not be painted.

There are rarities such as "The Sharpshooters," done in 1860 just before the start of the Civil War. If you own an 1860 "Farmer's Wife" or an 1862 "Camp Life" (sometimes called "Card Players"), you could do quite well financially.

Rogers is known to have made 309 groups, of which nine have never turned up. At the Vermont Country Store in Weston, owner Vrest Orton, sells a comprehensive booklet about Rogers and his work.

Russian Lacquered Boxes

The town of Palekh is about 180 miles northwest of Moscow in a flat, forest-studded countryside. Only about 4,000 people live there, 150 of whom are engaged in making papier mâché boxes painted with Russian folk art scenes. These boxes are quite popular throughout the world, and many are exported to this country. As early as the sixteenth century, this village was known for its icon painters. The revolution in 1917 brought to a close this chapter in religious paintings of any kind, so the artists turned their talents to boxes, placques, and the like.

Many boxes portray a scene from one of Pushkin's fairy tales. The noted Russian writer, whose works became known throughout the world, lived near St. Petersburg. The techniques of icon painting, such as in the intricate ornamentation and flowing elongated figures, are quite evident in this work. Colors are vivid, and many lines are hair thin. To make the tempera paint used on the boxes, dry pigments are added to a mixture of egg yolk and vinegar. The very fine, pointed brushes are often made by the artists themselves from squirrel tail fur. The papier mâché boxes are made from pressed cardboard, coated with black lacquer, then rubbed with pum-

Russian lacquered box from Palekh. The best are sent to other countries to sell for hard currency. Those in the Beriovska, or dollar stores, are not as high-quality.

ice, since colors cling better to a rough surface. The drawing is traced on with a zinc white. After the colors dry, coats of lacquer are applied and the box is rubbed with pumice. Then gilding or silver-looking aluminum is applied, and the boxes are lacquered and polished again.

The newer boxes are valid collectibles, as the work is hand-done and often quite good. Old boxes made before the revolution can be found as well—include these in your collection, too.

Santa Claus

One of our greatest folklore figures is Santa Claus. He has been reproduced in so many forms that collectors have many avenues of choice. They acquire Santa in any form they find him, and this makes for an interesting and what is growing to be a profitable hobby.

You can collect Christmas items of all

Santa Claus with oriental features, plaster, twentieth century. Most Christmas ornaments now come from the Orient. You can collect Santa in many forms, from many countries.

types. Santa himself can be found in ceramics, wood, plaster, and even in glass as a hanging ornament on a Christmas tree.

Since the advent of color lithography about 1870, he has been seen on postcards, advertisements, packaged products, and trade cards. He has been used to sell everything from cereals to automobile tires. Little did his nineteenth-century creators anticipate that he would be helping the commerce of the twentieth century, yet he is one of the world's best salesmen.

An interesting challenge is to seek out pictures, mostly on postcards, showing Santa arriving Christmas Eve by different means of transport. I have seen him not only in his sleigh, but also in a train, dirigible, or plane, on skis, in a touring car, trolley, ship, parachute, and just about any other form of transportation imagined. Putting cards together in a collage and framing them makes an interesting and fun wall hanging.

Some cards show Santa smoking a pipe, with the smoke spelling out the greeting. Though scarce, and out of step with our attitude toward tobacco today, they have not soared in price yet.

This is a fun area for your children and one which still is not too expensive.

Ship Models

Visitors to President Franklin Roosevelt's home at Hyde Park, New York, are always attracted to the ship models he collected. Ship models can also be found in abundance at marine museums. Most of these were never made to be sailed, but rather were created as presentation pieces at launchings, as advertising displays for shipping lines and travel agents, and just as decorative items for the office or home. Many were made by home craftspeople who treated this work as a hobby. Unfortunately, many junk models have been turned out over the years to appeal to the tourist trade in this and foreign countries. Doing appraisals, I have seen these in many homes. At times the owners, who

treasured them as family items supposedly made by a long gone grandfather or other member of the family, have been devastated to learn that a particular model is not valuable. As with all antiques, each must be seen to be valued.

Sailing vessels seem to be the favorites among models, although every branch of marine activity has been represented. The marine museum at Greenwich, England, has a superb collection of fighting vessels used in that country's many wars. In this country, naturally, models representing American ships are most desired. Collectors like models that show great activity, with figures on board doing something, much as in a genre painting. The more

Model of the nineteenth-century schooner Australia, *made by Raymond Pendleton. Mystic Seaport, Inc., Mystic, Connecticut. Photo by Mary Anne Stets.*

accurate and more true-to-life it is in detail, the greater the interest. The decks should have all the items that would normally be found aboard a ship of its type, and all models should be made true to scale. Best is the model with lifeboats aboard as well as a carved wood figure on the prow.

Snuff Boxes and Bottles

The use of snuff, a derivative of tobacco, goes back to biblical times and possibly before. It reached its height in the eighteenth and nineteenth centuries during the growing trade with the Orient. Many regarded it as medicinal, as one could clear out his nostrils with it very quickly, much in the manner of today's nosedrops. This was important in foggy and damp England.

Containers for snuff were made in all kinds of materials and in every nation where it was used. Orientals are known to have been big users as well as those who lived in countries that traded with them.

Containers ranged from simple boxes made of papier mâché to the gilt and jeweled examples made by Peter Carl Fabergé for the Russian royalty. In between are Battersea and Bilston enameled boxes made in England in the eighteenth century

Group of Oriental snuff bottles, carved from rock crystal and semiprecious stones. Nineteenth and early twentieth centuries.

and those of carved bone or ivory. The Orientals used the widest range of materials to make snuff boxes. Today, collectors prize early cinnabar lacquer snuff boxes. Bone and ivory snuff boxes were more common.

Many snuff boxes are made today in China and marketed out of Hong Kong and Singapore. Some are of old bone and ivory, which makes dating them difficult. A small spoon is attached to the top, so when the box is opened, one may spoon out a little on one's wrist to be sniffed from there. You will find snuff bottles in jadeite, semiprecious stone of all kinds, wood, crystal rock which looks like glass, and even metals. The old bottles are quite expensive today.

Stereopticons

Photography as we know it was perfected in 1839. Various people are credited with this exciting development, but most feel that Louis Daguerre made the first practical camera. By 1841, Charles Wheatstone was experimenting with stereo photography, insisting that if two pictures were taken from points equivalent to the distance between a person's eyes, one would see startling realism. I have several glass ambrotypes made in 1864 by this process, some taken at the top of Mount Washington in New Hampshire. From the 1850s through the 1870s, literally millions of stereo views were taken on both sides of the Atlantic. The noted justice Oliver Wendell Holmes is credited with making the best of early stereopticon viewers, many of which

still turn up at auctions today. The Shakers are known to have made a folding version of the viewer, which made it much easier to carry about. At last, people were able to get a three-dimensional view of places that most could never afford to see in person. Before the days of TV, radio, and phonographs, stereopticons were a favorite pastime for entertainment.

Most of the early stereo pictures were produced on glass plate negatives. Most of these have disappeared, leaving only the prints behind. However, there was a revival of interest in stereo when, early in the 1950s, David White of Milwaukee brought out the Stereo-Realist cameras, which are twin-lensed cameras that use 35mm film. A hardcover book was published on their use.

Stereopticon picture of the elegant Grand Union Hotel, at Saratoga Springs, New York. The structure was taken down in the name of progress after World War II. Stereo photo by Baker & Record of Saratoga Springs before the turn of the century.

Pentax offers a stereo adapter for many of its cameras. There are used stereo hand viewers and projectors still on the market.

One has to wear colored glasses to view them on a screen.

The Seven Household Gods

The seven household gods are considered in the Orient more as patron saints than as deities. Nominally, they are considered Buddhist, but three are derived from Brahmanic sources, three are Chinese, and one is Japanese. Even the ancients considered seven a lucky number. Each god personifies a type of good fortune.

Ebisu, the fisherman, provides for daily sustenance of the working man and is the god of fishermen and tradesmen. He carries a fishing rod and a Tai, which is a sea bream.

Daikoku is the god of wealth for the farmer. He is often depicted seated on bales of rice and holding a mallet or hammer, emblem of the miner and mineral wealth.

Benzaiten, the one feminine member, represents art, literature, music, and elo-quence. She plays on the Biwa, her favorite instrument.

Bishamon, the god of war, wears a suit of armor and carries a long spear. He is one of the guardians of heaven.

Hoti is the god of happiness and good luck. He has a body of generous proportions. He carries a bag loaded with gifts of good fortune.

Fukurokuju is the god of longevity. A Chinese philosopher, he is able to live on the mists of heaven and dews of earth.

Jurojin, the god of wisdom, is shown as an elderly man with a white beard and dressed in the robes of a scholar.

There is much symbolism in oriental carvings. If you learn the stories of what you buy and understand the message they carry, it makes ownership much more fun and rewarding.

The Three Stooges

Movie heros are the subject of much collecting today. Recent auctions of clothing, props, and memorabilia have caught the public's fancy. The sale of a pair of red shoes worn by Judy Garland in *The Wizard of Oz* for $60,000 shows how valuable and important some of these items can be.

Latest to join the parade of collectibles are items related to "The Three Stooges." This very mad threesome, which still entertains us via TV reruns, is the object of collectors and clubs all over the country. At a show in Philadelphia, several years ago, honoring Curly, Moe, and Larry, more than 3,000 attended to do business with 25 dealers. Old movie programs, posters, cue sheets as well as the old films themselves are eagerly sought. An LP recording, "Snow White and the Three Stooges," made some time ago, is a goodie to own. As early as 1959, the Three Stooges appeared on gum cards, some of which are worth well into the three figures now.

At one time, Publishers Clearinghouse advertising a guide to "The Stooges Lost Episodes," the fifty never-before-released films of the Stooge adventures.

Larry wrote a book called, *Stroke of Luck,* after suffering a stroke. Also look for *Curly: An Illustrated Biography of the Superstooge.* Also available are buttons, ties, stationery, buckles, hats, and shirts. Collect and have fun. That's the way they would want it.

Timepieces

Increased interest in clock and watch collecting has brought with it the usual reproductions and outright fakes, which means buyers must be on their toes. The proliferation of American dealers purchasing antiques in Europe has brought about misrepresentation in timepieces, with the mistakes usually being discovered after the item arrives, when it is much too late to do anything about it. Americans are regarded as "hot clients" for just about anything, and the poorer peoples of the world are wont to help us part with our dollars in a hurried and unwise manner. There are no rules to this game—you have to sharpen up on your knowledge and get up real early in the morning to outwit your counterparts overseas. Everyone is fair game.

Part of the problem in collecting pre-1800 clocks lies in making sure that the movements and case are original to each other. Many clockmakers engraved their names on the dials. The fakers have learned to grind off the names of lesser makers and replace them with famous names, like Thomas Tompion, Barraud, Perrigal, Dwerrihouse, and others. Some famous makers even bought inferior works and allowed their names to be engraved on them to keep up with the demand for their products. The old Stackfreed watches were imitated in at least three places in Germany, and recently in Belgium. Moving arm watches which were nineteenth-century reproductions of much earlier pieces were imported from France, and these are old enough to defy detection as to whether they are original. Water clocks are thought to be very old, but they were listed in a catalog of English manufacture as late as 1914, and many of these fakes are revered today as centuries-old originals. Some are stamped with the year 1640. When you know of the fakery going on, it can make you quite nervous when it comes to appraising and buying old timepieces.

There were clock and watchmakers in America early in the eighteenth century, but it was not until after the Revolutionary War that their output was significant. Anyone who has a timepiece of any kind made in America before 1800 has an important

Seventeenth-century wag-on-wall clock: a clock mechanism resting on a shelf. At the end of the century, the works were enclosed in tall cases to hide the mechanism.

where in the colonies. Try to determine whether the works were made by the clockmaker, since many grandfather clocks were assembled from parts bought elsewhere. Works and dials were imported from England, and many American makers merely made the weights and pendulums, had a cabinetmaker prepare the cases, and assembled the clocks for sale. Osborne's Manufactory in Birmingham, England, was a prolific concern, and many so-called American clocks house their works. However, as long as a clock is incorporated in an American case with native weights and pendulum, it is regarded as American. The desirability of these clocks is determined by whether the works came from England or were handmade in America, and the latter will command the most interest and value.

Until about 1850, clocks were powered by weights whose gravitational fall drove the hands and striking mechanisms. When the mass production of spring-wound

Connecticut peddler's clock by Seth Thomas, c. 1840. In small size they were carried by peddlers for sale in the country for only $10 each.

item indeed. Connecticut became the breeding ground for some of the best and most prolific makers, and after the beginning of the nineteenth century their impact was felt around the world.

Clocks

If you want to collect clocks of the late eighteenth and nineteenth centuries, you will do well to concentrate on those of American make. Piece for piece, they will command more money than their foreign counterparts. The tall or grandfather clock is one of the most desired, made every-

Left, *tall clock by Simon Willard of Grafton, Massachusetts*. Right, *tall clock by Abner Rogers of Berwick, Maine. In July of 1974, in Maine, the former sold at auction for $9,500 and the latter for $1,500.*

timepieces became practical, it was impossible to make a shelf clock that would run more than 30 hours with one winding due to the short distance a weight could fall. The tall clocks could run for eight days on one winding because of the long distance the weights could drop to the floor. Spring-wound mechanisms made the eight-day shelf clock a reality. Throughout the nineteenth century, various types of wall, shelf, mantel, and tall clocks were made, along with the clocks designed for commercial or industrial uses. Church and tower clocks were in demand, and many made way back in the last century are still keeping time.

CONSTRUCTION AND DESIGN

There are similarities between tall clocks made in Europe and those made in America. The Sheraton-style cases made in England are much the same as those made here, so it is advisable to check the works first to see if they are stamped with a maker's name. In upper New England, you will find that the makers used can-type weights made from tin, which were soldered after being filled with metal, stone, or even beach sand. Most of the many Pennsylvania clockmakers used solid cast iron weights in the manner of the English clocks. However, most of the Pennsylvania clocks are quite tall, some standing as high as nine feet, and the English clocks are more the height of those made in New England. So if you find a tall clock of New England height (in the seven-and-a-half-foot range) with iron weights, you could be looking at one made in England. Can weights are generally a good sign of American make, but you must realize that clock weights are interchangeable, so you must

A group of Connecticut clocks including the pillar and scroll, which is being reproduced today.

do some research to verify the place where the clock is reputed to have been made.

Mantel clocks took on different sizes and shapes. Most were made of wood, but marble, china, and iron cases are common. Some were made with scenes painted on the inside of the glass fronts, and this can heighten the value, especially if the work pictures some important place or person. Some had special movements or different means of powering the clock. One such device resembles a wagon spring—very few were made, and those appearing now command high prices. Some clocks were made with alarms, and these are of interest. The cases gradually evolved in style, keeping pace with furniture changes. Those made in the later nineteenth century in what is called "gingerbread" reflect the last true period change, that of East-lake. They were made in these fancy styles as late as the 1920s, with the designs often pressed into the wood by machine.

School and regulator clocks have experienced a revival, and those with calendar devices are interesting, but are in short supply. China cased clocks are often a product of foreign manufacture, notably German. Many have American works, however, which suggests that the cases might have been shipped here for final assembly. There are some French marble and iron-cased mantel clocks with American works, and you have only to read the dial to confirm this.

CLOCKMAKERS

Even if a clock is signed with the name of a noted maker, you must do a little more research to document it. Witness the case of the famous Simon Willard, who worked in the Boston area during the Federal period. A master clockmaker, he was responsible for training many apprentices. Those who came from his shop are regarded as

One of the most unusual clocks in the world is powered by steam. Gastown, Vancouver, British Columbia.

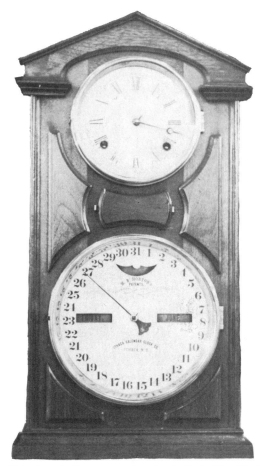

Calendar clocks were made extensively in New York State. Pictured is one from the Ithaca Calendar Clock Co., Ithaca, New York. The earliest patent date is 1865.

next to him in importance as craftsmen. Clocks by one such apprentice, Lemuel Curtis, often sell for more than the master's, but Willard is revered for his clocks and many fine ones grace homes and museums, not only in New England, but throughout the country.

Willard was known for creating masterpieces in unusual cases, such as his famous lighthouse clock, one of which is in the White House. Shaped like a lighthouse, this clock features a face at the top, surrounded by a glass dome, with the pendulum and weight hidden by the tall body. Some scholars wonder if he was actually responsible for such oddities as this, or if they were the creation of apprentices, with the works somehow appearing with Willard's name. In the absence of written proof, much of this was only conjecture until new evidence came to light.

An issue of the *Boston Evening Tran-*

script of Saturday, March 28, 1928, carries a revealing story about Simon Willard which should give rise to much conjecture and cause some uneasiness among owners of Willard clocks. It was written by a Charles Messer Stow, a highly regarded antiquarian of his time. He tells of visiting the showroom of Israel Sack, who was then in Boston, and he reprinted a bill of sale which was attached to the door of a tall clock. It read:

Clock Manufactory, Simon Willard, at his clock dial in Roxbury Street, manufactures every kind of clockwork, such as large clocks for steeples, made in the best manner and war-

Tall clock by Simon Willard sold at auction, May 17, 1975, in Massachusetts for $15,000. Bourne Auction Gallery.

Timepieces which run 30 hours and warranted, price 10 dollars. Spring clocks of all kinds, price from 50 to 60 dollars. Clocks that will run one year, with once winding up, with very elegant cases, price 100 dollars. Timepieces for astronomical purposes, price 70 dollars. Timepieces for meeting houses, to place before the gallery, with neat enameled dials, price 55 dollars. Chime clocks that will play 6 tunes, price 120 dollars. Perambulators are also made at said place which can be affixed to any kind of carriage and will tell the miles and rods exact, price 15 dollars. Printed by I. Thomas, Jun. Worcester.

The advertisement tells us of many items made by Willard that have not yet turned up. Where is a clock that runs one year on one winding, where is the clock that plays six tunes, where is the perambulator device that tells the miles traveled with the baby, who ever knew that Willard made such devices? What will give comfort to Willard clock owners if the following statement, printed by Willard, and inserted inside the same case, is true? It reads:

I believe the public are not generally aware that my former patent right expired six years ago, which induces me to caution them against the frequent impositions practiced in vending spurious timepieces. It is true these have Patent printed on them and some with my name and their outward appearance resembles those formerly made by me. Thus they are palm'd on the public. Several of them have been brought to me for repairs, that would certainly put the greatest bungler to blush. Such is the country inundated with, and such I consider prejudicial to my reputation; I therefore disclaim being the manufacturer of such vile performances. S. Willard.

When Willard retired from business in 1839, he sold his tools and goodwill to an apprentice, Elnathan Taber. Taber was allowed to print Simon Willard on the face of the clocks he made, and these were sold by Simon Willard, Jr., at his store in Boston. All of this should be cause for reflection by

ranted; price with one dial, 500 dollars; with two dials, 600 dollars; with three dials, 700 dollars; with four dials, 900. Common eight-day clocks, with very elegant faces and mahogany cases, price from 50 to 60 dollars. Elegant eight-day timepieces, price 30 dollars.

New Hampshire mirror clock, c. 1840, James Collins, Goffstown.

Eli Terry is credited with making the first Connecticut clocks with wooden works, 1808. Others made them as well until about 1838. Before buying one, make sure you know where you can have it serviced.

owners of "Willard" clocks, as well as dealers and appraisers. In light of the direct writing by Willard himself, you cannot be too careful in attribution to the master. You must apply some of this thinking to other makers as well.

Early in the nineteenth century, three noted clockmakers joined forces in one concern, though later they went out on their own. Each was a true craftsman and each left us a legacy in fine timepieces. Seth Thomas, Eli Terry, and Silas Hoadley made up this partnership and, along with other makers such as Chauncey Jerome and Joseph Ives, brought to the industry the mechanization that made volume production possible. The Connecticut ped-

dlers clock came into being—a shelf clock that sold for about $10 at a time when a tall one cost $100. These clocks were sold door-to-door, bringing a timepiece within the reach of almost everyone.

PERFORMING

Performing clocks are experiencing a revival. Years ago, just after World War II, cuckoo clocks were important collectibles. There was plenty of competition for those carved of walnut in fancy styles. Returning servicemen brought home many of them, which flooded the market, lowering the value of both old and new.

The cuckoo clock is said to have been invented about 1730 in Germany by a craftsman named Anton Ketterer. Most were made in the Black Forest region, a picturesque area along the Rhine. Perhaps they reached their peak in interest at the time of our centennial in the 1870s, when many were exhibited. Soon, almost every parlor had one, which is the reason so many turn up today. The huge output of new cuckoo clocks has reduced the value of old and new. Most hang on a wall, little used, as they have to be wound every day.

At auction recently, some of the earlier clocks in carved walnut, which match the

Commonly called "black" clocks, these were made c. 1880–1900. They are found in wood, marble, and iron. This one, with corner columns and brass feet and mounts, is quite fancy.

Brooks Palmer, author of the *Book of American Clocks*, the term was applied to many Connecticut-made clocks, many thousands of which were made. The octagonal frame around the face seems to have originated in the middle of the nineteenth century, though the greatest production came late in the nineteenth and early into the twentieth centuries. Hardly a school room or office was not equipped at sometime with a regulator clock. Some ran eight days on a winding, others were geared to thirty days.

Seth Thomas, with Eli Terry and Silas Hoadley in partnership, began making clocks in Greystone, Connecticut, about 1808. They made wood as well as brass movements. In 1813, Thomas sold out his interest to Hoadley and moved to Plymouth Hollow, where some of his most desirable clocks were made. In 1866, to honor one of its most popular residents, the name of Plymouth Hollow was changed to Thomaston, so it is reasonably easy to date his clocks, depending on the town name that appears on the label.

All regulators are quite desirable today, but those with names of the better

Eastlake period furniture, achieved prices not seen but a few years ago. None made after that time seem to complement the furniture of this century, so it may be a while before their turn comes.

REGULATOR

The word "regulator" was used to describe an accurate wall clock. According to

---

Orrery

An orrery is a clockwork mechanism that reproduces the daily motion of the earth and periods of the moon.

The idea was to show the sun and planets on the same plane with relative motions rather than showing their size and distance from each other. One can wind the clock mechanism and watch the revolving of the planets. Through scientific calculation it is also possible to establish their relationship to each other in future.

The first orreries were made by the noted English clockmaker Thomas Tompion and his nephew by marriage, George Graham. The first was made for Queen Anne. It was called a tellurium and was made of silver and ebony. Later models feature extended arms with planets and their satellites attached, showing their position at all times.

Orreries were expensive and were found at first only in wealthy homes. In time, less expensive models were designed for school use. By the middle of the eighteenth century they were quite common in the British Empire. The larger models are fixed; other models were designed to collapse and could be carried from place to place.

Most are wound with a hand crank, not a key. The better orreries are made of metal, but in the nineteenth century they were also made in wood, paper, and papier mâché. Variations of type are endless. Those made in England are the most collectible, so England is a good place to look for one.

Seth Thomas regulator clock, typically found in schoolrooms and offices. The term "regulator" denotes accuracy.

Howard watches and clocks of the nineteenth century are highly regarded throughout the world. Made in Boston, this watch movement found its way to the Museum Technesches in Vienna, Austria, where it is on permanent exhibit as an example of American workmanship.

makers, such as Thomas, are the ones sought by collectors. Oak cases are the best, and condition must be good. Copies of these clocks made in Japan have recently flooded the American market. Once in a while a cache of them turns up which had been stored away by some institution that replaced them with electric clocks years before. Quite interesting are those with an S and T forming part of the hands. These clocks were made in a variety of sizes; thirty inches was the standard size for schoolroom clocks. They keep good time, and the brass works in most will outlive any present-day owner.

Watches

Watchmaking hit its stride in the nineteenth century and watches were mass-produced to meet the demand. The maker who had perhaps the greatest influence in the industry was Edward Howard, born in Boston in 1813. At age 16, he was apprenticed to the noted Aaron Willard, Jr.,

whose father was Simon Willard's brother and a great clockmaker in his own right. He worked at Willard's company until 1842, when he left to form his own business with David P. Davis. During this period the clocks were labeled Howard and Davis. Howard was inventive and created a great deal of timesaving machinery during the growing age of industrialization. He joined forces with Aaron L. Dennison in 1848 to create the business that eventually became the Waltham Watch Company. It was known as Howard, Davis and Dennison in 1850; American Horologe Company, 1850; Warren Manufacturing Company, 1853; Boston Watch Company, 1853; Waltham Improvement Company, 1853–1857; E. Howard and Company, 1857; Howard Clock and Watch Company, 1863; E. Howard Clock and Watch Company, 1881. He retired in 1882.

Howard is best known for his commercial and industrial clocks. Rare was the bank, factory, or railroad station that did not boast one of his timepieces. He made banjo clocks in both wood and marble cases, ranging in size from 30 inches to 60 inches. These came in five sizes and collectors strive to get all five in each series. Many of his tower clocks are still used daily.

Howard made wall-hanging jewelers clocks—some with pendulum arms of different metals which would contract and expand with changing temperatures—in a manner to guarantee accurate timekeeping. His watches were the most elegant of his works, and it would be safe to say that an E. Howard watch in a gold case is the most desirable of the nineteenth-century production watches to collect today. They are still as accurate as the finest timepiece available to us at this time. Many railroads ran their trains by them. I do not know of any Howard timepiece wearing out and so they are perhaps the ultimate in American manufacture of all time. Howard movements from outdated cases are now being put into reproductions of dwarf (grandmother) and tall clocks. Rest assured that the timepiece will outlive you if you buy one today, even if the movement is already over a hundred years old.

Other good names in watches are Illinois, especially those with the superb 23-jewel movements, Waltham, Elgin, American Watch Company, and Hamilton. The value of most today is judged by the content of the gold in the case. Those with higher gold content naturally have greater value. The mark "20 Yr." or "25 Yr." indicated the length of time the gold plating was guaranteed. The mark "18K" or "14K" indicated the relative quantity of gold to alloy. Coin silver cases are so marked and will often be found on key wind watches, which were gradually phased out in the 1870s. Foreign watches of the seventeenth and eighteenth centuries are often quite spectacular and command high prices, as well they should. Collecting these is an entire study in itself.

You would do well to study Brooks Palmer's *Book of American Clocks* (Macmillan, 1950) since it cites the known and recognized makers and is a good reference for research on timepieces.

Toys and Puzzles

Early Toys

At flea markets and shows today, one can easily be shocked at seeing toys with which one played in the twenties and thirties. Not long ago good quality iron and tin was used to make toys, whereas today the plastics have taken over to provide us with little that will survive into the future. Toy makers were quite active in Ohio, Pennsylvania, Massachusetts, Connecticut, and New Hampshire late in the last century

---

Collecting Tip

Battery-operated toys are collected as well. It has been years since Mr. Machine, Great Garloo, and others made the scene, only to pass into history, which makes them quite collectible today. If you have some of these battery toys, do not discard them. Those of the fifties and sixties have risen considerably in value. The early radio-operated, cars, boats, and planes are good to save.

An excellent toy collection, with all items made by the Kingsbury Manufacturing Company in Keene, New Hampshire, is on display at the Colony Museum in that city. It is a good place to begin learning what is best in old toys.

Classic horse-drawn steamer, iron and tin. Late nineteenth century. Photo by Jim Hayman.

and through the forties, making the toys that are being collected now.

Those made of iron are more desired, and condition of paint is important. It is advisable not to repaint a metal toy as this offends the purist, who would most likely give the greatest amount for it. The metal of later tin toys was often lithographed to show ladders and men on fire trucks or designs on delivery wagons, racing cars, and aircraft. Completeness of a toy is important—if your firetruck has ladders and men missing, but has obvious holes and mounts intended for them, it would be wise to hunt for replacements at shows and markets. Wind-up toys should work.

Military Toys

TOY SOLDIERS

During the latter half of the nineteenth century, becoming a member of her majesty's armed forces was the highest as-piration for any British youth. The empire was at its peak with military scattered throughout the world. Military service offered an opportunity for travel as well as the respect of the populace, who looked upon members of the armed forces with respect and admiration.

In London in 1893, the William Britain firm decided to capitalize on this phenomenon and within a few years was offering complete sets of metal soldiers representing different regiments of the British and other Dominion forces. H. G. Wells wrote a book on model warfare, which heightened the interest in owning and playing with such toys. Gradually, the company broadened its scope by offering soldiers and other military items from nations on the continent. In fact, they made models of the soldiers who first served the Third Reich before any German maker offered any competition. After the coronation of Queen Elizabeth II in 1953, pro-

G.I. Joe

Every war has prompted the creation of toys related to it. Notable among them is G.I. Joe, who continues in popularity. First appearing in 1964, at the time of the Vietnam conflict, he seems to be the first military toy made to appeal to young children. About a foot high, he has movable parts. G.I. Joes were made to honor the four branches of the service—the army, navy, marines, and air force. They came complete with proper dress for all types of duty, from fatigues to dress uniforms. In 1965, a black figure was added. Jeeps, guns of all sizes, and other equipment appeared, and, later, Green Berets and helicopters.

Eventually, these were joined by forces from other nations who had battled with the Americans, and by frogmen, a firefighting unit, and desert patrol sets. Not to be chauvinistic, the makers created the G.I. Nurse in 1967, complete with various outfits. At the time of the Vietnam conflict, there was great division in the nation, so the sale of some war-related toys and other items fell to new lows. G.I. Joe took to the air as an astronaut. Various astronaut figures were made. By this time, however, the electronic age had arrived and something as provincial as military dolls and equipment took a back seat to the computer-oriented marvels. G.I. Joe is remembered today as a interesting collectible whose time has come in markets and shows. There is a wide range of collecting here, so the sky is the limit. At this time, the success of Desert Storm has not prompted a replacement. Perhaps the new phenonomen will be a version of "Stormin' Norman."

duction of the miniature military men ceased, causing immediate interest in collecting them. Prices have risen astronomically, so that some sell well into the three figures.

It is best to collect them by groups, such as an infantry platoon, a Red Cross unit, an artillery group, or a cavalry regiment. The sets should be complete, so one should learn what is in them before collecting. Original paint and color should be preserved. If they are in boxes, this will shoot prices sky high as the original boxes are highly prized. If the boxes are stamped on the base "Copyright Wm. Britain," they were made before 1912. From 1912 to 1937 they were marked "Britains, Ltd." After 1937, "Made in Britain" was added.

Play Money

There is still time to start collecting play money, an inexpensive collectible that can be found all over the country. Wooden nickels have enjoyed cycles of popularity as advertising gimmicks. They were passed

Much play money comes from cereal boxes. Paper bills, as well as metal and wooden coins, are collectible.

out and redeemed at places that issued them in lieu of real money. There is a wide range of pieces to collect—Burger King money issued in 1980; Bullwinkle Trading Coins; Cap'n Crunch coins, Hong Kong Candy Cash; and more.

If you enjoyed Post's Cocoa Pebbles and Fruity Pebbles cereal in 1974 and 1975, perhaps you saved your dinosaur coins. Pictures on them are of various members of prehistoric cultures and dinosaurs, such as the stegosaurus and edaphosaurus. Kiddy Cash was made in Hong Kong, notably for English use, but has turned up in this country. Moon Money features the landing of the lunar module, and Lucky Play Money features profiles of American presidents.

Play money seems to have made its first appearance in Germany about 1850. Milton Bradley, the noted game maker introduced cardboard copies of coins and bills around 1890 as a teaching tool for children. Our government became concerned and forced a growing group of manufacturers to put the word "educational" on all pieces, so there are two types to collect. Richard Clothier of Washington, Massachusetts, wrote a book on this type of collecting.

Puzzles

Puzzles can be found in almost any home. Simple puzzles are still used to educate children about the shape of our country and the world. Others show pets, homes, animal life, and landscapes of one type or another. Some were created as advertising tools, and they are among the most sought-after today.

Puzzles originated in Europe—some historians say in Germany; others, England. The first were handpainted and cut from thin wood. Color printing became possible about 1870. Some scenes were printed directly on the wood and others on paper glued to the wood before cutting. Later, the designs were printed directly on cardboard. This latter type is the most available among old puzzles. Puzzle boxes were decorated with chromolithography; having the original box heightens the value of the puzzle.

Back in the 1930s, the Par Company began to make puzzles. One could order a special puzzle to commemorate an event or to honor special people. These are quite rare, as most families regard them as heirlooms. Several of our big toy companies also made and marketed puzzles. One collector I know buys all she can. Most often, prices are low. She is tucking them away for what she sees will be a great demand for those made even since World War II.

If you locate a puzzle with pieces missing, perhaps it is best to leave it alone, unless it is a striking rarity. Finding pieces to fit means buying a similar one, and if rare, the odds are against you.

Typewriters

Typewriters go back to the 1840s, when an inventor in Germany brought out the first working model. It has wooden keys and carved wooden type. One of these is displayed at the Museum Technesches in Vienna. The type is inked by a roller, but did not really work well. It was not until later in the century that Hammond brought forth a typewriter that typed well. It featured the typing ball, which reappeared in the IBM machines after World War II as the latest thing in typing technology. The Hammond company failed because of a lack of financing, but the machine today is one of the most desired in a collection.

Another early typewriter that would be more available overseas is the Wheatstone, patented in England in 1851. It is unique in that the letters were typed on a tape. Some feel that early typewriters were designed and decorated to please women, who were likely to be the ones using them. The Wheatstone is a classic not only in its form, being built in a solid wooden case, but in the stenciled and painted decoration found on them.

The Blickensderfer is an oddity of the late nineteenth century as many were equipped with type that joined in a contin-uous line to look as if it had been handwritten. I used to type letters with one of these years ago to the amazement of friends who received them.

Most technology museums, which have been collecting for years, have all the examples they want. If you plan to deal in them, the market is limited. If you plan to collect them, concentrate on the nineteenth century.

Bibliography

Furniture

Boger, Louise Ade. *The Complete Guide To Furniture Styles.* Scribner's.

Butler, Joseph T. *Field Guide To American Antique Furniture.* New York: Facts on File, 1985.

Feild, Rachael. *Macdonald Guide To Buying Antique Furniture.* Radnor, PA: Wallace-Homestead, 1986.

Kayne, Myrna. *Fake, Fraud, or Genuine? Identifying Authentic American Antique Furniture.* Boston: Little, Brown, and Company, 1987.

Montgomery, Charles F. *American Furniture: The Federal Period.* New York: Viking Press, 1966.

Naeve, Milo N. *Identifying American Furniture: A Pictorial Guide To Styles and Terms, Colonial to Contemporary.* Nashville, TN: American Association for State and Local History, 1989.

Rubira, Jose Claret. *Encyclopedia of English Furniture Designs.* Sterling Publishing.

Santore, Charles. *The Windsor Style In America.* 2 vols. Philadelphia, PA: Running Press: 1981.

Smith, Nancy A. *Old Furniture: Understanding The Craftsman's Art.* Boston: Dover, 1992.

Swedberg, Robert W. and Harriett. *American Oak Furniture: Styles & Prices.* Radnor, PA: Wallace-Homestead, 1992.

———. *Furniture of the Depression Era: Furniture & Accessories of the 1920s, 1930s, and 1940s.* Paducah, KY: Collector Books, 1987.

Ward, Gerald W. R. *American Case Furniture.* New Haven, CT: Yale University Art Gallery, 1988.

Watson, Aldren. *Country Furniture.* Crowell.

Glass

Barlow, Ray, and Joan Kaiser. *The Glass Industry in Sandwich.* 4 vols. Windham, NH: Barlow-Kaiser Publishing Co. 1987.

Boggess, Bill and Louise. *American Brilliant Cut Glass.* New York: Crown.

Courter, J. W. *Aladdin Electric Lamps.* Published by author, 1987.

———. *Aladdin: The Magic Name In Lamps.* Radnor, PA: Wallace-Homestead, 1971.

Florence, Gene. *The Collector's Encyclopedia of Depression Glass.* 10th ed. Paducah, KY: Collector Books, 1992.

Heacock, William. *The Encyclopedia of Victorian Colored Pattern Glass.* 9 vols. Marietta, OH: Antique Publications.

Hollister, Paul. *The Encyclopedia of Glass Paperweights.* Paperweight Press, 1969.

Innes, Lowell. *Pittsburgh Glass, 1797–1891.* Houghton Mifflin Co., 1976.

Jenks, Bill, and Jerry Luna. *Early American Pattern Glass, 1850–1910.* Radnor, PA: Wallace-Homestead, 1990.

King, Thomas B. *Glass In Canada.* Erin Ontario, Canada: Boston Mills Press.

Lee, Ruth Webb. *Victorian Glass.* Charles Tuttle Co.

Luckey, Carl F., and Mary Burris. *Depression Era Glassware, Identification & Value Guide.* 2nd ed. Florence, AL: Books Americana, 1986.

McKearin, George and Helen. *American Glass.* Crown, 1975.

Thuro, Catherine M. V. *Oil Lamps: The Kerosene Era in North America.* Radnor, PA: Wallace-Homestead, 1976, price update 1992.

Wilson, Kenneth M. *New England Glass & Glassmaking.* Crowell.

Ceramics

Arman, David and Linda. *Historical Staffordshire: An Illustrated Check-List.* Canville, VA: Arman Enterprises, Inc., 1977.

Bagdade, Susan and Al. *Warman's English & Continental Pottery & Porcelain,* 2nd ed. Radnor, PA: Wallace-Homestead, 1991.

Barber, Edwin Atlee. *Marks of American Potters.* Southampton, NY: Cracker Barrel Press.

Chaffers, William. *Marks and Monograms on European and Oriental Pottery and Porcelain.* 14th ed. Los Angeles, CA: Borden Publishing Co.

Evans, Paul. *Art Pottery of the United States.* 2nd ed. New York: Feingold & Lewis, 1987.

Gates, William C., Jr., and Dana Omerod. "The East Liverpool, Ohio, Pottery District." *Historical Archaeology* (The Society for Historial Archaeology) 16 (1982) nos. 1–3.

Gaston, Mary Frank. *Haviland: Collectables & Objects of Art.* Paducah, KY: Collector Books, 1984.

Hamer, Frank. *The Potter's Dictionary of Materials & Techniques.* Watson Guptil Publications.

Kovel, Ralph and Terry. *Kovel's New Dictionary of Marks.* New York: Crown, 1986.

———. *Kovels' Guide To American Art Pottery.* New York: Crown, 1974.

Oates, Joan Collett. *Phoenix Bird Chinaware.* 4 vols. Published by author, 1984.

Van Patten, Jan F. *The Collector's Encyclopedia of Nippon Porcelain.* Collector Books Series, nos. 1–3. Paducah, KY: Collector Books.

Williams, Petra, and Marguerite R. Weber. *Staffordshire, Romantic Transfer Patterns.* 2 vols. Jeffersontown, KY: Fountain House East.

Metalwork

Silver

Belden, Louise Conwoy. *Marks of American Silversmiths.* Charlottesville, VA: University of Virginia Press, 1980.

Bradbury, Frederick. *History of Old Sheffield Plate.* Sheffield, England: J. W. Northland Ltd., 1968.

Fallon, John P. *Marks of London Goldsmiths & Silversmiths, c. 1697–1837.* Charles Tuttle Co., 1988.

Forbes, Dr. H. A. Crosby, John Devereux Kernan, and Ruth S. Wilkins. *Chinese Export Silver.* Salem, MA: Peabody Museum of Salem.

Kovel, Ralph and Terry. *American Silver, Pewter & Silverplate.* New York: Crown, 1974.

McClinton, Katharine Morrison. *Collecting American 19th Century Silver.* Schribner's.

Rainwater, Dorothy. *Encyclopedia of American Silver Manufacturers.* 3rd ed. West Chester, PA: Schiffer Publishing, 1986.

Wyler, Seymour B. *The Book of Old Silver: English, American, Foreign.* Crown, 1937.

Pewter

Cotterell, Howard. *Olde Pewter, Its Makers & Marks.* Charles E. Tuttle Co.

Jacobs, Carl. *Guide To American Pewter.* McBride Co., 1957.

Kerfoot, J. B. *American Pewter*. Bonzana, 1924.

Laughlin, Ledlie. *Pewter in America*. Barre, MA: Barre Publishers.

Montgomery, Charles F. *A History of American Pewter*. Weathervane Books.

Decorative Art

Currier, William. *Currier's Price Guide to American Artists, 1645–1945, At Auction*. Brockton, MA: Currier Publications.

———. *Currier's Price Guide to European Artists, 1545–1945, At Auction*. Brockton, MA: Currier Publications, 1989.

Fielding, Mantel. *Dictionary of American Painters, Sculptors and Engravers*. Apollo Books, 1983.

Howat, John K. *The Hudson River and Its Painters*. Apollo.

Johnson J., and A. Greutzner. *Dictionary of British Artists, 1880–1940: An Antique Collector's Club Research Project Listing 41,000 Artists*. Antique Collector's Club, 1976.

McKittrick, Rosemary and Michael. *McKittrick's Art Price Guide*. Dealers Choice, 1990

Theran, Susan. *Fine Art, Identification and Price Guide*. Avon Books.

———. *Leonard's Annual Price Index of Art Auctions*. 2 vols. Auction Index, 1981.

———. *The Official Price Guide to Fine Art*. 1st ed. New York: House of Collectibles, 1987.

Textiles

Anderson, Suzy McLennan. *Collector's Guide to Quilts*. Radnor, PA: Wallace-Homestead, 1991.

Dolan, Maryanne. *Vintage Clothing, 1880 to 1960: Identification and Value Guide*. 2nd ed. Florence, AL: Books Americana, 1987.

Johnson, Frances. *Collecting Antique Linens, Lace, & Needlework*. Radnor, PA: Wallace-Homestead, 1991.

Collectibles

Andacht, Sandra. *Oriental Antiques & Art: An Identification Value Guide*. Des Moines, IA: Wallace-Homestead, 1987.

Barlow, Ronald S. *The Antique Tool Collector's Guide To Value*. 3rd ed. Windmill Publishing Co., 1991.

Carnevale Jones, Diane. *Collectibles Market Guide & Price Index*. 10th ed. Radnor, PA: Wallace-Homestead, 1992.

Cunningham, Jo. *The Collector's Encyclopedia of American Dinnerware*. Paducah, KY: Collector Books, 1982, revised 1992.

Dennis, Lee. *Warman's Antique American Games: 1840–1940*. Radnor, PA: Wallace-Homestead, 1986, price update 1991.

Docks, L. R. *American Premium Record Guide: Identification and Value Guide 1915–1965, 78s, 45s, and LPs*. 4th ed. Florence, AL: Books Americana, 1992.

Foulke, Jan. *10th Blue Book Dolls & Values*. Cumberland, MD: Hobby House Press, Inc., 1991.

Franklin, Linda Campbell. *Identification And Value Guide: 300 Years of Kitchen Collectibles*. 3rd ed. Florence, AL: Books Americana, Inc., 1991.

Greason, Rebecca. *Tomart's Price Guide To Golden Book Collectibles*. Radnor, PA: Wallace-Homestead, 1991.

Hake, Ted. *Hake's Guide to TV Collectibles*. Radnor, PA: Wallace-Homestead, 1990.

Hake, Ted, and Russ King. *Price Guide To Collectible Pin-Back Buttons, 1896–1986*. Hake's Americana & Collectible Press, 1986.

Horsham, Michael. *The Art of the Shakers*. The Apple Press, 1989.

Johnson, Frances. *Wallace-Homestead Price Guide to Baskets*. 2nd ed. Radnor, PA: Wallace-Homestead, 1989.

Klug, Ray. *Antique Advertising Encyclopedia.* 2 vols. West Chester, PA: Schiffer Publishing, Ltd., 1978.

Kovel, Ralph and Terry. *The Kovel's Bottle Price List.* 8th ed. New York: Crown Publishers, Inc., 1987.

Lemke, Bob and Dan Albaugh. *Sports Collectors Digest Baseball Card Price Guide.* 2nd ed. Krause Publications, 1988.

Mace, O. Henry. *Collector's Guide To Early Photographs.* Radnor, PA: Wallace-Homestead, 1990.

Mallerich, Dallas J., III. *Greenberg's American Toy Trains.* Radnor, PA: Wallace-Homestead, 1990.

Maloney, David J., Jr. *Collector's Information Clearinghouse Antiques & Collectibles Resource Directory.* Radnor, PA: Wallace-Homestead, 1992.

Mascarelli, Gloria and Robert. *Warman's Oriental Antiques.* Radnor, PA: Wallace-Homestead, 1992.

McNulty, Lyndi Stewart. *Wallace-Homestead Price Guide To Plastic Collectibles.* Radnor, PA: Wallace-Homestead, 1992.

O'Brien, Richard. *Collecting Toys: A Collectors Identification and Value Guide.* 5th ed. New York: House of Collectibles, 1990.

Overstreet, Robert M. *The Overstreet Comic Book Price Guide.* 22nd ed. New York: Avon Books, 1992.

Rinker, Harry L., Jr. *Price Guide To Flea Market Treasures.* Radnor, PA: Wallace-Homestead, 1992.

Sargent, Jim. *Sargent's American Premium Guide To Pocket Knives.* Charles E. Tuttle Co.

Schiffer, Peter, Nancy, and Herbert. *The Brass Book.* Exton, PA: Schiffer Publishing Ltd., 1978.

Schugart, Cooksey, and Tom Engle. *The Official Price Guide To Watches.* 8th ed. New York: House of Collections, 1988.

Snell, Doris J. *Antique Jewelry with Prices.* Radnor, PA: Wallace-Homestead, 1984, price update 1991.

Sprigg, June, and David Larkin. *Shaker Life, Work, and Art.* Stewart, Tabori, & Chang, 1987.

Tempest, Jack. *Collector's Guide To Post-War Tin Toys.* Radnor, PA: Wallace-Homestead, 1991.